CLINT EASTWOOD'S
AMERICA

America Through the Lens
Martin Scorsese's America – Ellis Cashmore
Clint Eastwood's America – Sam B. Girgus
Alfred Hitchcock's America – Murray Pomerance
Spike Lee's America – David Sterritt
Steven Spielberg's America – Frederick Wasser

CLINT EASTWOOD'S AMERICA

SAM B. GIRGUS

polity

First published in 2014 by Polity Press

Polity Press
65 Bridge Street
Cambridge CB2 1UR, UK

Polity Press
350 Main Street
Malden, MA 02148, USA

ISBN-13: 978-0-7456-5040-1
ISBN-13: 978-0-7456-5041-8(pb)

A catalogue record for this book is available from the British Library.

Typeset in 10.75 on 14 pt Adobe Janson
by Toppan Best-set Premedia Limited
Printed and bound in Great Britain by T.J. International, Padstow, Cornwall

Poem quoted from *Clint Eastwood's America*:
By Kenneth Patchen, from SELECTED POEMS, copyright ©1957 by New Directions Publishing Corp.
Reprinted by permission of New Directions Publishing Corp.

The publisher has used its best endeavours to ensure that the URLs for external websites referred to in this book are correct and active at the time of going to press. However, the publisher has no responsibility for the websites and can make no guarantee that a site will remain live or that the content is or will remain appropriate.

Every effort has been made to trace all copyright holders, but if any have been inadvertently overlooked the publisher will be pleased to include any necessary credits in any subsequent reprint or edition.

For further information on Polity, visit our website: www.politybooks.com

To Scottie
Katya, Meighan, and Jennifer
Jeff and Ali
Arielle Gianni, Zachary Isaac, Mia Victoria, and
Maxwell Scot-Smith

Sam B. Girgus, August 2013
Photo: Zachary Arrington

CONTENTS

ACKNOWLEDGMENTS

After more than two decades, my students at Vanderbilt have worked with me through many classes and about a half-dozen books. I thank and appreciate them all. As Levinas says, "The presence of the other is a presence that teaches," and I have learned more than I can say from them. In the Department of English, I especially wish to thank Mark Schoenfield for his generous and steady support. Friends in the film studies community have been especially supportive of this project, starting with the newest of best friends, Cindy Lucia, and a long-term debating partner, Jerry Christensen, along with Peter Bailey, Rebecca Bell-Metereau, Jennifer Smyth, Colleen Glenn, Hunter Vaughan, Anne Kern, Krin Gabbard, Lucy Fischer, and Dudley Andrew. I would like to express my appreciation to Thomas G. Schatz for his critically and analytically astute reading of the original manuscript, which reflects his years of extraordinary contribution to film criticism, history, and scholarship. His thoughtful insights and informed suggestions proved of enormous help to me in editing and revising the manuscript. John Belton graciously read and encouraged me on an early draft of the introduction to the book as well as the completed manuscript.

Others who have proven so important through their friendship and support include Negi Darsess, Dan and Emily Vafa, Audrey Scot-Smith Shapiro, Ellen and Gene Winter, Joel Jones, Leah and David Marcus, Thadious Davis, Jonathan Lamb and Bridget Orr, Carol Burke, Beverly Moran, Robert Mack, Risa Arnold, Agnieszka Masica Supel and Ola Supel, Joe Fashing, Kent Barwick, Carol and Keith Hagan, Magda Zaborowska, Kelly Oliver, Tina Chanter Sara Cooper, J. Aaron Simmons, Cristina Giorcelli, Carola Chataway, Humberto Garcia, Cecelia Tichi, Dana Nelson, Michael Kreyling, Kathryn Schwarz, Teresa Goddu, Houston and Charlotte-Pierce Baker, Jay Clayton, Jennifer Fay, Anne Cook Calhoun, John Halperin, Gabriel Briggs, David Lewis, Sandy Stahl, Sara Bickell, Roger Moore, John Sloop, Martin Rapisarda, Karen Campbell, Carolyn Dever, Richard McCarty, Nick Zeppos, Gordon Gee; also Trey Harwell, J. Douglas Macready, Monica Osborne, Ira Allen, Col. Patrick Hampton and Gator, Tara Jacobs Castiglione, Jay Brown, Betty Davies, Danny Dalby, Jean and Phil Roseman, Capt. Tom Limbaugh, Brian and Judy Jones, Ken and Claire Darling, Allen Weitsman, Ed O'Neil, J. Delayne Barber, Stephanie Page Hoskins, Katie Ferguson, Oliver Luckett, "Brittwick" Strottman, Ginia McPhearson, Nicole Crane, Katy McCall, Katrina Markoff, Jacqui Leitzes, Peter Dale, Hill Perot, Kalan Contreras, Hayley Danner, Ashley Hedgecock, Jamie Mauldin, Julie Sharbutt, Sarah Louise Childress, Rachel Hodorowicz Hitt, Alison Barnes-Cohen, Adam Rabinowitz, Ben Scott, Amanda Grosse, Avi Ginzburg, Corwyn Ellison, Alyson Huff, Chad Gervich, Shirley Bolles and Angela Lopez, Rick and Christy Pearce, Nadia

Khromchenko Sikorshi, Jim and Martha Bomboy, Richard Bruehl, Tommy Haraway family, Vickie Williams, Natasha Brenna, Gentry Young, Nord Bathon, Natasha, Mary, Wade, Shannon and Anias, Chris, Patrick and Kate, Scott, Denise, Molly Ramsey, Melissa Childers, Roger Bishop, Bill Andrade, André Mouledoux Steve Ladd, Chad Given, Stephen Hendrix, Mickey Brathwaite, John Haley, Barry Coggins, Joe ("Pete") Ratliff, John Walker, Corey Spalding, Jill Furstenberg, Shannon Snyder, Steve Waterman, Paul Meyer, Jeremy Joiner & Co. The late Bob Sklar's name and work appear throughout this book. I miss his friendship and presence as much as the steady force of his brilliant and original film criticism.

Calista Marie Doll was of great help to me, as were other staff members of the Department of English, Administrative Assistant Janis May, Sara Corbitt, Margaret Quigley, and Donna Caplan. Chris Noel was especially generous and patient in giving me technical video assistance for the book. For other technological, administrative, and academic support, thanks to John Kilbourne, Chris Nold, Carol Beverly, Jamie Adams, Jeff Baltz, director Penny Peirce, Racquel Goff, Robyn Harris, Frank Lester, Ralph Schuller, and Holly Scott.

Calista Marie Doll was of great help to me, as were other staff members of the Department of English, Administrative Assistant Janis May, Sara Corbitt, Margaret Quigley, and Donna Caplan. Chris Noel was especially generous and patient in giving me technical video assistance for the book. For other technological, administrative, and academic support, thanks to John Kilbourne, Chris Nold, Carol Beverly, Jamie Adams, Jeff Baltz, director Penny Peirce, Racquel Goff, Robyn Harris, Frank Lester, Ralph Schuller, and Holly Scott.

It certainly was my lucky day when Andrea Drugan, a senior editor at Polity Press, talked to me about this book. I could not have asked for a warmer, friendlier, more support-ive and encouraging guide for the project. Her intelligence, editorial acuity, and critical clarity were of great importance at the beginning of the project. I was just as lucky that upon her leave of absence she was followed by editors with equal commitments to excellence and with similar levels of support, including Lauren Mulholland, Jonathan Skerrett, Helen Gray, Clare Ansell, Joe Devanny, and Elen Griffiths.

My daughters and their husbands and our grandchildren remain a source of unending joy and pride and the core of our purpose and being. Scottie helps to keep our households together with her love, care, sensitivity, informed and intel-ligent guidance, sparkling humor, generosity, and endless charm. The first and strongest reader, the best and greatest of friends, the person who fills life with love and meaning, she keeps, as a close friend noted, the "there" there.

ABBREVIATIONS

BS   Julia Kristeva, *Black Sun: Depression and Melancholia*, trans. Leon S. Roudiez (New York: Columbia University Press, 1989).

DF   Emmanuel Levinas, *Difficult Freedom: Essays on Judaism*, trans. Seán Hand (Baltimore, MD: Johns Hopkins University Press, 1997).

DL   Julia Kristeva, *Desire in Language: A Semiotic Approach to Literature and Art*, ed. Louis S. Roudiez, trans. Thomas Gora, Alice Jardine, and Leon S. Roudiez (New York: Columbia University Press, 1980).

FF   James Bradley with Ron Powers, *Flags of Our Fathers* (New York: Bantam, 2000).

GDT   Emmanuel Levinas, *God, Death, and Time*, trans. Bettina Bergo (Stanford, CA: Stanford University Press, 2000).

HF Julia Kristeva, *Hatred and Forgiveness*, trans. Jeanine Herman (New York: Columbia University Press, 2010).

IR Julia Kristeva, *Intimate Revolt: The Powers and Limits of Psychoanalysis*, trans. Jeanine Herman (New York: Columbia University Press, 2002).

LD Norman O. Brown, *Life Against Death: The Psychoanalytic Meaning of History* (New York: Vintage, 1959).

NMS Julia Kristeva, *New Maladies of the Soul*, trans. Ross Guberman (New York: Columbia University Press, 1995).

PH Julia Kristeva, *Powers of Horror: An Essay on Abjection*, trans. Leon S. Roudiez (New York: Columbia University Press, 1982).

PN Emmanuel Levinas, *Proper Names*, trans. Michael B. Smith (Stanford, CA: Stanford University Press, 1996).

R Paul Ricoeur, *Time and Narrative*, vol 3, trans. Kathleen Blamey and David Pellauer (Chicago, IL: University of Chicago Press, 1988).

RK Richard Kearney, *Anatheism (Return to God After God)* (New York: Columbia University Press, 2010).

RPL Julia Kristeva, *Revolution in Poetic Language*, trans. Margaret Waller, intro Leon S. Roudiez (New York: Columbia University Press, 1984).

INTRODUCTION: EASTWOOD'S
AMERICA – FROM THE SELF TO
A WORLD VIEW

The Making of an Artist

The transformation of Clint Eastwood into one of America's
most significant directors stands as an extraordinary achievement in film history. After decades of acting and directing
that gained him success and fame but little recognition for
his film art, Eastwood's emergence as a major creative and
artistic force in film came as a surprise with *Unforgiven* (1992).
Film critics, scholars, and the public, as Edward Buscombe
writes, have discussed the significance of *Unforgiven* as a work
that changed film and cultural history with its unique revision
of the Western genre.[1] What could not be known at its
release was how much change *Unforgiven* would initiate by
opening a series of major transformational films by Eastwood
that engage the ethical and moral crises of our times. *Unforgiven* and the works that followed it constitute a vital and
original addition to American and world film art from an

unexpected source to proffer new ways of looking at and thinking about modern experience.

Unforgiven reintroduced Eastwood to film culture and the world. The film instigated the change in the meaning of the name "Clint Eastwood" from being a label or brand for a popular American film hero and a marketable film commodity to signifying not just excellence in film-making but a film art and ethical consciousness that exceed and transcend simple definition and categorization.

In the film that arguably revivified the modern Western while changing popular and critical perceptions of Clint Eastwood's artistic sensibility and ethical consciousness, William Munny (Eastwood) in Unforgiven *searches his soul and ponders his destiny.* (Unforgiven, *1992, Warner Bros, Malpaso Productions, dir. Clint Eastwood.*) (*All images are screen captures produced by the author.*)

Building on his considerable film experience at the time, Eastwood in *Unforgiven* and then in the major works that follow it explores new territory for art and meaning. Like *Unforgiven*, subsequent films revise film genres. *Mystic River* (2003) turns a crime and detective story into a modern drama of vision and ethics. *Million Dollar Baby* (2004) revivifies and transforms the dormant sub-genre of the boxing film. The joint venture of *Flags of Our Fathers* (2006) and *Letters from Iwo Jima* (2006) not only revolutionizes the concept of the war film; the films become a consciousness-altering cultural endeavor to suggest the fear and repulsion of the stranger and the other as a source of death and violence. The war films indicate that such fear requires new thinking about difference as a basis for a culture of strangers.

Accordingly, Eastwood should receive critical attention as a director for taking film as an art form to new horizons of meaning as part of a dedicated ethical and spiritual quest. Eastwood has found the means of mind, imagination, and artistic will to create films that provoke new thinking, especially regarding ethical relationships and responsibility. For more than a century of film, directors have told viewers what to think about life, sex, love, relationships, society, and the inexorable complexities of experience. Eastwood, however, has become part of that special group of directors who makes viewers think. His anti-violence Western ends in a massacre; his film of transformative love in which the word becomes flesh in the boxing ring ends with a form of human sacrifice in the name of a transcendent and redeeming care; his crime story of perversion, murder, and revenge insinuates a deific power of witnessing that propounds the promise of an ethical vision of transcendent responsibility to the other; his unprecedented venture of filming both sides of a horrible battle, the Battle of Iwo Jima, goes beyond the espousal of peace to make the stranger, the foreigner, the outsider, and the history of the other the material and structure of film art. The intellectual courage and ethical imagination of the Iwo Jima films directly challenge the stereotype of Eastwood as a political reactionary that goes back to his early roles in film.

Hailed as masterpieces, Eastwood's mature works comprise a cinema of thought. They incite the ethical imagination to seek alternative possibilities in relationships, while stirring the artistic sensibility to appreciate new forms for examining and expressing experience. In these films, Eastwood's film art and his persistent drama of the ethical cohere. His art becomes more than a vehicle for ideas. Artistic tensions and ethical relations engage in an ongoing exchange between form and meaning.

In his films of artistic, intellectual, and ethical maturity, Eastwood fulfills what had been incipient in his early work as a director, namely, a search for meaning in human relationships in which ethics entails a transcendent responsibility to the other greater than the self and more than a negotiation or discourse on values, interests, and power. Antiinstitutional and rebellious to his core, Eastwood conveys in the later films a form of religious consciousness regarding radical moral and ethical responsibility.

In inchoate form in his early Westerns – especially in *High Plains Drifter* (1972) and *Pale Rider* (1985) – the redemptive impulse calls for "regeneration through violence." In these and other early films, Eastwood tended to embody the regenerative in a transcendent, superheroic figure.

In contrast, Eastwood's mature films suggest the infinite in the human that exceeds knowledge and certainty but still demands absolute responsibility in intersubjective relations. The films look toward Emmanuel Levinas's anarchic ethical time before synchronic time, "to a past that was never present," a time of "a deference of the immemorial to the unforeseeable," a paradox that "inscribes the glory of the Infinite."[2]

Moreover, Eastwood's focus as a director on reconsidering masculinity and male responsibility in relation to the feminine originates in his first film, *Play Misty for Me* (1971). This project develops concomitantly with the maturation of Eastwood's ethical vision and his art into a sophisticated sensitivity to the work of the body in the construction of subjectivity, social identity, and moral and ethical relationships. In Eastwood's films, the organization of the drives of the body and the psyche into social and cultural structures and relationships parallels the violence associated with the denial, disavowal, and fear of feminine sexual space, and sustains the countermovement to fill the void of being with family-centered love.

Thus, starting with *Play Misty for Me*, gender and sexuality in Eastwood's films have been the focus of debate by scholars such as Dennis Bingham, Drucilla Cornell, Adam Knee, Christine Holmlund, and Tania Modleski, among others.[3] In many of his films, Eastwood confronts the violence and fear related to the feminine and maternal for the purpose of transforming the naked energy of internal drives into a source for love and parental care and responsibility. Interestingly, acclaimed actress Meryl Streep recently asserted in Richard Schickel's *Eastwood Directs: The Untold Story* (2012) that Eastwood has "a female sensibility in many ways."

As Eastwood's film-making progressed, he contrived his own directing style of building narrative tension to climactic scenes of tightly compressed emotion and meaning in carefully constructed frame spaces and images that dramatize his ethical vision. Eastwood's mature directing style of cuts, montage, parallel editing, dynamic composition and framing, and fast filming present a cinema of ethical and moral complexity in a context of psychological uncertainty and social instability.

Eastwood's cinema of thought compares to feminist philosopher and psychoanalyst Julia Kristeva's "culture of revolt," becoming artistically, philosophically, and socially a film aesthetic of questioning and intellectual unrest. For Eastwood, the cinema of thought and revolt constitutes neither a structured philosophic system nor a totalizing ideology but a cinema of oppositional images and impulses that counters what Kristeva terms the society of the "total spectacle" of social, intellectual, and political conformity.[4]

Accordingly, with *Unforgiven*, the beginnings could be discerned of the changes that would become Clint Eastwood over the next decades. Of significance, Richard Schickel notes of Eastwood and *Unforgiven* that "critical recognition of his achievement was unhesitating." He says, "It was almost as if that 'revisionist' tag they hung on the film was their way of saying that Clint was obviously a new man, some sort of born-again filmmaker." Schickel observes that "implicit in the film's critical reception" resides a "forgetting that Clint had been working his way toward this apotheosis almost since the beginning of his career."[5]

As the culminating, triumphant works of more than four decades of directing, the films of the "new man" and the "born-again film-maker" that Schickel describes compel further study for Eastwood's artistic originality, intelligent exploration of the complexities of modern experience, and passionate ethical vision.

Film Art and Ethical Vision

Over the years, Clint Eastwood's America usually has meant just that, America through the psyche, vision, voice, and imagination of Eastwood, often as represented on the screen by an Eastwood performance under Eastwood's direction.

For several decades, when you looked through Eastwood's lens to see America, you probably saw Eastwood. Eastwood's face and body in close-ups, closer close-ups, medium shots, and long shots often have been the focus of his version of the story of America. Ordinarily, such narcissism might seem somewhat strange in a grown man.

In retrospect, however, it can be seen that Eastwood the director has endeavored to put his films and himself as an actor in challenging and meaningful social and cultural contexts. It also can be understood with hindsight that a serious search for ethical and moral meaning provides much of the impetus for Eastwood's film-making enterprise. Eastwood, as John Belton says, enacts "a unique moral vision" in his films. In a similar vein, Drucilla Cornell writes of Eastwood, "He grapples with all of the most significant ethical issues of our time: war, vengeance, the role of law, relations between the sexes, the meaning of friendship, and indeed with what it means to lead an ethical life as a good man in late modernity." Sara Anson Vaux also persuasively insists that Eastwood's films exhibit a powerful "ethical vision."[6] As such comments suggest, in his extended body of work as a director, Eastwood has developed his ability to relate his story through film as a quest for individual redemption in the context of the struggle for social redemption.

Eastwood's work as a director has gone through three fairly obvious overlapping narrative modes and artistic styles. In the first stage that starts with Eastwood's inaugural film as a director, *Play Misty for Me*, he learned to direct in part by directing himself. In this largely narcissistic period, Eastwood usually focuses on the self. Eastwood's *Unforgiven* begins his second stage as a director in which he continues to star and direct himself in his films but evidences a growing maturity in terms of both his art and ethical consciousness, including the development of relations to others. Eastwood opens yet a third creative mode with *Mystic River*. In this mode of his directing, Eastwood departs as an actor from his own work. A continuing movement away from the self toward the other as an ethical and philosophical proposal characterizes this phase.

In the films of his first 20 years of directing, Eastwood solidified marginalization and border identity as a defining theme. He directs himself as the liminal man with a threshold existence, entrenching his character's lone identity on the border between rigid resistance to and anticipation of radical social change. With roots in the era of assassinations, Vietnam, and Nixon, Eastwood's marginalized hero in the films of this first stage resonates with the fragmentation and chaos of that time. In his films and in the country, it was a time of basic changes regarding sexuality and gender as well as in other areas of values, beliefs, and behavior. In the films of this mode, Eastwood tends to rely on filming himself for narrative continuity, dramatic development, and psychological intensity. Noteworthy films in this mode include *Play Misty for Me*, *High Plains Drifter*, *The Outlaw Josey Wales*, *Bronco Billy* (1980), *Honkytonk Man* (1982), *Sudden Impact* (1983), *Pale Rider* (1985), and *White Hunter, Black Heart* (1990), a provocative and compelling effort by Eastwood about director John Huston. Anticipating some later films, Eastwood does not act during this period, in *Breezy* (1973), a winter–summer love story starring William Holden, and *Bird* (1988), an excellent film about jazz great, Charlie Parker, with Forest Whitaker. *Bird* also illustrates Eastwood's passion for jazz and the blues and his inclusion of African-American actors and issues in his films.

In the films of the first decades of directing, Eastwood steadily acquired and developed expertise and confidence as a director. He exercised his creative imagination and his powers of film construction. From his first films to his most recent work, Eastwood has never stopped working, learning, and growing.

Eastwood emerged from this extended early stage of directing to make his revisionist Western, *Unforgiven*, the film that establishes a new stage of maturity in his film-making. Following *Unforgiven*, films in which he also stars include another celebrated masterpiece, *Million Dollar Baby*, and other works of considerable artistic merit and strength, including *A Perfect World* (1993), *The Bridges of Madison County* (1995), *True Crime* (1999), *Gran Torino* (2008), and some less notable efforts. In this period, he directs but does not act in *Midnight in the Garden of Good and Evil* (1997) with Kevin Spacey, John Cusack, Jude Law, Lady Chablis, and Alison Eastwood.

In these more mature films, Eastwood continues to cast himself and others on the threshold as the outsider but with a new emphasis on the search of the self or subject for meaningful relationships. Still on the margin socially and on a psychological threshold existentially and temporally, a mature Eastwood demonstrates greater awareness of the ethical, moral, and social meaning of separation. In these films, Eastwood works within a *mise en scène* of intense relationships in social and cultural contexts of increasing ethical complexity. Inevitably the subject of attention as the star, Eastwood nevertheless shares a broader, deeper, and darker scene of moral and ethical action with others. Dramatic tension, story coherence, psychological intensity, and ethical conflict tend to be shared with others for sustaining action and thematic development.

As Eastwood continues to direct, he renews himself and his career once more in his third artistic phase of directing films without acting in them, including several master-pieces, *Mystic River* and *Flags of Our Fathers* and *Letters from Iwo Jima*. Again in *The Changeling* (2008), *Invictus* (2010),

Hereafter (2010), and *J. Edgar* (2011), he makes powerful and provocative films that add substantially to his years of dramatizing issues of children, women, and family along with race, death, and American character.

The Self-Made Man: A Hero of Revolt

From the very beginning of his acting career, Eastwood proved brilliant in creating and re-creating himself, starting literally from nowhere with little more than his own innate resources. Eastwood epitomizes the struggles of the self-made man, although for many years of his youth and early manhood, he clearly was unsure of what to make of himself. He came from Oakland, California, a place that Gertrude Stein famously described with the phrase, "There is no there, there!" His parents were loving and stable but struggling in his youth with the family's serious economic troubles during the Depression. He worked hard at various jobs, including in the timber industry of the forests of the Northwest, but as an enlisted man in the army he was assigned duty that enabled him to meet several actors and to get a notion of a possible acting career for himself. At times he tried community college on the GI Bill as he also aspired to get acting roles. Ironically, in spite of his obvious good looks and charisma, Eastwood struggled to create his own presence, stature, and identity. He eventually managed some minor parts in small movies until he got his role as ramrod Rowdy Yates in *Rawhide*, the 1960s hit CBS television series, which marked the beginning of his fame.

As an actor from the mid-1960s to the early 1970s, Eastwood achieved superstar status based on his image first as "The Stranger" – "Il Magnifico Straniero" – or "The Man With No Name" in Sergio Leone's "spaghetti Westerns" and then as "Dirty Harry" Callahan in Don Siegel's films. In films such as *The Good, The Bad, and The Ugly* (1966/1968) and *Dirty Harry* (1971), he was at once very visible and out of place standing in a dusty poncho, smoking a cigarillo, and killing everyone in sight under a burning Spanish sun or hovering over San Francisco's worst criminals with a beautiful California sky behind him. In these roles, he looked extreme, perhaps sometimes silly and eccentric, especially to some eastern establishment critics such as Pauline Kael of *The New Yorker*.[7] At that point in his career, he did not have serious exposure to art or the life of the mind. He also did not have extended rigorous training for acting like Marlon Brando or Montgomery Clift in the Actor's Studio. A developing actor, he was learning to direct on his own in bits and pieces. But he kept pushing on like the cattle driver in *Rawhide*. For years no one noticed the strength of his commitment to directing. Ultimately, Eastwood snuck in under the radar into the realm of greatness as a director.

Accordingly, in the first decades of his career as both a director and actor, Eastwood could be described as something of a peculiar phenomenon of American film and popular culture. Given his background and image, many at the time failed to foresee that the initial phase of Eastwood's directing would serve as a period of artistic incubation. Critics such as Kael thought that noting the superficial when looking at Eastwood and his films meant everything to understanding him. In fact, Eastwood was nurturing his apparent and his hidden strengths and abilities of mind, imagination, and character. Born on May 31, 1930, Eastwood was already in his early forties when he directed *Play Misty for Me* and could have continued with relative ease with his directing career by staying in familiar film-making territory.

Instead of being complacent about his success, Eastwood renewed and transformed his work as a director in part by assimilating the volatile energies of violence and destruction in his first-phase films with what he learned during this stage about film-making and about life. In the films of his artistic maturity, Eastwood maintains the focus of his earlier films on mental crisis and ethical challenge. The later films, however, incorporate the violence, disjuncture, and death of the earlier films into broader and deeper contexts of ethics, values, and human relationships. As Cornell emphasizes, the trauma of the tension between psychological impulse and ethical demand constitutes a major force throughout Eastwood's work, beginning with his early films.[8]

As a superstar and celebrity, Eastwood's life and career have been documented in close detail in many books, most importantly, thoroughly, and lastingly by Richard Schickel. What comes through in all of the books about Eastwood centers around the deep sense of him as the rebel and outsider. This drive for independence manifests itself in his decision relatively early in his successful movie career to create his own production company, Malpaso, named after a creek by his home and property in Carmel, California. This entrepreneurial move toward financial and artistic independence and control occurred with the production of *Hang 'Em High* (1968).

Emphasizing the prominence of rebellious independence in Eastwood, Schickel repeats an Eastwood statement about himself. Eastwood said in an interview, " 'There's a rebel lying deep in my soul.' " Similarly, Schickel quotes Eastwood's first wife Maggie Johnson Eastwood as saying to *Playboy* in 1974, " 'He had this thing about being a loner, like I kind of didn't exist sometimes. He's a very complex person.' "[9]

It can be argued that Eastwood's penchant for rebellion and independence in his films goes beyond the ordinary understanding of the idea of the rebel. The rebel usually engages in anti-social activity as a challenge to authority and conventional rules of behavior. The rebel disdains conformity to develop an independent style and attitude.

While Eastwood and his movie characters certainly typify such nonconformist rebellion, he exceeds this model of behavior and thought to engage in a form of existential revolt involving the ethical and social relationship to others. Eastwood becomes what in the light of Kristeva's work could be called a hero of revolt.[10] Eastwood in his films occupies the position of the artist of modern revolt, becoming a voice for challenging the ethical and moral order of existing ways of thinking and living.

As further indication of Eastwood's awareness of the importance of the ethical and moral dimension to his work, Schickel reports and paraphrases another important comment by Eastwood that "the body of his work adds up not to a politics but a morality."[11] In this moral sense, Eastwood as a serious director and as an American artist injects a moral and ethical sensibility into his work, a sensibility imbued with the dilemmas and challenges of modernity and the American imagination.

Eastwood and Eastwood

In the special director–actor dynamic that informs many of Eastwood's films, the actor becomes the embodiment of the director's intent and purpose. Actor Eastwood functions in these films as the exterior representation and the performing self for the director. The actor Eastwood fulfills the role of director Eastwood's alter ego. The actor provides a narrative through performance that structures, expresses, and unifies Eastwood's meaning. In many Eastwood films, the screen presence of the actor externalizes and articulates an internal journey of engagement with violent psychological forces, often regarding sexuality, women, manhood, and guilt.

It would be a mistake, however, to confuse the Eastwood character on the screen with the Eastwood behind the camera or, for that matter, the Eastwood producing and helping to manage his overall film-making enterprise. Eastwood the director and the actor operate in something like a dialectic relationship of difference and sameness. In spite of their different functions, they remain dependent upon each other. The dynamic of director Eastwood and actor Eastwood in the same film entails an inherent tension between distancing and intimacy. The duality of director and actor in one person imposes a sense of self-enclosure. The cohesion of director and actor as the same suggests the possibility of intellectual and artistic narcissism. The fusion of the two functions in one person can limit diversity, difference, and dissidence.

At the same time, this duality of director and actor in one person also creates a divided subjectivity, a double vision and consciousness that can engender complexity, heterogeneity, and multiplicity. Such double consciousness can create the means for escape, for breaking out beyond barriers of rigid identity. The dual vision of director and actor, therefore, provides a structure for both revivifying change and stultifying repetition. The tensions of a self divided between acting and directing find expression in a kind of master–slave relationship.

In fact, it could be argued that especially in his early films as a director, the rigid, hard, reactive masculinity of the on-screen Eastwood face and persona may tyrannize over the director. Not considered the most nuanced of screen performers, especially at the beginning of his career, Eastwood's face, body, and overall performance to a certain extent define the psychology and personality of his characters on the screen, sometimes reducing complexity of meaning.

In his mature mode and stage of directing and acting, however, Eastwood generally exploits the highly identifiable signs and qualities of his physical appearance to create a sense of greater complexity in his roles. Age, maturity, and experience give a new depth and solidity to his performance. The unstable and reversible positions of dominance between actor and director achieve partial resolution for Eastwood with a new purity of emphasis on directing in his films, in which he removes himself as an actor and focuses on others. Suggesting psychological growth in the mature phases of his work, Eastwood has developed the structured duality of director–actor to go beyond immediate, ephemeral success to become an authentic artist and felt force in cinema.

An American Journey: Issues and Themes

Eastwood's films have been consistent over the decades in their concern about the direction and meaning of American culture. Issues about American culture and character in the early films become part of a more complex discussion in the later films of America in the midst of interminable change and crisis. A continuity of concerns about the state of mind and life of America connects Eastwood's films.

Revolutionary changes in the place and situation of women, people of color, lesbians, and gays during Eastwood's lifetime transformed America into a different and better country. Such changes came during decades of ongoing turmoil and crisis. As demonstrated most recently in *J. Edgar* but throughout Eastwood's work as well, turmoil and transition as a way of individual and social life create not only an opportunity for needed reform but also a situation of insecurity and instability. Eastwood's films generally do not so much document these times as dramatize the mental, emotional, and ethical conditions they suggest. His films to a considerable extent have been about the search for meaning in the midst of such transition, challenge, absence, and loss.

Significantly, throughout his career, Eastwood instinctively challenges the arrogance of self-appointed and privileged elites who claim moral and ethical superiority over others. He excoriates the custodians and guardians of morality who dissimulate the complexities of moral and ethical experience with easy and self-righteous platitudes and moral rigidity. For Eastwood, fixed rules often vitiate true ethical commitment that involves personal reflection, critical thinking, the courage to stand alone, and the inner strength to sacrifice. He disdains institutions – religious, social, and cultural – that prejudge people and thereby fail to clarify situations of moral and ethical crisis.

Reflecting his propensity for originality and difference, Eastwood's best films resist reduction to one simple theme or conflict. From the beginning, themes commingle, interact, contend, contradict or sustain each other. These basic themes and subjects pervade his films. They also guide his perception and understanding of an America that frequently has seemed under siege by strife and transition. The themes include:

The rebel and outsider: Eastwood invariably either plays or gives to other actors the crucial role of the rebel and outsider in his films. The rebel acts as the Stranger, a mythic figure to challenge the ethical assumptions and moral behavior of the community. He takes on the community to challenge, condemn, and ultimately to save it from itself.

Liminality: An extension and element of rebellion and alienation, liminality as a threshold existence, mentality, and position helps structure relationships and situations in Eastwood's work. Liminality means operating in the indeterminate space of social change and transition between the old and the new.

Women and sexuality: In the two films Eastwood initially directed, *Play Misty for Me* and *High Plains Drifter*, women and sexuality prove vexing and complicated. Women and sexuality retain their importance and prominence throughout his work. In *High Plains Drifter*, Eastwood opens with a rape scene that even by today's standards still shocks and disturbs, while in his first film, *Play Misty for Me*, he plays the lead role as the victim of a psychotic woman who wants to kill him out of jealousy and pathetic obsession. In *Play Misty for Me*, however, he also films himself, as Adam Knee indicates, as doubled in shots where his masculinity gets muted and feminized.[12] So, from the beginning, sexuality and relations with women involve violence, conflict, and ambiguity.

Family, children, and community: With the emphasis so solidly on the rebel and outsider in Eastwood's work, a contrasting focus occurs in his films on the desire and need for family and community. The pain and sorrow of separation from family and community dramatize the power, attraction, and centrality of these institutions. Eastwood characters in their dark alienation lose, pick up, subvert, and honor families. Also, throughout his films, caring for children becomes a central issue as the measure of values and character. Eastwood regularly emphasizes the vulnerability of children and the need for being responsible for them. He often casts his children in his movies, a situation that can increase the importance of their roles in his films for developing narrative and character.

Race and ethnicity: From the beginning of his directing, Eastwood exhibited sensitivity about issues of race, even when criticized by some for his portrayal of people of color. In addition, he invariably places a priority upon putting African-Americans and other minorities in the forefront of his filming.

Western and urban frontiers: Eastwood tends to dramatize both environments of the Western frontier and the city as places of threat, danger, and violence that require intervention through heroic action.

Failure: The dread and the reality of failure pervade Eastwood's films. Eastwood's heroes at times ambiguously confuse failure with independence and rebelliousness. His Bogart-like penchant for losers who function outside of society raises the question of the real meaning of winning and losing, succeeding and failing in corrupt, dishonest, and dysfunctional societies.

Invincibility and vulnerability: The mythic wish for invincible power and omniscience suggests the awareness of danger, destruction, and debilitation in his films.

Humor and irony: Humor and irony help structure, balance, and assuage the intense oppositional relationships that pervade Eastwood's work, whether such tensions occur between people or as part of dramatic and thematic development.

Religion: A bias against organized religion occurs in Eastwood's work. He tends to see institutional religion as hypocritical and dishonest. Yet his cynicism and disillusionment suggest the deeper passion and pain of a true believer.

Justice: The demand for justice over corrupt and evil individuals and societies becomes mixed with the wish for vengeance and retribution in Eastwood films.

Love: Love and the inability to find it, feel it, or know it, and the dilemma of the impossibility of living a worthwhile life without it suffuse Eastwood's films.

Ethics and redemption: Ethics as the emphasis on the other and redemption as the search for a meaning to life greater than the self emerge as motivating themes in Eastwood's work. Indeed, ethics and the journey for redemption propel the narrative in much of Eastwood's mature work.

Death and transcendence: Death proves paradoxical in Eastwood's films as the end of physical being, but also as the
mysterious power that forces questions about seeking different paths for finding meaning to life.

Rethinking and Reviewing Eastwood: Ethics and Psychoanalysis

In his search for meaning in a postmodern, post-Holocaust
age that tolerates genocide among other horrific evils,
Richard Kearney commingles the work and thought of
several major continental philosophers to articulate a coherent intellectual position for an ethics that proposes the
promise of renewal through the relationship with the other.
Emmanuel Levinas, Julia Kristeva, and Paul Ricoeur, among
other thinkers, investigate for Kearney, "a dimension of transcendence in the other that – in part, at least – exceeds the
finite presence of the person before me." In their different
ways, Levinas, Kristeva, and Ricoeur enable Kearney to articulate an ethics of the relationship of the finite individual to
the infinite realm of transcendence and responsibility. These
three among others for Kearney construct a meaningful and
usable philosophy for the transcendence, transformation, and
redemption of the individual in relation to the other. They
sustain Kearney's wish to "wager on the stranger – as infinite
Other incarnate in finite others." Kearney reads the teach-
ings of these thinkers as "a phenomenological testimony of
goodness."[13] These thinkers, including Kearney himself, can
inform and enlighten the meaning of the ethical and psychological drama of Eastwood's films.

Kristeva professes and practices a philosophy of psychoanalysis that proposes spiritual as well as psychological healing
by transforming the body's inner drives and impulses into

forces for the renewal of the flesh and the "soul." Levinas sees death in its relation to the infinite as providing meaning through the possibility of turning our temporary existence as strangers on earth into an opportunity for transcendence by placing absolute priority on the other. Ricoeur proposes the power of language, metaphor, and narrative for structuring time and identity with the meaning and purpose of ethics and responsibility. Such thinkers speak to moments of crisis and transformation that occur throughout Eastwood's major films.

The writings and analytical thinking of Kristeva, Levinas, and Ricoeur, among others, enable a fuller and deeper exploration of the significance of Eastwood's artistic and cultural achievement. They help explain the evolution of Eastwood's rhythm and time as a director into an art form that shifts from simply photographing physical faces, or the visage, to presenting the human face in all of its ethical drama of vulnerability, love, and transcendence.

A Pilgrim's Progress

The story of the evolution of Eastwood's art and ethical vision dramatizes a pilgrim's progress through the changing American social and cultural landscape. The connection of Eastwood the creative artist, ethical consciousness, and public personality to America constitutes a vital narrative of the relationship between a maturing and developing individual and the social and cultural crises of his times.

The long, steady rise of Eastwood's career has occurred in parallel with a pressing desire in the country for a figure and a story of purpose and redemption. Eastwood not only has told and filmed that story of the search for regeneration, but he steadily has come to embody it for many, both in his public image and film persona. Certainly, as often portrayed in the media, Eastwood represents values, ethics, and qualities of character of importance to diverse groups of people in America. Even after the controversy of his shaky appearance at the 2012 Republican National Convention, he can continue to claim a depth and intensity of aura, charisma, and glamor with much of the general public that no longer seem so available to other stars and celebrities of any generation.[14] The very decision to invite him to the convention testifies to his prominence and aura that had been confirmed just months before by the earlier reaction in the media and from the public to his commercial for Chrysler, entitled "It's Halftime in America," during the 2012 Super Bowl.[15] The commercial's theme of a comeback for the auto industry, in fact, resonates with the meaning of Eastwood's most powerful films that project the challenges and paradoxes of the search for individual and national regeneration.

Thus, for a significant number of Americans, Eastwood in many of his films creates a bridge over the ever-widening, frightening gap in the country between the near desperate need for security and the anxious awareness of a world that has seemed out of control economically, ecologically, politically, morally, and culturally. Eastwood responds to a national yearning for a vision of individual action and initiative, personal responsibility, and a potential for renewal. Eastwood's work over time dramatizes that search for meaning in America.

Eastwood's triumphs as a director confirm the continuing saga of his own development, not only as a director and artist but arguably also as a thinking, feeling, and loving human being. Eastwood's recent films continue to provoke and move audiences and touch people's lives in profound ways. In *Changeling* (2008), for example, Angelina Jolie (Christine Collins) achieved an intimate connection with some in her audience with her portrayal of a woman who loses her child

and then must contend with powerful forces and circumstances arrayed against her. As Sara Anson Vaux writes,
"*Changeling* touched my heart. After watching the movie for
the first time, I sat for an hour in the bar attached to the
cinema scarcely able to breathe, the sorrow for my lost children released at last. The little baby who disappeared under
the ground – would I ever see him again?"[16] In an essay-
review on *Mystic River* in *The New York Review of Books*, Geoffrey O'Brien writes that Eastwood "challenged his own
resources as a director and met the challenge with tremen-
dous success." O'Brien adds that "nothing in Eastwood's
earlier work quite prepares one for the unrelieved sadness of
the world he evokes in *Mystic River*."[17] Similarly, David
Denby in *The New Yorker* states that in Eastwood's early
movies "outsider heroes operated with an unshakable sense
of right." Denby then goes on to note that as his career progressed, Eastwood showed "twinges of doubt and self-
reproof" that were accompanied by "a broadening of interest
and a stunning increase of aesthetic ambition."[18] Considering
where he started in the eyes of the custodians of contemporary culture, Eastwood must derive some measure of satisfaction in gaining praise and recognition from writers working
in the inner sanctum of the New York intelligentsia and
publishing elite.

As both articles suggest, Eastwood's journey has taken him
in a direction distinctly away from making the kind of movies
that pander to the apparent preferences and predilections of
most general audiences for spectacles, low-level comedies,
unrealistic action films, and sci-fi thrillers. What Denby
terms Eastwood's "aesthetic ambition" melds with a spiritual
quest in his films, a search for ethical priorities and meaning.
Eastwood's years of film-making attest to his commitment to
this cause of aesthetics and ethics on a field of battle for the
hearts and minds of a distracted and anxious public.

Also, a recent discussion with Eastwood of his ideas about directing reflects the ever-growing concern in his films with the views and contributions of others. In a Director Series conversation with director Darren Aronofsky at the Tribeca Film Festival (April 9, 2013), Eastwood said that in contrast to "the auteur theory," he saw the director as a "platoon captain" working in a "collaborative" effort with an "ensemble." He maintained the director's right to take from others. He said that when a good idea came up, "You have to be smart enough to grab it."

In the spirit of his individual and collaborative search involving art and ethics, Eastwood the director moves on. Looking back over the territory he already has traveled as a director, artist, and man, it becomes clear that Eastwood executed one of the most amazing transformations in film history. Not content with what he had achieved in the first decades of directing, Eastwood graduated almost unnoticed from his comfortable celebrity status to become a major American film-maker of more than 30 films, several of them recognized as masterpieces. In this process of radical transformation as a director and creative consciousness, Eastwood became an artist, discovering the means to reimagine and reinvent the world on film as opposed to merely copying it or following the work of others.

1

THE FIRST TWENTY YEARS:

BORDERLINE STATES OF MIND

A Western State of Mind

The Western part of Clint Eastwood's decades-long struggle into the upper echelon of leading American and world directors begins with a long ride on a dapple-gray horse into the town of Lago in *High Plains Drifter*. To many, becoming a director of outstanding artistic achievement seemed like the last place Eastwood was headed at that point in his career, at least as based on the evidence of this particular Western, his second effort as a director following *Play Misty for Me*.

An international celebrity with great box-office appeal for his roles as "The Man With No Name" in Sergio Leone's spaghetti Westerns and as "Dirty Harry" in Don Siegel's films, Eastwood generated attention for directing and acting in his own films. Although *High Plains Drifter*, like *Play Misty for Me*, clearly exhibits the flaws of a new director, in this Western, the ride into Lago not only advances a journey of redemption that continues for the rest of Eastwood's career as a director; it also develops an artistic process for structuring and enacting the complex ethical geography of his artistic imagination. On this aesthetic and ethical venture, the Western becomes more than a classic genre and narrative form that Eastwood can tinker with, from *High Plains Drifter* to *Unforgiven*. The Western as a projection of the American and world imagination sustains the contours and development of Eastwood's world view.

So, for Eastwood, the Western provides a structure for the expression of the border state of mind that characterizes much of his work. Moreover, Eastwood's West as a border state of mind can be enlightened by discussing it in terms of Julia Kristeva's extensive examination throughout her work of the meaning of borders. As different as they are, Eastwood, the iconic rebel American roughneck, and Kristeva, the quintessential European thinker of seminal importance to the world of ideas, intersect at crucial points. Eastwood and Kristeva can inform each other. As an acutely modern artistic and cultural consciousness, Eastwood in his work dramatizes a border state of mind that explores much of the same philosophical and psychological condition of borders that Kristeva expatiates upon with persuasive eloquence and systematic analysis.

The concept of borders and boundaries suffuses Kristeva's writings. Kristeva maintains "border states of the mind" include "borderline personalities," more specifically the modern narcissist for whom "subject/object borders" collapse into a "border region" of reality and fantasy "that is psychosis."[1] She says modern man "is a being of boundaries, a borderline, or a 'false self'" who is part of "the growing number of narcissistic, borderline, or psychosomatic patients."[2]

Admittedly, Eastwood's Western state of mind at first seems quite removed from Kristeva's theory. At its most

immediate level of meaning, the West as a border state of
mind for Eastwood retains the conventions that historically
have defined it in the literary and cultural imagination. The
West cultivates independence, self-reliance, hostility toward
civilization, alienation, and violence. The West develops a
border personality type with a divided psyche that reflects
the untamed, unruly environment.

The West of Eastwood's early films, however, also intimates other levels of meaning. A closer look at the West as
a state of mind in Eastwood reveals a psychic and cultural
space that boils over with ambiguities and tensions that
reflect modernity. Questions of religion, naming and language, sacrifice, unspeakable emotion and violence, purification, gender identification, sexuality, murder, and death
infuse this Western state of mind in Eastwood's films, all also
essential matters of intrinsic importance to Kristeva's project.
Images and signs in Eastwood's films resonate with meaning
related to these same subjects in Kristeva's writings.

The transcendent nature of Eastwood's Stranger hero in
High Plains Drifter, *Pale Rider*, and in other films as well
exemplifies the border state of mind and being. Eastwood's
use of transcendent figures resembles Mark Twain's attraction to superhuman figures who transcend the limitations of
mind, spirit, and character of ordinary human beings.[3] For
Eastwood, the Stranger's identity, mind, and body entail a
borderline between the human and the superhuman, between
immanence and transcendence. The ontology of the Stranger
is problematic. Without a known name and place of origin,
he lacks a clear empirical identity. He exceeds existential
boundaries.

Eastwood's representation as director and actor of such a
transcendent figure in *High Plains Drifter* keeps the film
together as an artistic totality. Eastwood's Stranger provides
continuity for the film, often making up through the force

of his presence and personality for incoherent, awkward, and undeveloped aspects to the film such as the surreal atmosphere of Lago in the opening sequence that seems more bizarre than authentic as a rendering of the town's psychology. Perhaps the Stranger's superhuman powers explain how he overcomes and kills others without being hurt himself. He also escapes bullets fired directly at him while he bathes by Callie (Marianna Hill), whom he earlier raped. He eludes the bullets by simply immersing himself in the water so that only his cigarillo peeks out above the water like a weird periscope.

Eastwood associates the Stranger in *High Plains Drifter* with a vague form of divine power that entitles the transcendent figure to stand in judgment of the people. After demanding that the townspeople paint the entire town red, the Stranger leaves Lago behind with a sign that changes its name to "Hell," reaffirming the people's collective guilt, shame, and punishment, as well as the Stranger's power to condemn them to a living purgatory.

The Stranger's putative godlike power resonates through his parting words at the end of the film to Mordecai (Billy Curtis), the midget who has become his agent and ally in the town. Mordecai says, "I never did know your name." The Stranger responds, "Yes, you do," presumably hinting at his connection to an other-worldly force.[4]

Entering Lago from the high desert like some kind of dedicated prophet on the margin of society, the Stranger embodies the outsider, appearing initially in a long shot out of a misty, hazy background, accompanied by an eerie soundtrack. The image and sound immediately implant an aura of suspenseful foreboding about him. He arrives to punish the community for their corruption and bad deeds, as seen in flashbacks of the whipping and killing of a Marshal Duncan, who in fact may be related by family and name to the Stranger. He soon demonstrates a primary concern with his own moral authority as opposed to any responsibility for the reform of others, although some appear ready for an ethical turn that distinguishes them in Lago. The narcissism, self-indulgence, and self-absorption of the transcendent Stranger ultimately will change in Eastwood's later films to evidence the experience and ability to escape from the enclosure of the same to concentrate on the relationship and the importance of the other.

In her ethical and psychoanalytical theory, Kristeva delineates historic rituals for meaning that also can be discerned in Eastwood's journey of the Stranger, elements that have been dramatized and narrated in the Bible and other cultural sources. Kristeva helps to place events, occurrences, and relationships in *High Plains Drifter* in a greater context of meaning for the film. She articulates the psychoanalytical roots of the ethical endeavor.

Kristeva argues that throughout history the essential purpose of "sacred literature" has been to "use various forms of sacrifice" as a means "to enunciate *murder* as a condition of Meaning" (*NMS*: 119–20). Similarly, Kristeva writes elsewhere that at the "dawn of religion, the sons of the primitive horde commemorated their share in the Death of the father by partaking of a totemic meal. In fact, the father's Death was a murder denied."[5]

Such defining murders and acts of cleansing and purification soon occur in *High Plains Drifter*. In an early sequence, the Stranger's killing of three thuggish, bullying cowboys constitutes, in Kristeva's terms, the sacrifices and murders that create meaning. The Stranger's shootings follow the process of basing a new beginning on slaughter. His actions continue the pattern of murder and sacrifice set by the town with the killing of Marshal Duncan for trying to stop pervasive illegal activities.

Eastwood as the mysterious Stranger with transcendent powers in
High Plains Drifter *begins his journey of reform and retribution.*
*(*High Plains Drifter, *1973, Universal Pictures, The Malpaso*
Company, dir. Clint Eastwood.)

The Stranger also immediately mixes murder and purification at the beginning of the film. He enacts a crucial ritual of purification that will distinguish him from the profanity of others. After having a drink at the bar where he encounters the three thugs he soon will kill, he leaves the bar and crosses the street to the barber's shop for a shave and a bath, followed by the thugs. Covered by the barber's sheet and shooting from the barber's chair, the Stranger kills the three men. The dramatic action of killing in the midst of the shave to be followed by a bath, as described earlier, has special significance, emphasizing the Stranger's ritual of purification and murder.

In terms of the rituals of meaning in *High Plains Drifter*, the shave and bath as a process of purification constitute the abjection and distancing that Kristeva describes as basic to creating identity. Cleansing inheres in the sacred. She writes, "The Bible's obsession with purity seems then to be a cornerstone of the sacred. Nevertheless, it is merely a semantic variant of the need for separation, which constitutes an identity or a group as such, contrasts nature with culture, and is glorified in all the purification rituals that have forged the immense catharsis of society and culture" (*NMS*: 116).

In *High Plains Drifter*, cleansing also helps define the Stranger's killings as sacrificial murders to sanction his power and actions. Through a kind of metonymy, killing the thugs extends the cleansing and purification process from the self to a new social authority. The killings certify through blood the Stranger's transcendence to another realm of meaning and approval beyond the ordinary. Thus, in a discussion of the relationship between purity and sacrifice, Kristeva emphasizes that in Leviticus in the Hebrew Bible "a communication from the Lord seems to indicate that the sacrifice 'in itself' cannot assume the status of a divine covenant, unless the sacrifice is *already* inscribed in a logic of pure/impure distinction."[6]

By condoning the Stranger's actions, the town leaders accede to the moral and ethical superiority of the Stranger's transcendent powers and being. Their sanction confirms the murders as sacrifices for the safety of the community, thereby attesting to the Stranger as a special presence in Lago. Kristeva argues the law "curtails sacrifice" and "restrains the desire to kill" so that "homicide becomes the object of a *sacred* law that changes murder into defilement." She says, "The sacrifice has efficacy then only when manifesting a logic of separation, distinction, and difference that is governed by admissibility to the holy place, that is, the appointed place for encountering the sacred fire of the Lord Yahweh" (*PH*: 97, 112).

Leaving the barber's shop after the shootings, the Stranger encounters Callie, who had noticed his arrival and seems intent on a mean argument with him that leads to her rape. The rape, which begins with Callie's furious resistance but ends with her obvious sexual satisfaction, becomes a kind of public event in that Mordecai the dwarf, who assumes a clownish, childlike role for the Stranger, enjoys secretly witnessing the act.

Given his childlike body, Mordecai, hiding in the shadows of the barn, can be seen as re-envisioning on a psychoanalytical level a parental scene, a family re-enactment, that injects meanings into the sexual assault that complicate its significance as a sexualized counterpart to murder, both being acts of ultimate violation and domination. The situation projects Oedipal issues onto the Stranger's actions. The violence also unsettles the meaning for Eastwood in this film of male subjectivity and sexuality and the situation of women and the feminine in his world view.

One obvious question stands out. Other than being a largely gratuitous sign of extreme, transcendent masculine domination and power, what serious value could there be in such a horrible rape scene? Callie, allegedly the town whore, proclaims with justified outrage, "Isn't forcible rape in broad daylight still a misdemeanor in this town?" Even Eastwood has come to separate himself somewhat from the act, confessing that, as Schickel says, "He has no good explanation for why he went ahead with the sequence anyway." His admission that he knew while making the scene that it was "'politically incorrect,'" hints at his own puerile wish to shock and offend and perhaps to directly challenge the growing feminist movement at that time. He told Schickel, "'I might do it differently if I were making it now. I might omit that.'"[7] One sign of Eastwood's maturation can be found in his next Western, *The Outlaw Josey Wales*, in which Josey (Eastwood) demonstrates a charisma for attracting outcasts, such as Lone Watie (Chief Dan George), and enables them to form a family that replaces the family he lost in the beginning of the film in a Civil War massacre.

The unmitigated violence of the rape scene in *High Plains Drifter* contrasts with the Stranger's relationship with Sarah

Belding (Verna Bloom). The wife of one of the men most responsible for the murder of the marshal and for the town's corruption, Sarah sleeps with the Stranger, in part as a demonstration of her contempt for her husband. The Stranger's influence encourages her to leave her husband to start a new life as the one other person in town beside Mordecai with a sense of conscience and moral awareness of the town's bloody past. Sarah's conscience and responsibility contrast sharply with Callie's crude indifference to others.

The scene between the Stranger and Sarah, however, plays as awkwardly in its own way as the earlier rape scene. She clearly desires him and wakes up with him in the morning with a renewed sense of her own body and being. They have become intimate in more than a physical sense, but the scene fades into self-conscious banality. A superhuman figure requires a compatible feminine counterpart in an accommodating situation to make the relationship credible. Eastwood at this stage of directing the Western was not creating female figures with the same energy and imagination that went into his development of his dominant male protagonist, the transcendent Stranger.

It took Eastwood 12 years to complete the early phase of his work as a director of the Western that started with *Pale Rider* and the failure to relate to the feminine as a key to the search for renewal and meaning in life. The raw, unassimilated themes and experience of the feminine that play out awkwardly in *High Plains Drifter* achieve fuller, more coherent treatment in *Pale Rider*, although still somewhat tentatively and self-consciously.

The respectful homage *Pale Rider* pays to George Stevens's Western classic *Shane* (1953) has been noted and appreciated since its release. In *Pale Rider*, Eastwood uses the foundational popular myths of the West as dramatized in *Shane* to develop the myth he initiates in *High Plains Drifter* of a transcendent, godlike hero of superhuman powers and authority. In *Pale Rider*, no doubt obtains as to the film's association of the stranger-hero with divine power. *Pale Rider* marries the myth of the Western adventure to the myth of a divinely inspired transcendent hero.

Thus, the Stranger figure in *Pale Rider* quickly becomes dubbed "Preacher" because of his turned-around collar, although any actual religious or institutional affiliation seems unlikely for him. Schickel succinctly describes the development and nature of Eastwood's superhero in *Pale Rider* as a figure who embodies and enacts multiple myths and meanings, including the religious and divine. He says, "To some degree this is *Shane* with a supernatural twist, except that the Preacher is an even more magical figure – perhaps even a Christ-like one, enjoying a resurrection."[8] Such associations define the important dynamics of the relationships Preacher will develop in *Pale Rider*.

In *Shane*, Alan Ladd as Shane in buckskins plays the mythic hunter-killer with an altruistic heart who rides onto the farm of Joe (Van Heflin) and Marian Starrett (Jean Arthur) and their young son Joey (Brandon de Wilde) to help them fight the ranchers who wish to expel them. Eastwood moves the story to the Carbon Canyon in the Sawtooth Mountains of Idaho where "Tin Pans," legally encamped gold miners, struggle against a ruthless industrial miner, Coy LaHood (Richard Dysart), who wants to vent his voraciously acquisitive instinct for more by evicting the miners so he can expand and intensify his ecologically destructive hydraulic strip mining.

In *Shane*, an important secondary theme concerns the sexual tensions between Shane and Marian. The Freudian "family romance" intensifies with Shane's position as the dominant male. Observing the adult drama of egos and desire, young Joey undergoes his own struggles with identity and manhood.

In *Pale Rider*, Preacher also becomes part of a family under duress. In this film, however, the role of the young boy gets taken over by a lovely, pubescent young girl, Megan (Sydney Penny), and the sexual drama erupts from its latency in *Shane* to become central to the story as both Megan and her mother, Sarah Wheeler (Carrie Snodgrass), speak and act on their competing desires for Preacher.

In contrast, therefore, to the distortion of the Freudian family drama of *High Plains Drifter* with its hidden dwarf-child, the Eastwood hero in *Pale Rider* dives right into the Oedipal imbroglio. Moreover, he does so as an emissary of God. In *Pale Rider*, Eastwood returns to and develops the mixture of the sexual with the sacred and transcendent that he introduces in *High Plains Drifter*.

Moreover, in *Pale Rider*, Eastwood politicizes and social-izes the sexual by developing the metaphor of the feminine landscape. Eastwood in *Pale Rider* updates the feminine influ-ence on the images of the landscape in *Shane* by placing a patina of contemporary concerns about ecology and the envi-ronment over the land in his film. He contrasts Lahood's industrial rape of the lush, mountainous wilderness of the film's setting with Preacher's desire and responsibility to love Sarah and to protect the vulnerable and innocent Megan, most especially in a climactic moment of rescuing her from an attempted rape by Lahood's son Josh (Christopher Penn) and his gang. The son's sexual violence enacts and confirms the ethical and psychological disaster of the father's example and influence.

Thus, in *Pale Rider*, Eastwood makes a politically astute version of the classic *Shane* that reflects the growing ecologi-cal awareness at the time of the need to protect the environ-ment. The film clearly advocates reform. Breaking with preconceived notions of Eastwood's rigid conservative views, he told Schickel, "'I think the bureaucratic workings of nations and corporations have encouraged people to form counter-societies. It seems like the growing complications of our lives have made us wonder if there isn't some way to cut out all of that."[9]

Before Preacher's arrival, the only man in this family group, Hull Barrett (Michael Moriarty), lives and boards with Sarah and her daughter, and, as a hard-working Tin Pan, strives to care for them in hopes of eventually marrying Sarah who had been abandoned by her husband soon after Megan's birth. Interestingly, after a wild group of thugs rides through the Tin Pan "colony" to destroy it and frighten the miners, Barrett decides to make a gesture of manly defiance by riding back into town in spite of the danger of confronting and further antagonizing the violent men. On his way out of the camp, two men use the word "dumb" to him to describe his decision to go into town alone after previous incidents there at the hands of the thugs, thereby dubbing him with an epithet that solidifies his image as a weaker, stubborn, slower character in comparison to Preacher.

In the light of Preacher's development of the Stranger's mission and search for the sacred, it can be argued that the most brilliant and creative innovation in *Pale Rider* involves the roles of Sarah and Megan. The mother and daughter add a special dimension of meaning to Preacher's quest and narrative on many levels, religious, spiritual, and psychoanalytical.

Mother and daughter bear witness to Preacher with a physical, emotional, and spiritual devotion and intimacy that surpass the experience of others in *Pale Rider*. Their relationship to him occurs on a deeply personal level that intensifies and channels their view of him as a kind of savior figure whom they must share with each other and with others in the squatter community. Like Hull, who sees Preacher's wounds when he cleans up and changes for dinner, only

Sarah will have access to him to notice his back scarred with bullet holes, wounds most probably inflicted on him years before by the same Marshal Stockburn (John Russell) whom LaHood hires to kill Preacher, only to be outgunned and outfought by Preacher in a standard Eastwood conclusion of carefully choreographed violence and death. Mother and daughter respond to Preacher in a way that creates an exchange between them of negotiated meanings that deepen and complicate his role and significance in *Pale Rider*.

In effect, while their devotion to Preacher deepens and intensifies his psychoanalytical and religious significance, Sarah and Megan compel him to deal with them as different, as the other. From their positions as mother and daughter, they view his paternal and divine function in terms of the feminine, motherhood, and love that dramatically recontextualize and reconceptualize his meaning in the film. Preacher in turn must learn to question and counter the tyranny of the phallus in his relationship with the feminine as exhibited in *High Plains Drifter*.

Sarah and Megan open a new territory for the exploration of the borderline state of mind in Eastwood's Western. With them, several border states overlap. The boundaries indicate a Kristevan crisis of subjectivity. The borders involve the feminine body and mind, the relationship between mother and daughter, and the tension between the sacred and the profane. These lines of demarcation intersect on the bodies and minds of the girl and her mother and in their relationship to each other and to Preacher and Hull.

The lines of tension achieve fresh focus and new intensity with the insertion of Preacher into the story. By feminizing the construction of the subject in *Pale Rider*, Sarah and Megan create the potential through their presence and influence to revolutionize the significance of Preacher as a representative of the divine to ethics, transcendence, and the other.

As in classic quest journeys, a young maiden, Megan, initiates the greater meaning of *Pale Rider*, if not the action itself of the narrative. Her words and feelings signify the introduction of the sacred into the story. She helps to make the story a ritual narrative of redemption and love.

For Megan, the ritual of invoking the sacred begins with a sacrifice, not of a goat or a lamb as in biblical times, or a lawman or thugs as in *High Plains Drifter*, but of her mutt dog, Lindsay. The dog is shot and killed by one of the gang of cowardly and cruel raiders, who begin *Pale Rider* with an overheated, excessively long ride and assault on the Tin Pan camp.

Terrified by the killing and destruction, Megan manages to retrieve her dead pet amidst the chaos of the attack. The film then cuts to a dark shot through the fog and mist of the lush mountainside as she appears to bury Lindsay. In this setting of fear and loss, Megan prays, reciting the Twenty-third Psalm. In an interesting innovation, Eastwood directs her to intersperse her recitation of the psalm with questions and comments. Her words indicate her independent mind and the beginning of her maturation as a young woman, as well as Eastwood's notorious skepticism.

As Megan prays for a "miracle" to save them all from death, the camera cuts to Preacher, like the Stranger before him, riding a wonderful pale-gray horse in a rhythmic lope. As in classic quest myths or even fairy tales, Megan calls, and he appears. Megan's call and prayer designate Preacher immediately as chosen to lead and inspire. She helps to create Preacher's role and position in *Pale Rider* through her combination of vulnerability, innocence, intelligence, and faith. Her prayer and voice and his image mark the film's clear assertion of his divine mission.

In the following scene, Preacher appears in a long shot and then rides into town to quickly pulverize the bullies who have been beating Hull. Wearing a signature flat hat and a long coat and showing a slight growth of beard, Preacher hides any sign of his divine connection. The two men ride off together, Preacher on the extraordinary horse with the Appaloosa markings and Hull on his simple wagon.

Realizing Preacher has nowhere to stay, Hull invites him to move into an extra room in his place that he shares with Sarah and Megan, but he apologizes for the modest accommodations. He says, "All I got is a kind of fiancée is all."

A little later he explains to Preacher that he lives with Sarah and Megan "not in sin" but only to protect them. Hull's self-description solidifies his role as a humble Joseph figure in the film's version of a holy family.

Hull's gesture of welcoming Preacher into the house carries much significance with it. For philosopher Emmanuel Levinas, such an invitation constitutes the very basis of the religious impulse in that it follows the dictates of the Talmud to put the stranger, the homeless, and orphan first.

The religious or spiritual significance of such kindness, however, also has other implications for the film. The very notion of the dwelling resonates for Levinas with the feminine body as home. In *Totality and Infinity*, he describes woman as "the condition" of "the interiority of the Home and inhabitation."[10] As a caring and loving Joseph figure, Hull not only opens his dwelling to Preacher but also leads him to his place with the women.

Thus, like John Ford and Michelangelo Antonioni in such films as *The Searchers* (1956) and *L'avventura* (1960), Eastwood assumes the domesticated interior dwelling space as feminine, and like these classic directors, he endeavors in *Pale Rider* to film the visual metaphor as the feminine itself.[11] By crossing the borderline of the dwelling, Eastwood imagines the borderline of the feminine. This borderline leads to multiple borderlines and border states of mind regarding the feminine, motherhood, sexuality, love, and religion.

The cutting, editing, movement, and balance of sound and vision in the sequence when Preacher arrives at the home stand as a true achievement for Eastwood during this phase of his work and constitute a seminal moment of cinematic expression for him. Eastwood fills the sequence with tension, meaning, and promise. The religious and psychoanalytical elements of the relationships in *Pale Rider* cohere in these shots as a promise of future brilliance in film-making for Eastwood. The scene constitutes a major advance on Eastwood's journey to a greater understanding of his themes of transcendence and redemption and to his steadily growing powers and capabilities as a director.

For a visual expression in the scene of the idea of the borderline, Eastwood uses the kitchen window of the dwelling as the boundary between interior domestic women's space and the outer environment of danger, between the internal psychology of mother and daughter and the social order, and between the safety of the same and the danger of change and the other. The window opens to the promise of a transcendent power.

As Preacher and Hull make their way toward the house that Hull shares with Sarah and Megan, an interesting sound bridge of Megan's voice connects the men to Sarah and Megan in the house. Once again Megan recites from the Bible, this time from the Book of Revelations. Her carefully spoken words infuse the kitchen and the house with a sense of the religious and spiritual, helping to make the activities that occur there part of a ritual process that will become related to the appearance of Preacher. The meal that Sarah prepares as Megan speaks takes on a special meaning as the kind of dietary event that Kristeva mentions as part of a religious ritual to signify the sacred. Although Sarah does not realize it yet, this meal will become a means of welcoming and celebrating Preacher's arrival.

Eastwood makes outstanding use of Bruce Surtee's photography to create a visual poetry for the kitchen scene to match the significance of Megan's Bible reading and the symbolism of the film narrative. The look of the scene establishes a precedent that will be used to similarly powerful effect with a different director of photography, Jack N. Green, in *Unforgiven*.

In the case of *Pale Rider*, the extreme darkness of the scene emphasizes the kitchen as interior bodily space, a visual metonymic womb image that represents the mother and daughter relationship and that foreshadows the eventual intrusion into the home of the competing father figures, Preacher and Hull. The balancing of interior degrees of darkness and shadow utilizes the blazing light through the window to give the scene a religious quality of revelation. The light streaming through the window represents spiritual and sexual force.

Reading from Revelations, Megan describes the opening of the seals and says, "And there was given unto him, a great sword." As she reads, Sarah responds, "Very good" and works on dinner, interrupting Megan to ask for help to get some softly suggestive syrup and butter. Rising and helping, Megan continues to read. She says, "And I beheld, and lo, a black horse . . ." The view outside the window reveals a bit of the work, activity, and community of the miners.

Then a sudden change attracts Sarah's attention to the window. Megan says, "And when he had opened the fourth seal, I heard the voice of the fourth beast say, 'Come and see.'" A horse whinnies as though calling to Sarah. Sarah moves toward the window. Megan reads, "And I looked and behold a pale horse . . ." With Sarah at the window, Megan looks up as Hull on his wagon and Preacher behind him on his horse both appear. Megan's words match the vision of Preacher framed by the window in powerful, symbolic light. Megan says, "And his name that sat on him was death."

Megan rises, moving just in front of her mother. Their bodies align perfectly together, forming a fluid being. They both look. Preacher stops by the window. A low-angle shot tightens in on him. Megan says, "And hell followed with him." Preacher turns his head ever so slightly and gives them a brief, penetrating look and rides on.

The interior movement in the kitchen between Sarah and Megan has been up close and personal. The scene with mother and daughter has been set up and shot as a movement of dark colors and shadows that cohere into a whole but divided entity at the window. The colors flow and commingle

Eastwood as Preacher enters into the lives of a mother and daughter in Pale Rider *to the words from Revelations, "And I looked and behold a pale horse. . . . And his name that sat on him was death."* (Pale Rider, *1985, The Malpaso Company, dir. Clint Eastwood.*)

like rich, soft, and syrupy fluids into a vital force of the mother and girl in anticipated oppositional tension with the figure on the pale horse outside the window. Their faces gleam in illumination from the piercing light outside the window. Their dark eyes shine as they look out at the Preacher.

The two-shot of Sarah and Megan offsets and matches the paternal ferocity of Preacher. The shot resonates with powerful symbolic significance as a visually dramatic statement of the vitality of the female body and the feminine. The visual rhythms of the colors, light, shadows, and spoken sounds resonate with the strengths of the feminine and maternal.

The interaction between Sarah and Megan dramatizes what Kristeva terms "a primal mapping of the body" as a pre-linguistic learning that builds the foundation for the future. Calling this mapping "semiotic," Kristeva describes an "authority" that "shapes the body into a *territory* having areas, orifices, points and lines, surfaces and hollows, where the archaic power of mastery and neglect, of the differentiation of proper-clean and improper-dirty, possible and impossible is impressed and exerted" (*PH*: 72). This "maternal authority" as the "trustee of that mapping of the self's clean and proper body" operates differently from the "paternal laws" of language acquisition and social authority (*PH*: 72).

In *Pale Rider*, Megan's place by Sarah signifies precisely such a process of mapping the externalization of interior drives and impulses. Together by the window, their bodies, dresses, and faces follow a design of the feminine exhibiting what Kristeva terms "the continuum of the body," not just individually but together between each other as mother and daughter.[12] Megan's body becomes "articulated as an organized discontinuity, exercising a precocious and primary mastery, flexible yet powerful over the erotogenic zones, blended with the preobject, the maternal Thing" (*BS*: 62).

Megan and Sarah act out Kristeva's psychoanalytical theory of the daughter's pre-linguistic, pre-symbolic focus on the mother for directing the chaotic drives of the "semiotic" into an organizational form that ultimately also will deal with the paternal authority of language and symbolization. The "monopolizing" mother as the pre-object of psychic needs and affection invariably leads to an irresolvable conflict between desperate dependence and repulsion of the mother, creating *"impossible mourning for the maternal object"* (*BS*: 9, 78). The body mapping with the maternal expresses a deeply rooted crisis that never quite ends. Kristeva explains that "the body of her mother is always the same Master-Mother of instinctual drive, a ruler over psychosis, a subject of biology" (*DL*: 239). Such mapping highlights Kristeva's work as a persuasive delineation of Eastwood.

In *Pale Rider*, the sensuousness of the movements, colors, and rhythms of the kitchen scene articulates the semiotic power of interior forces and impulses between Sarah and Megan. At the same time, the colors and rhythms of shadow and dark not only flow and interact; they also evoke the internal tensions of authority, position, and power between a single mother and adolescent daughter that will grow more intense and divisive with the emerging prominence of Preacher.

While Kristeva's theorizing brilliantly enlightens the forces that operate and construct meaning for the border states of mind in *Pale Rider*, she becomes especially helpful in connecting this psychology to the borderline between the sexual body and the sacred. Kristeva conjectures a source of religious consciousness and sensibility in the very turmoil of the pre-linguistic semiotic that acquires initial meaning in the mapping of the body with the maternal.

Kristeva's ideas of the intrinsic connection between the divine and the semiotic provide insight into the centrality of the kitchen scene to the interaction of the sacred and the body in the film. Explicitly relating the "sense of the divine or the sacred" to the semiotic rushes of interior drives and impulses that interact with the maternal, she writes, "The semiotic, with its maternal dependencies, seems to me to be the distant horizon to which thought gains access when it tries to think of itself at the borders of physis and being immersed in it" (*IR*: 260). From a Kristevan perspective, *Pale Rider*, especially in the kitchen scene, could be viewed as a dramatic exemplification of her belief that "this new millennium, which seems so eager for religion, is in reality eager for the sacred" (*IR*: 260).

Kristeva jumps several borderline hurdles and states of mind. She goes from the maternal and semiotic to language and symbolization, and from there to the border between the physically human and the search for meaning in the sacred, and then in a sense, she returns to the sacred maternal as the source and basis of it all. She writes, "Seen in this way, as the emergence of meaning, the semiotic seems to me to stir up the metaphysical dichotomies (body/soul, physical/psychical)" (*IR*: 260).

Eastwood cannot go as far as Kristeva at this point in his work on the Western state of mind in *Pale Rider*. He can show the word made flesh when Preacher appears to Sarah and Megan in the window. In portraying Preacher, however, Eastwood has not yet made the leap to love and the maternal as a response to death. Even as a divine figure, Preacher as the Stranger remains, as stated in Revelations, the agent of death to kill death.

At the same time, in *Pale Rider*, the dynamic configuration in the house by the window of Sarah and Megan constitutes a visual statement of the feminine and maternal that fuses psychology and the sacred. Given the religiosity of the scene and the moment with Sarah and Megan, the film insinuates a possible if loose association with Mary and Saint Anne.

As Sarah and Megan leave the window to continue the preparation for dinner, Hull enters. He has just shown Preacher his room and observed Preacher wash for dinner. Preacher thereby repeats the gesture of purification and cleanliness that occurred in *High Plains Drifter*. In the washing scene, Hull noticed the six bullet holes in Preacher's back. The scars clearly suggest signs of stigmata and martyrdom. The holes also symbolize the fragility of the body, as Kristeva argues, as a kind of unsealed, porous container with open boundaries between inner and outer spaces.

When Preacher enters for dinner wearing his priest's collar, the table recognizes the sacredness of the moment, especially as Preacher says grace. As Freud would predict, however, the search for the sacred soon becomes confused and submerged by the desire both Sarah and Megan have for the transcendent father figure.

With Preacher's insertion into the kitchen and the family scene, the pre-verbal semiotic sexual drives and impulses that Megan maps in the context of her mother's bodily and maternal care become mobilized toward him as dictated by her emerging, adolescent sexuality. Sarah becomes for Megan "the two-faced mother" (*PH*: 158) who loves and nurtures but also dominates and controls and even sometimes suffocates with love and discipline. Megan must invest her innate spunk and energy to become "autonomous" as "she disengages from the maternal figure," literally and imaginatively separating herself from her mother's body and control to become what Kristeva terms a "liberated subject."[13]

Thus, in intertwining one story of a young girl's sexual awakening and coming of age with her mother's story of her own revivified sexuality with Preacher, *Pale Rider* complicates the film's impulse toward the sacred. A transcendent and mysterious being like the Stranger in *High Plains Drifter*, Preacher in *Pale Rider* in his role as a divine figure must embody an intersection of worldly linear time and the time of transcendence and the infinite. The other Eastwood Western during this early phase of his directing, *The Outlaw Josey Wales*, avoids this crisis of different temporalities by keeping the story within the realm of conventional linear time and historical narrative. Josey stays content as a heroic figure with very human qualities and vulnerabilities.

In concentrating on Sarah and Megan's amatory feelings toward Preacher, *Pale Rider* demonstrates, as Kristeva says, "this slide from the sacred to sensual pleasure" (*HF:* 73). Megan's latent sexuality becomes manifest when she offers herself to Preacher, arguing that she is almost 15, the age her mother married. Megan, therefore, identifies with and emulates her mother even while trying to supersede her. She blatantly and emotionally expresses her sexual desire for Preacher in terms of her jealousy and competition with her mother. She says that she has seen how they look at each other. In an exchange that fails to mollify Megan's youthful yearning and passion, Preacher declines, offering her platitudes on love and the future that do not explain her feelings to her in a meaningful way. Her hatred changes when Preacher rescues her from being gang-raped by LaHood's son and his thugs, a scene, as in *Sudden Impact*, perhaps designed as an apology for the rape scene in *High Plains Drifter*.

Sarah and Preacher, however, consummate their relationship but in an encounter that diminishes them both. She explains she did not want to deny herself the experience with Preacher but will be reconciled to a life with Hull. As a paternal figure, Preacher's denial of sex with Megan saves them both from violating the incest taboo, but perhaps sex with Sarah is meant to bestow a form of grace upon her for both physical and spiritual fulfillment.

In its presentation of Preacher as a figure of divine paternal transcendence, *Pale Rider* suggests a potential for him as a savior for Sarah and Megan. As such, Preacher would enact an idea Kristeva cites repeatedly from Freud – *"Vater der personlichen Vorzeit"* – the " 'Father in personal prehistory' " or "an Ideal Father, the Imaginary Father in prehistory" or, more specifically, "not as the mother's phallus, but as that ghostly third party to which the mother aspires, as a loving version of the Third Party, a preoedipal father 'who first loved you' (according to the Gospels), a conglomeration of both genders (as Freud suggests). 'God is agape' " (*NMS:* 65, 121, 180).[14]

In *Pale Rider*, Preacher embodies such a personal father outside of ordinary time. Preacher intimates omniscient fatherhood. Propounding the importance of the sacred in human affairs, Michael Butler and Dennis Shryack's screenplay for the film persistently extols values of "conscience," the soul, and spirituality.

Thus, *Pale Rider* dramatizes the Western as a borderline state of mind between bodily desire and spiritual transcendence. Even with the film's tentativeness at times about its own religious and ethical purpose and assumptions, *Pale Rider* demonstrates the challenge to Eastwood of integrating the sexual and the sacred and the body and the spirit into a coherent artistic entity. The film positions Eastwood to advance toward reaching that objective of artistic creativity and intellectual integrity in later phases of his unique achievement as a director.

For Kristeva, omniscient paternity would prove meaningless alone. Kristeva's interpretation of Freud's statement of the "Father in personal pre-history" melds father and mother in a pre-oedipal organization of love that prefigures psychic constructions of language and symbolization. It proposes a psychological basis of a transcendent force outside of ordinary, linear time. She proffers such a time as a transcendent temporality of love and the sacred that emanates from the feminine, the maternal, and the paternal. For Eastwood, the search continues for such a time and condition of ethics, transcendence, and redemption through other films in the three stages of his directing.

On the Road

Eastwood the director and Kristeva the philosopher-psychoanalyst meet on other borders and borderlines than the Western. They cross on points that dramatize and inform each other's body of work. Kristeva on comedy helps explain the importance of Eastwood's two early-stage comedies, *Bronco Billy* and *Honkytonk Man*, to the overall development of his career as a director. For Eastwood, laughter opened the door for him to re-examine basic issues of mind and body that were of concern to him from the beginning of his directing and stayed with him throughout his career. Comedy enabled him to revivify his creative imagination and fulfill his artistic potential. As comedies, *Bronco Billy* and *Honkytonk Man* prove especially useful, therefore, for helping to explain the making of Clint Eastwood into a modern artist of cinema.

Bronco Billy and *Honkytonk Man* can be characterized as variations of the road film sub-genre, movies in which the structure of road travel proves significant, almost as though Eastwood as a director was using the road-journey narrative to externalize and focus his internal journey as a director and a man. In *Bronco Billy* and *Honkytonk Man*, the comedic road film becomes an effective vehicle for his transition toward true artistic achievement as a director. The comedies suggest changes in the construction of the subject, identity, and the relationship to the other. These changes constitute the beginning of a new foundation of meanings upon which Eastwood would continue to work and build with great critical and popular success.

For Kristeva, the heterogeneity of the signifying process generates change. Through ongoing actions of negativity and rejection, the continuing transformation and interaction of semiotic impulses into the symbolic and linguistic engender the potential for overcoming one-dimensional subjectivity and intellectual rigidity. Kristeva's project of dissolving and decentering a subject through the signifying process informs Eastwood's work on subjectivity, including in his comedies.

The original subject of the early Eastwood films resembles Kristeva's "atomistic subject" in Marxist thought.[15] The usual Eastwood character resembles the Cartesian, Kantian subject of independence and autonomy. The early Eastwood hero of the West and of city streets especially typifies this figure of autonomy and independence.

In his comedies, however, Eastwood radically disrupts his general signifying practice and troubles the position and meaning of the autonomous subject. By questioning his usual practice of creating a self-enclosed, autonomous hero in the mold of the classic isolated American, whether on the Western frontier or urban concrete jungle, Eastwood experiments with core values and attitudes about masculinity and identity.

Comedy for Eastwood introduces self-reflection and contradiction into his construction of subjectivity and identity. Laughter intimates the possibility of renewal. Interestingly, the effort to change and renew through the comedic for Eastwood begins in somewhat infantilized and feminized body conditions in *Bronco Billy* and *Honkytonk Man* that enact Kristeva's theory of the comedic interaction between the semiotic home or psychic *chora* and symbolization.

Kristeva sees humor as innate in the pre-linguistic semiotic stages. Humor helps make the separation from the semiotic stage possible. She writes, "A sense of humor seems to
build up, beginning with such semiotic underpinning, both
upon the inhibition of autoeroticism (prescribed by parents)
and upon its removal within childhood situations where
parental authority or its substitute is weakened" (*DL*: 285).
Helping to orchestrate a balance between "the ego as falter-
ing" and the demands of the super-ego, comedy establishes
some distance for inhibition to occur without destroying the
semiotic source of that inhibition.

For Kristeva, the semiotic *chora*, which refers in Greek to
the womb, becomes a kind of comedy theater in which drives
focus around the mother in the process of dealing with the
outer world and its laws. Humor structures the interaction
between the inexpressible semiotic drives and the mother.
She writes, "Those scattered and funny moments become
projected – archaic synthesis – onto the stable support of the
mother's face, the privileged receiver of laughter at about
three months" (*DL*: 283). At this point "the narcissism of
the initial mother–child symbiosis slips toward autoeroticism" so that the body emerges as "parcelled into eroticiza-
ble" parts in a process that precedes and anticipates the
mirror stage from which Lacanian identity and difference
will occur (*DL*: 283).

Accordingly, for Kristeva, humor becomes crucial in the
development of the individual subject from the situation of
the semiotic *chora* to achieving the distinction between the
self/Same as opposed to the Other. She writes:

The imaginary takes over from childhood laughter: it is a
joy without words. . . . During the period of indistinction
between "*same*" and "*other*," infant and mother, as well as
between "subject" and "object" . . . the semiotic *chora* that

arrests and absorbs the motility of the anaclitic facilitations relieves and produces laughter. (DL: 283–4)

Clint Eastwood's humor in his return to childhood, youth, and the vulnerabilities of the body, in *Bronco Billy* and *Honkytonk Man*, enacts the drama of laughter and humor in the semiotic *chora* that Kristeva describes. Like Kristeva, for Eastwood, laughter animates the potential for rethinking the patriarchal intervention of language and authority. Laughter not only energizes the semiotic activity toward maturity. It subverts the symbolic and the law, opening what Kristeva calls a "dialectical" encounter for possible change. Kristeva writes, "There is one inevitable moment in the movement that recognizes the symbolic prohibition and makes it dialectical: *laughter*" (RPL: 222).[16]

Encapsulating in two words much of her complex philosophy and its relationship to both humor and to modern thought and structures, Kristeva writes that in the modern Western world, "laughter dethrones," meaning that it subverts entrenched truths and conventions. Kristeva argues that laughter ensues from "the *arbitrariness of the break establishing meaning*" (DL: 181, 182). For Kristeva, laughter sets forth alternative epistemologies to what we know and how we know it.

Accordingly, humor fuels the effort to fill the infinite gap between drives and meanings.[17] As part of Kristeva's program of inner "intimate revolt," the energy hermeneutic of the open gap draws on the power and imagination of what could be called a humor hermeneutic.

Partly through laughter in *Bronco Billy* and *Honkytonk Man*, Eastwood rethinks the relationship of the vulnerable body to subjectivity. The vulnerability of the body as a center of resistance to a hostile world sparks a reconsideration of the relationship of the individual to others. Laughter in these

films enables a fundamental rethinking of the self's entrapment by its own interior forces of violence and aggression.
Laughter for Eastwood exposes the origins within the self of
the stranger and the foreigner. Laughter turns a light on the
enemy within, the stranger in the self.

Even before *Bronco Billy* and *Honkytonk Man*, Eastwood
experimented with comedy in film. In *Every Which Way But
Loose* (1978), Eastwood shared the screen with a pet orangu-
tan named Clyde in what turned out to be a very popular,
commercially successful comedy. Eastwood went into this
project, which was directed by James Fargo, largely on his
own and in opposition to most of his advisors with the
exception of his lover and frequent co-star during this period
of his life, Sondra Locke. *Every Which Way But Loose* was
widely seen and reviewed as an effort by Eastwood, as
Richard Schickel notes, to "openly send up his image" to
counter the public perception of him as limited as a performer and character to tough-guy roles.[18] Certainly the
comedy worked for Eastwood's purpose of altering his image
with the public.

In contrast, the comedies Eastwood directed and starred
in during his first phase of directing, *Bronco Billy* and *Honkytonk Man*, dramatize interior searches for peace and identity.
Thus, Gene Siskel in the *Chicago Tribune* observed that in
Honkytonk Man, "Eastwood successfully played a character
similar to Red Stovall in *Bronco Billy*, which is my favorite
Eastwood-directed film. Billy, like Red, was a bit of a char-
latan and dreamer, but one never doubted that he existed."[19]
In *Bronco Billy* and *Honkytonk Man*, Eastwood acts and directs
himself as a grown man who regresses psychologically into a
near-infantile state of physical and emotional fantasy and
dependency. Both films dramatize escapes from reality that
could be viewed as defying credibility and verisimilitude but
also seriously suggest the acting out of deeper psychic forces

that involve more than a strategy to advance his career and public image.

Leading film critics such as Siskel tended to see both *Bronco Billy* and *Honkytonk Man* as reasonably successful efforts at Eastwood's image-building. They declared the films acceptable representations of a strong film personality who understandably wanted to change his image and prove his versatility as both an actor and director by working and succeeding in different genres. Eastwood up to the point of these two films gave them scant reason to foresee his ultimate transformation as a director and artist.[20]

In the context of Kristeva's work, the films dramatize the potential through humor for ameliorating and healing psychic division. In *Bronco Billy*, Eastwood plays Billy, who somehow found the means to change from being a shoe salesman in New Jersey to starring in and managing a Wild West road show that consists of a motley group of itinerant, unpredictable, sometimes charmingly eccentric performers. In the film, little ironic distance obtains between Eastwood and Billy. Billy immerses himself in a kind of pre-verbal childhood that eradicates the line between fantasy and reality. As Maslin notes, the film's screenplay describes Billy as "a big kid in a man's body."[21]

In Billy's make-believe world, the circus tent for his show becomes a form of semiotic *chora* that Kristeva postulates, a theater of laughs and the fantastic. Billy goes from his New Jersey shoe store to throwing knives with pinpoint accuracy at women such as Antoinette Lily (Sondra Locke) for the amusement of small rural audiences. As Bronco Billy, he speaks and functions on the level of the very children he entertains. At one point, desperate for money for the show and the performers, Billy leads his gang of misfits in a failed train robbery. The seriousness and intensity of Billy's efforts to execute this robbery of a high-speed modern train emphasizes a separation from reality that challenges the film's credibility.

The rhythms and movements of *Bronco Billy* in the form of Billy's riding and shooting as well as the pulsating sounds of the country music performed by Merle Haggard and Ronnie Milsap present a semiotic alternative to stable, mature conventional adult manhood. Billy prefers the false security and fantasy of his circus tent. Such persistent childishness maintains an element of mirror-stage narcissism in Billy's character. Both the story of his wife's adultery years before with his best friend and his relationship with Antoinette, a spoiled, affected heiress who gets caught up in his world, suggest Billy's cowboy act of targeting women with knives expresses conflicted feelings of childlike dependence and hostility toward women.

While *Bronco Billy* dramatizes the centrality of comedy and laughter to prolonged infantilism, *Honkytonk Man* emphasizes the need to break out of that protective enclosure of the maternal body and *chora*. In *Honkytonk Man*, Eastwood plays Red Stovall, a self-centered, self-indulgent, and irresponsible but charismatic country-and-western songwriter with dreams of success in Nashville as a singer. Red personifies the stereotype of the hard-drinking, womanizing vagabond songster of the road. With the possibility before him of an audition for the Grand Old Opry in Nashville, Red sets out on the road from Texas during early Dust Bowl days, accompanied by his nephew Whit, played by Eastwood's fourteen-year-old son, Kyle, and Grandpa (John McIntire). As Schickel says, the three of them "have many perilous, yet comic, adventures on the road."[22] Marketed on the DVD as part of a "Clint Eastwood Comedy" collection, the film ends sadly with Red dying painfully of tuberculosis without being able to fulfill his dream.

Yet the film corresponds to what David Robinson describes as a comedy film form that Charlie Chaplin pioneered in making from the beginning of his career, "a comedy with a sad end."[23] Like Chaplin and Woody Allen, who often temper energetic comedy with undertones of trauma, Eastwood in *Honkytonk Man* uses the comedy of a picaresque narrative of episodes and misadventures to delineate themes of importance to him involving loss, vulnerability, and death. The protagonist's name of Red obviously signifies the blood that he coughs up painfully from his sick, tubercular body. The spurting blood suggests a form of abject feminization of Red. Indeed, Red often enacts the maternal function in the film in his relationship to Whit. Red's fatal sickness and character flaws insinuate Whit's need to break through the semiotic *chora* of infantile dependence in his connection to Red. Whit must think for himself and initiate the separation that occurs with language and the knowledge of difference.

Thus, the break between Red and Whit that indicates Whit's growth and maturity happens through processes of what Kristeva calls abjection, rejection, and negation. Hence, the role of Whit the nephew in *Honkytonk Man* becomes quite significant in the film. As Whit both emulates and distinguishes himself from Red, he enacts the rupture, as explained by psychoanalysis, from the narcissistic mirror stage. Their relationship exemplifies the paradoxical engagement between the same and the other.

In a brilliant touch, Red undergoes a process of physical and spiritual purification that supports and parallels Whit's experience of initiation. As Siskel smartly notes, "The trip turns out to be as much of a rites-of-initiation journey for Whit as it is a purification ritual for Uncle Red."[24] This double journey involves a version of horror that enacts the signification and dissipation of the body in its relationship to the self and others. Red's sick body steadily deteriorates during his journey as Whit grows stronger. Through such changes, Red and Whit enact a form of split subjectivity that proffers the possibility of the new.

While Red's bloody ritual of purification dramatizes the horrors of loss and death, his bodily condition also accentuates the significance of the life processes of transition as Whit enters into manhood. Through various humorous episodes, Whit learns about life, independence, courage, sex, and women, ultimately going off with a young woman, Marlene (Alexa Kenin), in a culminating act of separation and maturation after Red dies. Yet Whit and Red remain part of each other even with Red's death, as Whit's words echo the kinds of ambitions and plans he learned from his uncle, his alter self.

Thus, humor facilitates the new by mockingly subverting the same. Laughter becomes part of the process for discarding the old to create the new. Red's death opens the possibility for Whit to achieve his own identity and subjectivity. The presence and disappearance of Grandpa, who ultimately goes off on his own, sustain the film's drama of life's changes. The generational relationship of the three males conveys the significance of time in the narrative of self, identity, and change. Gaining his own mind, language, and time in his break from the past, Whit goes forward on the open road.

On psychological and philosophical levels, the humor of *Bronco Billy* and *Honkytonk Man* energizes journey narratives for exploring the possibility of constructing an identity and subjectivity with another meaning than detached autonomy. Just as Eastwood had hoped, the comedies helped him redesign his image and refocus his career. Such creative venturing into new art forms, however, involved deeper and more significant changes than even he may have fully appreciated. Like the character Whit as played by his son Kyle, Eastwood was moving toward a new future with renewed creative power. The interior psychological journeys in both films required a confrontation with forces of the body, love, hate, and renewal that opened the possibility for a greater, freer expression in later films of lasting artistic and cultural significance.

"Black Hole": Love, the Feminine, and the Other

In her discussion of the state of mind and condition of a female client named "Isabel," Kristeva uses the image and metaphor of "*a black hole*" to connote feminine depression, melancholia, and "living motherhood." She writes, "A nothingness that is neither repression nor simply the mark of the affect but condenses into *a black hole* – like invisible, crushing, cosmic antimatter – the sensory, sexual, fantasy-provoking ill-being of abandonments and disappointments." Kristeva goes on to describe a psychic state of mental and physical mutilation. She writes, "Narcissistic wounds and castration, sexual dissatisfaction and fantasy-laden dead-ends become telescoped into a simultaneously killing and irretrievable burden that organizes her subjectivity; within, she is nothing but bruises and paralysis; outside, all that was left to her was acting out or sham activism" (*BS*: 87–8).

In the concluding sequence of shots in Eastwood's *Play Misty for Me*, the camera moves in slowly upon a bedroom doorway. The camera freezes on the absolute pitch blackness framed by the door. The shot intimates a threshold to utter nothingness, danger, and despair. Not technically or artistically very exciting in itself, the shot still stands as a crucial psychological and aesthetic moment for Eastwood. It becomes Eastwood's "black hole" of the feminine, a Pandora's box that has been a key source of energy, danger, and imagination in his work as a director ever since. For Kristeva and Eastwood, the threshold into the darkness of the feminine constitutes the mother of all borderlines and border states of mind. For Eastwood this shot also signals the exploration of the feminine in the male.

Eastwood's mistakes in this first film as a director made him the object of criticism by reviewers and scholars such as Paul Smith.[25] The film revolves around Dave Garland (Eastwood), a very cool late-night disc jockey at a jazz radio station in Eastwood's home base of Carmel (radio station KRML) and Monterey. Dave becomes the deadly obsession of a fan, Evelyn Draper (Jessica Walter), who tries to take over his life after a one-night stand that she instigates. Behind the darkened doorway toward the film's conclusion, Evelyn captures and wants to kill Dave's girlfriend, Tobie Williams (Donna Mills), and then Dave after already killing a detective, Sergeant McCallum (John Larch), and wounding Dave's friend and cleaning woman, Birdie (Clarice Taylor). As a character, Dave gets compared to Eastwood's role as John McBurney in *The Beguiled* (1971) that was directed by Eastwood's mentor Don Siegel, who plays a bartender (Murphy) in *Play Misty for Me* to support Eastwood in this film. The film provides something of a model for the far more commercially successful *Fatal Attraction* (1987).

It has been noted that Eastwood mistakenly obsesses in *Play Misty for Me* on beautiful but excessively long shots of the northern California coast; overly romanticized and lengthy love scenes with Tobie; an ill-fitting documentary-style shooting of the Monterey Jazz Festival that he admired and supported as a music and event fan; and a song he used to establish the feeling and mood for the film, Roberta Flack's rendition of Ewan MacColl's "The First Time Ever I Saw Your Face." With the benefit of consistently beautiful weather, he shot the film in sequence. The end product includes other filming, editing, and continuity mistakes that critics cite.

While making one flawed film in the order of the events of the plot, Eastwood also was shooting what can be viewed and interpreted in retrospect as an interior film with, in Kristeva's phrase, an "internal vision" (*IR*: 46). Vivid visual images, pulsating musical rhythms, and eerie sounds of the great white caps of the Pacific pounding the rough and rocky coast relate the story and feeling of the interior film. The inner film intimates the complexity of feminine spaces, both the infinity of interior darkness and the pleasure and joy of endless external light and renewal. The inner film of images and sounds resonates with the semiotic and choratic rhythms of the feminine.

Play Misty for Me projects meanings of sexuality, mother-hood, and the female body in one of its opening scenes after a long sequence of Dave driving his convertible Jaguar along the coast. When he arrives at the radio station another disc jockey, Al Monte (James McEachin), men-tions a woman, Madge (Irene Hervey), who has been helping Dave to develop his career and "pull it all toge-ther." When Al Monte teases him about the woman, Dave calls her a "grandmother," emphasizing her maternal power to describe their relationship.

Beginning his broadcast, Dave recites from Kenneth Patchen's poem "O Fiery River" as a lead into his music for the evening. Lines from the entire poem ask, "What has made these men sick rats/That they find out every cheap hole?" These lines and the lines Dave recites readily resonate with Kristeva's imagery of the depth, power, and crisis of the feminine in relation to the corrupting influences of the male. Dave reads, "Men have destroyed the roads of wonder,/ And their cities squat like black toads/ In the orchards of life./ Nothing is clean, or real, or as a girl,/ Naked to love, or to be a man with."[26] Patchen's poem, therefore, also speaks to the concern in *Play Misty for Me* and Eastwood's other films for making the connection of the feminine to the search for cleanliness, purity, and the sacred. Such a connection opens a path for a love that turns the physical into a meaningful practice of both the body and soul.

So when Patchen discusses "the roads of wonder" that have been destroyed by the violence and wastefulness of men, he also addresses a central theme of Eastwood's work. The search for "wonder" as the desire for the sacred that occurs in the early Westerns starts here in the darkness of the feminine in *Play Misty for Me*.[27]

Also interesting, Patchen as a poet noted for the surreal and for Dadaistic influences wrote a form of visual poetry, very much like the kind of film art Eastwood at times would strive to achieve throughout his career, including in *Play Misty for Me*. Eastwood reportedly sacrificed his actor's fee to get the backing of Universal to direct *Play Misty for Me*, tangible and material proof of the depth of his seriousness about directing. His commitment to film as an art form becomes apparent in studying the interior, psychological film of *Play Misty for Me*. Rather than relying solely upon denotative referentiality and conventional plot and character development, he also works to create an interior psychological film of visual images and audial resonances.

In *Play Misty for Me*, the semiotics of an interior film that vibrates to Errol Garner's "Misty" and Flack's singing enacts on a level of emotional immediacy the psychoanalytical and philosophical issues of the dark infinity of the feminine. The inner, psychological film in *Play Misty for Me* struggles to integrate the semiotic and the symbolic in the construction of both male and female subjectivity through the exploration of the feminine.

Eastwood begins his serious directing career in *Play Misty for Me* with a hero who embarks on a road that differs from his early signature examples of male hegemony and aggression, such as the Stranger and Preacher in his Westerns, or as "Dirty Harry" in his development of that city character in *Sudden Impact* (1983).

Play Misty for Me propounds and propels the challenge to Eastwood of transforming the energy of the semiotic into a symbolic system of love, the sacred, and belief. As Kristeva says, "What appears on the psychological level as omnipotence *is the power of semiotic rhythms, which convey an intense presence of meaning in a presubject still incapable of signification*" (*BS*: 62). The black hole image of the darkened threshold signifies the process in *Play Misty for Me* of what proves to be a psychologically dangerous and life-threatening effort to balance the semiotic and symbolic through the engagement with the feminine. The images and sounds of Eastwood's pre-symbolic semiotics must convert to the symbolization of language, sexual difference, and the ethical relationship to the other.

The melodramatic plot of *Play Misty for Me* concludes with the violent resolution of Dave's relationships with Evelyn and Tobie. Toward the end of the film, Evelyn fakes her identity and enters into Tobie's home as a new roommate, subsequently assaulting and binding Tobie and taping her mouth, leaving her hostage in the bedroom. In another use of poetry in the film, Dave figures out clues about the situation that Evelyn has given him, based on Edgar Allan Poe's "Annabel Lee," and races to the house to save Tobie. At the house, Dave overcomes a bloody assault by a scissor-wielding Evelyn, hitting her across the face so hard that she crashes through glass windows to her death on the rocky ocean front below.

On the near side of the darkened doorway, a severely bloodied and wounded Dave drags himself to the bedroom to see if he arrived in time to rescue Tobie. He emerges with her from the darkened bedroom and door. The blood and

wounds that cover Dave's injured body signify the sacrifice
of the body to the processes of language and maturity. They
indicate a new negotiation with the darkness of the feminine
in acquiring identity and the self. The body sacrifices the
security of immersion in the feminine for a measure of
painful, mature detachment.

Evelyn's combination of infantilism and adolescent rage
enacts an aspect of the depression of the black hole of the
feminine that Kristeva describes. The list of Evelyn's infantile
actions reads like a case study in mental illness: rages and
violent outbursts; attention-getting games like taking Dave's
car keys; utter dependence on Dave in spite of his insistent
denial of an emotional commitment to her; disturbing verbal
repetitions of words, phrases, and vulgarities; reversion to
childish behavior with a Snoopy doll; jealously intruding on
Dave's business lunch; and drawing an unwelcome lipstick
heart with both of their initials in it on his mirror. Evelyn's
sexual masochism grows more aggressive with Dave's rejection of her. She exhibits a needy, demeaning eagerness to
return to him for sexual "seconds" that intensifies with his
resistance. In one scene, she arrives unannounced at his place
naked beneath her coat. Such behavior demonstrates a kind
of nymphomania that numbs the body to satisfy unappeasa-
ble psychological needs.

Evelyn's condition and her relationship to Dave suggest a
fantasy belief that Kristeva describes as "an imagined partner"
with the false power of giving freedom from the melancholia
of interior feminine space. Evelyn's feminine depression and
melancholia worsens to the point of psychopathic violence.
Jessica Walter's provocative performance of Evelyn's feminine narcissism and depression establishes a pattern for
Evelyn that leads to violence and relates to Dave's character.
Evelyn also functions in the film as a metonymical extension
of Dave's narcissistic personality. Much of the film's story

becomes Dave's reconsideration of his narcissistic behavior and his rethinking of masculine subjectivity in his exploration of the feminine in the light of Evelyn's example.

Dave's first meeting with Evelyn at Murphy's Bar immediately establishes an important connection between them that relates to the "narcissistic wound" for each of them that, according to Kristeva, institutes subjectivity and signification. As Kristeva explains, "evocations of narcissistic wounds" identify "subjects who are constituted by a narcissistic wound" (*NMS*: 121). The bar scene situates that narcissistic wound for both of them in terms of interior feminine space.

Eastwood visually constructs and dramatizes feminine space as the context for the wound of absence and lack that inflicts such damage to narcissistic self-content. In the scene and shot at Murphy's Bar, Eastwood positions Evelyn visually between Dave and Murphy in a kind of deep hole in the background at the end of the bar. She literally appears seated in such an interior space formed by the shot of the men who talk and play a game together in the foreground at one end of the bar, while Evelyn drapes herself on her seat at the other end. The shot accentuates the feminine space with the exposure of her legs. The composition, too, clearly suggests interior sexual feminine space. The outsider, she slowly, tentatively walks down the bar to the men.

As Dave and Evelyn sit together at the bar, the camera makes a crucial but subtle point that Eastwood insinuates about them. Dave and Evelyn look alike. Their haircuts, coloring, and even the structure of their faces as the camera covers the two of them intimate profound similarity. The cut of Dave's hair, its length, style, and wave form a kind of shag that replicates Evelyn's own look. The look feminizes Dave. The cut for both Dave and Evelyn suggests the physical manifestation of the narcissistic wound, as Kristeva describes it, to both the ego and body that instigates subjectivity.

Haircuts, coloring, and facial structure create a similarity between Eastwood as Dave Garland and Jessica Walter as Evelyn Draper in Play Misty for Me. *(Play Misty for Me, 1971, Universal Pictures, The Malpaso Company, dir. Clint Eastwood.)*

Interestingly, a visual similarity also occurs between Tobie and Dave. With a rounder, softer facial structure, Tobie's shag of a hairstyle and cut again mirrors Dave's look. Significantly, in the concluding scenes of the film, Evelyn ties up Tobie and threatens her with her scissors, asking if Dave loves her hair and if he runs his fingers through her hair. Threatening her eyes as well, Evelyn snips at Tobie's hair so that Dave will find her ugly.

Thus, Eastwood indicates the cutting of hair as a narcissistic wound that connects Dave to both women. Looking like both women, Dave explores his own being through the feminine. Interestingly, in one earlier visual sequence when Dave and Tobie go off together to a hillside meadow by the woods, the camera shoots them in profile, facing each other in a kind of diptych composition that emphasizes the similarity of their faces as though they are related. The camera then zooms in on Evelyn's face as she spies upon them from her hiding place in the woods. The intrusion of Evelyn's distant face into the scene between Dave and Tobie indicates how Dave operates and moves through the feminine between both women, looking like each of them. Even in the distance, Evelyn's face cuts between them. Dave finds himself living between and manipulated by the visions and gazes of two women who replicate him in facial appearance, one a psychotic killer and the other a romantic artist.

Dave's face becomes fetishized. Camera close-ups continue eroticizing Dave's face, ultimately leading to Evelyn's vicious, tearing attack on a portrait Tobie made of him. The scissors attack manifests what had been latent in much of the film, the dread, denial, and disavowal of castration and emasculation. The slashing scissors attack symbolically climaxes the assault on Dave's sexuality.

An object of distorted affection, the fetishized face dehumanizes Dave and the women. It gives an ironic twist to Flack's song, "The First Time Ever I Saw Your Face." The fetishized face signifies misdirected love and subjectivity. Wounding and abjection must occur to break the sameness of the narcissism of the fetishized feminized face.

In their shared wounding and struggle for subjectivity, Dave and Evelyn also signify the processes of negation and disavowal, of *Verneinung* and *Verleugnung*, which Kristeva develops from Freud. Negation and disavowal characterize Dave's escape from relationships and responsibility and Evelyn's refusal to face reality. Kristeva writes, "*Negation* will be understood as the intellectual process that leads the repressed to representation on the condition of denying it and, on that account, shares in the signifiers advent. According to Freud, *denial* or *disavowal* (*Verleugnung*) refers to the psychic reality he deemed to be within the realm of perception" (*BS*: 44). Such denial defines Evelyn's behavior from the beginning with Dave, while his "splitting in the subject" (*BS*: 44), which occurs as his negation of intimacy, also characterizes Dave's actions in relating to both Evelyn and Tobie. Tobie broke off her relationship with Dave before the action of *Play Misty for Me* because of his persistent unfaithfulness.

Indeed, the motivating impulse behind Dave's story centers on his expressed desire to Tobie to be better, so to speak, to forgo the self-indulgence of impulsive recreational sex for more meaningful relationships. The story begins with his wish to renew his connection to Tobie in a more serious and committed way. To an extent, his immediate failure to evidence significant concern for Evelyn helps explain her anger toward him in spite of her denials about expectations or "strings" to keep them together. As Cornell notes, Dave fails "to read the signs of her anguish, of her growing desperation – a failure premised on his inability to understand what it might mean for a woman to take on a sexual relationship with a man."[28]

Dave's effort to heal the split within his own psyche by achieving a mature masculinity develops through further exploration of the feminine in his relationship with both Tobie and Evelyn. Through Tobie, he endeavors to improve, to effect a process of eroticization of the body that allows for the synthesis of the semiotic and symbolic, a process that in turn will engender a situation of love and healing. In a sense, Eastwood incorporates within the body of Dave what Kelly Oliver terms the "double-binding" of the feminine in the need to maintain the maternal and feminine while also establishing subjectivity, language, and signification.[29] Trapped in her own darkness, Evelyn can never achieve, as Kristeva says, "the speaking being as separated by sex and language" (*PH*: 83), while Dave seeks such maturity in his renewed commitment and connection to Tobie.

In an extensive love scene between Dave and Tobie, Eastwood suggests the possibility of moving through narcissism to a mutually loving relationship. In a long shot, Dave and Tobie at first still somewhat resemble each other. The long shots and medium shots and closer shots show them making love in a deep stream with a waterfall, in the Pacific forest in proximity to the ocean. Their bodies are immersed in water, once again indicating the importance of cleansing and purification as part of the sacred and love to Eastwood. The ambiance of the forest and water associates their love with nature and the forces of birth and renewal as they also make love on the forest floor. In this scene, Roberta Flack's song accentuates the rhythms of the semiotic in their lovemaking. The music works with the timing of the visual sensuousness of the overlapping images and shots of the love scene. To Eastwood, such music becomes more than an ancillary audial enhancement to a scene but crucial to its fulfillment. Eastwood's appreciation for music and jazz subsequently impelled him to make and direct *Bird*, his well-received film about Charlie Parker, an interest that probably accounts for the housekeeper's name in *Play Misty for Me*, Birdie. Although too slow and too long, the love scene still makes Eastwood's point about finding a spiritual and sexual love.

The love scene between Dave and Tobie parallels the story of Dave and Evelyn as contrasting explorations of love, the body, and the feminine. The contrast between Dave's relationships with Evelyn and Tobie dramatizes what Kristeva explains as two different kinds of jouissance or feminine pleasure and fulfillment. She writes:

> Two forms of jouissance thus seem possible for a woman. On the one hand there is phallic jouissance – competing or identifying with the partner's symbolic power – which mobilizes the clitoris. On the other hand, there is an *other jouissance* that fantasy imagines and carries out by aiming more deeply at psychic space, and the space of the body as well. (*BS*: 78)

For Kristeva, the distinction between kinds of jouissance involves seeking the possibility of recognizing the near "sacred value" of jouissance for achieving "a new life." She writes that "if men and women endow the *other jouissance* with nearly sacred value, it is perhaps because it is the language of the female body that has temporarily triumphed over depression" (*BS*: 78, 79).

For Eastwood as a director, the question of such "sacred value" and love through and with the feminine begins then with his first directing effort, *Play Misty for Me*. For Kristeva, such love demands the courage of "a face-to-face confrontation with the abject" (*PH:* 209), the kind of confrontation that Dave experiences with Evelyn and Tobie. Kristeva here approaches the Levinasian focus on the face of the other as the source of the human and the ethical. Thus, *Play Misty for Me* ultimately implies a profound significance to Roberta Flack's song and celebration of the face as the sign of love and meaning.

One meaningful close-up of the fetishized Eastwood face suggests a movement of the face in the direction of the other. It occurs after Dave has been forced to stay at home and miss a crucial evening with Tobie in order to care for and watch over the sick Evelyn who has sliced her wrists in his bathroom. As Evelyn sleeps, the camera closes in on Dave's tortured face in the dark interior of his house. His face becomes barely visible in the dim light and dark shadows, a dark scene that evidences Eastwood's developing film-making style of darkness and shadow.

The face suggests not only Dave's fear and desperation over his situation of being entrapped by Evelyn but also a new awareness of the human and the costs of the responsibility for the other, even the sickest and most deadly of others. Eastwood as director and actor manages to convey both expressions at once, responsibility and hatred. The look in

Dave's eyes, the tension of his facial muscles, the shadowy darkness, and the movement of the camera impressively dramatize interior ethical and emotional conflict between the narcissism of the same, and the responsibility for difference and the other.

The two faces of Eastwood in the close-up, the face of rage over lost independence and the face of passive awareness of responsibility to the other, will recur in conflict and engagement in other Eastwood films. The two faces visually dramatize the ethical conflict that helps to define the meaning of his films. One face reaches for transcendence and redemption; the other sees and lives for the immanent moment.

Significantly, the two faces suggest a division in attitudes toward masculinity that Eastwood explores by proposing that mature masculinity eschews macho overcompensation for recognition of the feminine in the self. Thus, in his first film, Eastwood proffers a challenge to what has become perhaps the greatest stereotype about him, that of masculine insensitivity and aggression toward the feminine.

2

UNFORGIVEN: THE SEARCH

FOR REDEMPTION

On Death and Transcendence

Emmanuel Levinas concludes one of his introductory lec-
tures and notes with an especially acerbic and pungent statement. He says, "We encounter death in the face of the other."[1]
Characteristically both profound and ambiguous, Levinas
encapsulates in this brief sentence the interconnections in his
philosophy of death, love, and the self in the context of his
transformative ethics of the inescapable responsibility for the
other. Developing the ancient insight from Epicurus that " 'If
you are there, then death is not there; if it is there, you are
not there,' " Levinas maintains that the face of the other
teaches us about the meaning of death and the possibility of
redemption through love (*GDT*: 19). Citing another ancient
source in the Hebrew Bible's "Song of Songs," Levinas says
"we come back to the love 'as strong as death.' " He says, "It
is not a matter of a force that could repel the death inscribed
in my being" (*GDT*: 105).

For Levinas, the ineluctable challenge to come to terms with death compels appreciating the power of love for embodying the subject's infinite potential of regeneration through love of the other. Challenging what he sees as Heidegger's thinking of "time on the basis of death" (*GDT*: 106), Levinas writes, "Time is not the limitation of being but its relationship with infinity. Death is not annihilation but the question that is necessary for this relationship with infinity, or time, to be produced" (*GDT*: 19).

For Levinas, then, love overcomes death for the subject by animating and structuring a rethinking of the relationship of time and the infinite to death. He asserts that "death is powerless over the finite life that receives a meaning from an infinite responsibility for the other." He says, "It is here, in ethics, that there is an appeal to the uniqueness of the subject, and a bestowal of meaning to life, despite death."[2]

Levinas's words could provide an interesting and provocative if complex preface to Clint Eastwood's masterpiece, *Unforgiven*. In *Unforgiven*, Eastwood's hero undergoes an extended search for moral and ethical meaning that transpires over different time periods. The search begins with questions and ends with more questions. As such, the position of this searcher in *Unforgiven* contrasts with the certitude and moral supremacy of the Stranger-Preacher-Killer of Eastwood's earlier Westerns. On a quest from the beginning for a meaning to his existence and his place in the world, the Eastwood hero in *Unforgiven* wants to fulfill his responsibility for those he loves. He detours on his journey of redemption, finding himself fighting death with more death. To protect those in his care, he propels and energizes forces of physical and emotional repression that feed the very evils and dangers he most fears. A possible paradigm for America today, the fortress of his body engages in a prolonged war with itself until it unleashes death on all he sees.

In *Unforgiven*, Eastwood films a story of death and defecation. He proffers a disturbing religious and psychoanalytical portrait of life as "shit" and money as the epitomization of death in life. In his search and struggle for a meaningful and understandable redemption, the hero of *Unforgiven* becomes death itself.

Eastwood's face at the beginning of *Unforgiven* immediately dramatizes a change from the imperial persona of previous films to a portrait of a man in crisis. Lines, crevices, and signs of wear, including thinning hair and a small circle of baldness, inscribe a painful past and an eventful history, but also an uncertain future.

Eastwood's face in *Unforgiven* resonates with Levinas's words of the construction of the subject in relation to death. Not just biological aging but a kind of existential death as in alienation and estrangement from the self and others occurs on this hero's face in *Unforgiven*.

Death, however, hints its presence in Eastwood's face in *Unforgiven* as the opening to the possibility of the infinite. From a Levinasian perspective, therefore, the encounter with death in Eastwood's face in *Unforgiven* also suggests the engagement with the infinity of hope and love, what Levinas frequently intimates as the ineffable and unspeakable. For Levinas, "the face is meaning of the beyond." He says the "uniqueness of self" becomes possible because of "the epiphany of the face."[3]

Eastwood achieves such an epiphany in *Unforgiven*. The film suggests the power of the flesh and the body to welcome the infinite and the transcendent in the encounter with death and the responsibility for the other. He also envisions the death of love in the death of the body. The struggle between life and death, love and murder, plays out on Eastwood's face and body and resonates in the performances of the stellar cast.

The Feminine Frame

Unforgiven opens and closes with the story of Claudia Feathers, the deceased wife of William Munny (Eastwood). Once a notorious killer and thief, Munny now struggles in poverty to support his young son and daughter on his pig farm on the Kansas plains. Claudia's story frames the film. The sunset, which occurs, as Edward Buscombe notes, at the very beginning and the end of the film, signifies Claudia's influence on Will as a dark force that encloses him under her influence even from the grave.[4] Claudia's frame story that constructs an enclosure for *Unforgiven* replicates on the narrative level the psychological encirclement of the feminine in the film. The entire film occurs within the confines of this feminine-maternal space and feminine frame of reference. Even as the complex stories in *Unforgiven* develop and unravel through time and different locations, the overall feminine enclosure or consciousness of the wife's story remains. The feminine narrative works, in Kristeva's phrase for the female body, as "the maternal container" for the film.[5]

Moreover, the instigating event and action of *Unforgiven* of the facial slashing of a prostitute named Delilah Fitzgerald (Anna Thomson) reinforces the focus on the feminine body and space in the film. The film expands the feminine "container" to Delilah and the other prostitutes who work with her in Big Whiskey, Wyoming, miles away from the site by Munny's pig farm in Kansas where he digs his wife's grave in the film's opening image. Significantly, the film links violence to sexuality as a basis for the relationship between men and women. The film makes this sexual and psychological encounter part of a search for ethical meaning. The reputed anti-violence message of the film, as discussed by scholars and maintained by two of its stars, Gene Hackman and Morgan Freeman, follows the questions raised in other Eastwood films about the relation of the body and violence to the feminine and maternal.[6] The film problematizes its putative anti-violence arguments by suggesting the source of violence as rooted deeply in the psyche and intertwined with the most basic of impulses in the relation to parents, instincts, and sexuality. This immediate linkage in the film of violence and sexuality and the aggression of men toward women emphasizes the complexity in *Unforgiven* of the construction of ethical subjectivity. It also suggests the complexity of Will Munny's ethical endeavor.

The violence against the prostitute Delilah turns Munny's journey into a moral mission to compensate for the wrong done not only to the woman known as the "cut-face whore," but also for the other prostitutes who are mistreated and demeaned by men in the film. The opening sequence of events and meanings of *Unforgiven* establishes the ethical imperative of the film. It presents the challenge to articulate, as John Belton says, "a larger moral economy," one that no doubt begins by ending the treatment of women as animals and slaves.[7]

Thus, the journey of Will Munny involves not just the external challenges of danger and violence, but also an internal quest through the relationship to the feminine that structures the self in engaging the psychological and ethical challenges that come with the attempt to be human, to create a meaningful identity and subjectivity.

Unforgiven makes clear that Munny has been invested from the beginning in trying to rebuild his identity, to reform, and to find himself primarily by adhering to the harsh punitive ethical and moral expectations of his deceased wife. The cutting of the face of a prostitute by an angry cowboy that results in Munny's journey of retribution and justice to

Wyoming in some ways enacts the tensions of Munny's own ambivalence toward the suffocating encirclement he feels about the feminine force of Claudia.

Opening Scenes: A New Artistic Sensibility

Buscombe maintains that, in *Unforgiven*, Eastwood "brings to the composition of the visual image his own highly distinctive style."[8] It could be argued that Eastwood actually finds "his own highly distinctive style" in *Unforgiven*. The timing, pacing, organization, and structuring of the opening scenes and sequences in *Unforgiven* immediately propose a new beginning in intellectual complexity and film art for Eastwood. *Unforgiven*'s complex construction of images, shots, and frames supports the new complexity of thought in the film. The compressed depth of detail in the opening scenes establishes a basis and momentum that the film sustains.

In the new stylized art of *Unforgiven*, Eastwood guides and suggests meaning. Instead of largely concentrating in his directing on a rigid continuity of actions and events that emphasize close adherence to causal connections in plot, character, and theme, the new Eastwood relies more on building associations of images and juxtapositions with parallel editing and thought-provoking transitions. He puts new concentration and thinking into each frame and image as a work of multidimensional art, creating a rhythm of meanings in his jumps or moves to new frames, images, and scenes.

A suggestive but inconclusive crawl of letters accompanies the establishing shot that opens *Unforgiven* of a man in the distance digging under a lone tree as a bright sun fades over the horizon. It reads:

She was a comely young woman and not without prospects. Therefore it was heartbreaking to her mother that she would enter into marriage with William Munny, a known thief and murderer, a man of notoriously vicious and intemperate disposition. When she died, it was not at his hands as her mother might have expected, but of smallpox. That was 1878.

The soft, sorrowful tones on the guitar of the original Lennie Niehaus musical score accentuate the somber mood of loss and burial.

The simplicity and sobriety of this opening image of *Unforgiven* clashes with an unanticipated change to another establishing shot of loud thunder and storm clouds gathering over beautiful distant mountaintops. Writing on the screen reports Big Whiskey, Wyoming, 1880, although the film setting was Alberta, Canada. The brightness of the Western scene then dissolves into a thunderous night scene of torrential rain engulfing the streets of Big Whiskey as the camera shows a lamp lighting up a sign for Billiards Upstairs, meaning the whorehouse at Greely's Beer Garden.

The quick scenes that follow show the interruption of vigorous sexual action between a cowboy, Davey Bunting (Rob Campbell), and Strawberry Alice (Frances Fisher), the whorehouse madame, by screams from a neighboring room from Delilah Fitzgerald, who cries, "Please, no," and the shouts of an enraged cowboy customer, Quick Mike (David Mucci), "Damn it! Brand you like a damn steer, bitch!" The inexperienced Delilah, the cut-face whore, has enraged Mike by laughing at the size of his penis. Mike slashes viciously at her bleeding face with a long barlow knife, not stopping even as Delilah hurls the contents of a chamber pot at him and Alice struggles with him from behind.

Shots from behind Mike reveal Delilah's horribly bloodied face in sudden light and a reverse shot from her point of view shows the ugly rage and anger on Mike's face. Then the sound of the cocking of a gun pointed to Mike's head freezes the violence. Skinny Dubois (Anthony James), the owner of Greeley's, holds the gun to Mike's head and says, "Get offa her, cowboy."

The special importance of the opening scenes and sequences of *Unforgiven* comes from the deliberation East- wood put into them. The depth, detail, and careful composi- tion of the scenes saturate the screen with significance. A careful use of lighting, positioning, and spacing articulates relationships and meanings as much as verbal expression. Multiple perspectives articulate a complexity of ethical con- nections. Even the care with which Eastwood shoots Alice as she races from her room behind Davey down a hallway toward Delilah entails a form of narrative positioning and ethical articulation. She instinctively switches from horizon- tal labors to maternal urgency and care.

Thus, with the arrival from the rain-soaked street of the sheriff, Little Bill Daggett (Gene Hackman), and his deputy, Clyde Ledbetter (Ron White), Eastwood sets up a powerful visual tension between the men and the women. Little Bill finds the room with several stunned and horrified women in it, all trying to nurse the severely cut-up and bleeding Delilah. From the door, in the now well-lit room, the women become a composite of separate but united figures, a pathetic sister- hood of abused and violated women of different ages and types.

The subtle, understated use and work of Hackman in the opening moments of the film beautifully offset the intensity of the women and the horrible act of cutting the prostitute. He stands as a center of stability in contrast to the despair of the assembled women and the chaos and pandemonium that brought him there.

Hackman's presence in the hallway and at the door, observ- ing the girls, transforms the moment into his time and place.

The power Hackman emanates comes in part from the authority of his physical presence and bearing, but also from its opposite, his detachment, his lack of commitment, the ethically fatal flaw, as Levinas would say, of "indifference" to the other. He sees the women as objects, products, commodities, damaged goods. One of them simply has gone from damaged to ruined. He has never seen Delilah's face in the Levinasian sense of her vulnerability and humanity, but only as an item in a human package that has now been defaced, so to speak. He will need to assess the amount of damage and how to deal with it as the ultimate authority in the situation. The high-angle shot from behind Daggett into the room establishes Daggett in a privileged station that creates and maintains a boundary of legal and personal authority for him. Daggett casually asks, "She's gonna die, huh?" And Alice answers bitterly while attending to her, "She's gonna live."

The shot from Daggett's perspective in the doorway entails a visual narrative in itself that testifies further to the detail, precision, and care of the artistry and content of Eastwood's filming. The shot from over Daggett's shoulder literally re-enacts male entry into female space. Eastwood creates a circular opening of space over his shoulder into the room. The women, including Alice and Delilah, are framed within this iris-like circle that clearly insinuates entry into the female body. In the middle of the small group of women and toward the bottom of the iris that also takes the shape of a keyhole rests a basin of blood from Delilah's cut-up face, the blood and the basin once again signifying the female body and its abuse.

The verbal exchange between Little Bill Daggett and Alice centers on Quick Mike's thrusting penis or, more precisely, the lack of it. She says, "She didn't touch his poke. . . . All she done was . . . when she seen he had a teensy little pecker . . . she gave a giggle. That's all. She didn't know no better."

The camera then replicates the sexual act by zooming in and out between Alice and the other women and Daggett in the doorway.

Among the prostitutes, fifteen-year-old Little Sue (Tara Frederick) stares questioningly at Little Bill with the particularly cold ferocity of angry adolescents, demanding some form of justice that she cannot describe or even imagine. Alice says, "You can hang him, Little Bill." Alice's lips suggest just a smirk and touch of pleasure at the thought of such a punishment. The other women stare in silent, closed-mouth pain at Little Bill.

Without assertive facial expression, Hackman brilliantly manages to indicate more than a combination of disdain and disgust; he also conveys dismissal and condescension. Hackman's face and eyes literally evoke the abjection of the feminine space and position that Kristeva discusses. His attitude and actions dramatize hatred and fear of the feminine and female space. As Little Bill walks off, an outraged Alice follows him.

Hackman's actions, demeanor, and voice in the following scene solidify Little Bill's position of privileged authority and power as a form of patriarchal law-giver and sovereign over this little frontier domain. Eastwood cuts to a setting that sustains Bill's power and authority. The camera pulls back to what has become a makeshift primitive court. Bill descends the stairs from the rooms above the bar. Mike and Davey have been tied together back-to-back around a pole, Davey naked and Mike in his leggings, both men terrified. Their distance from the stove indicates that they shiver from fear and the cold.

As Bill prepares to punish the cowboys with a whipping, Skinny holds up a document and says, "This here's a lawful contract . . . betwixt me an' Delilah Fitzgerald, the cut-whore. Now I brung her clear from Boston, paid her expenses an' all, an' I got a contract which represents an investment of capital."

The discussion between Bill and Skinny takes away any remnant of Delilah's humanity and dignity. Her only value comes from her body and her sexuality. Bill says, "Property," and Skinny confirms, "Damaged Property. Like if I was to hamstring one of the cow ponies." Little Bill says with callous insouciance, "You figure nobody'll want to fuck her."

Skinny's words put a thought in Bill's head that constitutes the greatest insult. He decides to forgo the whipping and just penalize the boys by making them give up five ponies in the spring, three from Mike who "done the cutting" and two from Davey who held her. The ponies go to Skinny as restitution for the damage done to his property. When Alice, who has been observing this horrible action from the stairway, cries out in rage, "You . . . you ain't even gonna . . . whip 'em?" Bill responds smartly, "I fined 'em instead." Alice exclaims, "For what they done? Skinny gets some ponies an' that's . . . ?" Hackman then manages a look of exquisite perversity in its indication of the pleasure Little Bill derives from taunting Alice with his own contrived notion of justice and from reasserting his elevated position as supreme authority and law-giver of the community.

Unforgiven in its entirety will make it clear how Munny and Little Bill complement and fulfill each other in a deeper purpose of the film as the story of control through repression and suppression. They operate in their own ways to advance different forms of regulation and restraint in the higher service to death.

Little Bill and Munny desexualize and therefore dehumanize and abstract the body for higher causes, William Munny to maintain his promises of redemption to his late wife, and Little Bill, to exercise absolute authority over others in the name of law and order. Little Bill's disdainful denigration and dismissal of the prostitutes indicates a core of sexual tension and denial to his sadism and violence. While Will Munny smothers the life out of the physical and sexual body, Little Bill wars against the community. They each engage in a form of social pathology that enacts the psycho-sexual sources of violence and aggression. They dramatize the importance of creating a new ethics beyond the aggressive morality of repression and the intimidating police power of suppression.

In another form of attack on the women, Little Bill treats Alice as the guilty party for wanting harsher punishment for the boys. Taking Alice by the arm and walking her from the stairs, he says, "Ain't you seen enough blood for one night? Hell, Alice, they ain't loafers nor tramps nor bad men. They're hard-workin' boys that was foolish. Why, if they was given over to wickedness in a regular way . . ."

"Like whores?" Alice fires back at Bill, finishing his thought and acknowledging Bill's insinuation of his contempt for the women.

Alice's frustration over the many injustices done to Delilah and the other women soon causes her to conspire with them to put together from their earnings and then publicize a reward of $1,000 for killing Davey and Mike. She says to the other prostitutes, "Maybe we ain't nothin' but whores, but by God we ain't horses."

Eastwood signals the growing complexities of ethical and moral balances and relations in *Unforgiven* when he cuts from Alice and the women of Greely's in Wyoming to William Munny's hog farm in Kansas. Munny and the children remain mired there in the frustration, poverty, mud, and filth of working with fever-ridden hogs.

The camera's focus on Eastwood on the hog farm in *Unforgiven* emphasizes the physical changes from the actor's earlier starring roles. Older, sour, tired, beleaguered,

Eastwood's Munny struggles to survive in the dirt and provide for his children in the midst of his failure and loss. Sick pigs squeal and oink their discontent and disrespect and even drag him through the mud. The helpless and distraught children look on, trying to understand as they report the spread of fever among the pigs. As Munny struggles, a messenger arrives to initiate changes to come for Munny.

The intruder, known as the Schofield Kid (Jaimz Woolvett), invites Munny to join forces with him to kill the offending cowboys from Big Whiskey and split the $1,000 reward offered by the prostitutes. A deeply flawed and immature braggart with grand illusions about himself, who proves unable to see distances but has ambitions to become a notorious gunman and killer, the Kid explains how he heard about Will Munny. Inside the sod hut of the farm away from the children outside, the Kid says to Munny, "Yeah, well, Uncle Pete says you was the meanest goddamn son-of-a-bitch ever alive an' if I ever wanted a partner for a killin' you were the worst one. Meanin' the best. On account of you're as cold as snow an' don't have no weak nerve nor fear." The Kid's description of Munny's legendary past as a cold-blooded killer living an event-filled life of murder, mayhem, and alcohol contrasts with the disorder, darkness, and poverty of the hut.

The low-angle profile shot of Munny deep in thought demonstrates Eastwood's new patience and skill as a director and actor, as he dramatizes through a sustained take on his face the complexities and ambiguities that confront his ambivalent hero. The shot exhibits a figure of pain, age, and vulnerability. The camera lingers on his face to register the imprints of doubt, fear, anxiety, all as inner feeling. In response to the Kid, Munny says, "I ain't like that anymore, Kid. Was whiskey done it as much as anything else, I guess. I ain't had a drop in over ten years. My wife, she cured me of that . . . cured me of drink an' wickedness."

A second shot, an exterior close-up of Munny looking toward the horizon and following the Kid with his eyes as the Kid rides off to the West to do his killing, continues to suggest the emergence of a new Eastwood protagonist and director. The shot maintains the intimation of the profile shot in the hut of a fresh depth and intensity of introspection and self-reflection in the Eastwood character.

The Journey and the Flesh Trade: The Ethical Cost

Like classic Homeric journeys in antiquity to adventure narratives in modern times, the journey in *Unforgiven* operates through many symbolic and ethical spheres.[9] The genius of *Unforgiven* in part entails the brilliance of its intertwining of the interior psychological journey, the drama over conflicting morals and values, and the spiritual search with the physical adventure in the West.

A scene beyond Munny's vision illustrates the moral and ethical meanings of his quest. The scene suggests that he embarks on a journey greater than his immediate understanding. The film dramatizes the persistent tension between Munny's narrow purpose of his own solitary interest in providing for his family and the greater meanings of the narrative that involve justice in the context of the dehumanizing treatment of the women in the film. A cut to Delilah's scarred face encapsulates the multiple meanings of the film. The camera closes in on her face and the patchwork of scars with their raised flesh that contrasts with the Levinasian message of her eyes of beauty and vulnerability. Then Delilah and several of the other prostitutes slowly and in turn notice the arrival of the cowboys, Quick Mike and Davey Bunting, on the way into town to comply with Little Bill's order to pay Skinny the whore master with several ponies for his loss of

Delilah's sexual value to him. Skinny says to them, "You boys took a while. Couple more days and I was gonna call on the Sheriff." When Skinny moves to take the best pony, a spirited chestnut with a white blaze down its nose, Davey refuses, indicating he intends to give the horse to Delilah, "the one my partner cut." Davey's sense of guilt constitutes one of the film's special touches and surprises that in this case adds depth and some measure of sympathy to his character in anticipation of events to come, but without unduly exaggerating any moral change in him.

The immediate reaction of the women to the boys and to Davey's gesture adds to the power and depth of the film's ethical discussion. They hurl mud at the cowboys. Two signs in the background behind the cowboys advertise a "Meat Market," making the less than subtle point about the treatment and the value that has been placed upon the women and their flesh. Davey indirectly appeals for forgiveness by saying of the pony, "It's the best of the lot. . . . She could sell it or . . . what she wants." He still hopes to cleanse his conscience by equating a horse with a face and life.

Alice responds in a rage. "A pony! . . . She ain't got no face left an' you're gonna give her a goddamn mangy pony." Davey's weak, almost whispered response with its hint of new courtesy and respect, as the whores continue to fire mud and abuse at the cowboys, summarizes the impossibility of the situation. He says, "He ain't mangy, ma'am, he . . ."

A perfectly timed series of intense close-ups and intercuts of the faces of the women, especially Delilah, articulates the ethical and psychological meaning of the scene and testifies to the brilliance of Eastwood's direction, Joel Cox's editing, and Jack N. Green's cinematography with Henry Bumstead's production design. The close-up of Delilah's torn face and sad eyes, as she looks at Davey with his pony riding away from the belligerent prostitutes, expresses the pain she never utters about her isolation and her future as a prostitute with a mutilated face.

Eastwood extends the meaning of moral economy from female flesh to animals in a following scene when Munny embarrasses himself before his children by trying to mount his horse to go on his journey. After years of use as a farm animal rather than a saddle horse, the animal resists Munny's awkward, clownish efforts to mount him. He tells the children, who have been instructed on how to care for the animals and the farm in Munny's absence, how the horse was paying Munny back "for the sins of my youth." He says, "I used to be weak mistreating animals. . . . Horses and hogs getting even with me now." He says that he is getting his "comeuppance for my cruelty." Before departing, Munny ponders a photograph of his wife, brings flowers to her grave, and reminds the children how "your departed mother, God rest her, showed me the error of my ways."

Thus, Eastwood significantly expands the moral economy of the film by associating the treatment of women at Greely's as animals at a meat market with Munny's guilty conscience over similarly mistreating and even no doubt slaughtering animals and eating their flesh. The broadening of the ethical argument by Eastwood testifies to the seriousness of his effort in *Unforgiven* to go beyond the reliance on psychology and narrative to serious ethical discussion.

The Sick Soul: Conscience, Death, and Repression

Unforgiven fulfills in a new way, Eastwood's long project of using the body, as Paul Smith suggests, as a stage for enacting and projecting these life-and-death struggles.[10] In *Unforgiven*, the actual time of the body for the aging Eastwood becomes a visible force in the struggle to overcome death with love as the body becomes the center of repression, love, aggression, and regeneration.

Munny's continuing relationship with Claudia of emotional dependency and moral need even after her death really determines the contours of what he must overcome to achieve self-definition and self-creation on his journey. Claudia in death solidifies her hold on him. Claudia takes Munny in the grave with her, sequestering him in the security of an existential, psychological, and sexual death. This relationship of death with Claudia establishes the basic boundary of his life that requires adjustment and change. The infusion of a repressive morality of death into the psycho-sexual dynamic of forces in *Unforgiven* originates and remains with Claudia's domination of the maternal and feminine space of the film.

Kristeva helps to explain Munny's mindset and place in *Unforgiven*, especially in his relationship to Claudia. In a comment about mystics and death that also obtains for Munny, Kristeva writes, "They identify with death, which is fundamentally the separation from the maternal container; they confuse themselves with lack." Similarly, Munny's relationship with what Kristeva calls "the lost mother" helps to explain him (*HF*: 298). Like a vampire, Munny functions in and out of the grave he shares psychologically with Claudia throughout the film as he tries to establish his subjectivity and place in the world.

From the grave, Claudia enacts her influence and hold over Munny as the enforcer and representation of his emasculation, the crucial lack from the film's beginning of masculine authority and presence, a lack that he dramatizes on his farm by being unable to shoot straight, mount his horse easily or control his farm with its sick pigs and troubled children. The more Munny claims to be reformed by his wife, the clearer it becomes that he needs to construct new boundaries and meanings for himself. The psychology of his moral masochism and his sexual masochism indicates his impulse for self-punishment and self-denial in his desire for redemption on the path Claudia set for him.

Kristeva describes the complex psychological processes that Munny exhibits in his relationship to Claudia of lack, abjection, repression, and sublimation, which keep him from establishing a secure sense of subjectivity and consequently from achieving his goal of regeneration. These processes structure his role and power as an agent and embodiment of psychological, social, and intellectual death. As a fitting description of the meaning of Munny's lingering connection to Claudia both alive and dead, Kristeva argues that the "experience of lack, which follows separation" leads to understanding "that the only psychosexual significance of *lack* . . . is abjection." She maintains, "That is, abjection is the only possible narrative of the experience of lack. Isn't this precisely what literature, religion, and mysticism tell us?" (*HF*: 186).

For Kristeva, we recall, abjection describes the processes of expulsion, demarcation, revulsion, and rejection that separate the subject for the construction of a distinct subjectivity.[11] Appropriately in Munny's case, Kristeva explains that "the mother object is the first result of the process of expulsion" so that in "abjection, the mother becomes the first 'abject' rather than object" (*HF*: 12). She writes, "I am driven to expel my progenitors and in this way I begin to create my own territory, bordered by the abject" (*HF*: 186). Lack and abjection, thereby, constitute a means to explain how the individual negotiates and constructs the borders for individual subjectivity, place, and identity.

Harkening back to earlier discussions of Eastwood characters as marginalized figures, liminal members on the threshold of society, Kristeva's theory of "these borders of one's own that are the abject and abjection" also points to

Munny in *Unforgiven* (*HF*: 186). Especially relevant to Munny and his late wife, abjection indicates a haziness in distinguishing between subject and object that confuses identity. A situation of fluid boundaries, the abject instigates forms of repression and sublimation, precisely modes of thinking and acting that help define Munny. Thus, for Kristeva, abjection in conjunction with other psychic operations such as repression and sublimation embed lines of "demarcation" for subjectivity (*HF*: 187).

Interestingly, Munny's partner on the journey to kill the cowboys becomes a kind of surrogate Claudia for Munny, in his combination of painful conscience and maternal care. Over the clear objections of his wife, an old friend and partner in mayhem, Ned Logan, as played brilliantly by Morgan Freeman, joins Munny on the journey. Ned immediately ventriloquizes Claudia's conscience. At the suggestion of becoming a third partner on the errand, Logan says, "We ain't bad men no more." Munny reminds him, "We done stuff for money before." Ned, however, gets the better of the argument by noting that they only "thought" they simply acted that way for money, but most importantly, he says, "If Claudia was alive you wouldn't be doing this."

Thus, even while joining Munny on the journey, Ned reinforces Munny's internalization of Claudia's moral voice but with crucial differences that become increasingly complex as the film develops. Ned not only functions as an interior voice reminding Munny of conscience; he also works as a kind of negotiator of the viciousness of the internalized super-ego in urging another form of ethical subjectivity and behavior involving love, sacrifice, symbolization, and renewal.

Encouraged by Logan, Munny insists throughout the journey that the intervention of Claudia into his life 11 years earlier changed him. Munny remarks on how Ned's Indian wife, Sally Two Trees (Cherrilene Cardinal), gave him "the evil eye" for taking Ned away on the journey. Munny says, "She knew what a no good son-of-a-bitch I was then," meaning the old days of violence and killing. But Munny insists, "I ain't like that no more." He feels Sally "won't allow how I've changed . . . I ain't like that no more." Ned agrees that "You ain't like that no more," and Munny tries to convince himself, "I'm just a fellow now." Munny continues, "Claudia, she straightened me up . . . cleared me of drinking whiskey an' all."

Significantly, even in the first stages of the journey, it becomes clear how Claudia's idea of conscience has failed to protect Munny from his deepest fears. He fears his own death, the death of others, and the death he will inflict on others. He rationalizes to Ned as they sit by a campfire, fighting the cold and the discomfort of the ground. He says, "Just 'cause we're going on this killin' that don't mean I'm gonna go back to the way I was. I just need the money . . . Get a new start for them youngsters." Munny's face in the light of the campfire expresses his fears. He asks Ned, "Remember that drover I shot through the mouth? His teeth came out through the back of his head. I think about him now and again. He didn't do anything to deserve that shot. At least nothing I could remember when I sobered up."

Munny's fear and guilt over death becomes most intense when the Kid, Munny, and Logan arrive at Greely's after riding for a long time in a terrible rain that thoroughly soaks them. In one of Munny's ironic moments that demonstrates the consistent strength of Peoples' script, Ned asks Munny as they ride through the rain if he still thinks "it'll be easy shootin' them cowboys?" Munny answers, "If we don't drown first."

Shots of Munny on horseback, clutching himself, shivering, gnashing his teeth, and pinching his shoulders forward against the relentless hammering of the rain, indicate his growing physical distress and discomfort that worsen into a serious fever and sickness.

At Greely's, Munny's illness and fever express the internal fever of guilt. Alarmed, Logan says, "Jesus, Will, you look like shit." As the two wait at a table at the bar of Greely's for the Kid to return from enjoying the prostitutes in the rooms upstairs, Will asks Logan, "Do you remember Eagle Hendershot?," a dead man. Munny shocks and frightens Logan by saying, "I seen him. . . . No! I seen him Ned . . . His head was all broke open. You could see inside of it. . . . Worms were running out."

When Ned then leaves Will alone with his fever and fears to join the Kid and the prostitutes, Munny falls victim to Little Bill, who enters the bar to punish Will and anyone else available as a warning to others who want to come to Whiskey to earn the reward for killing Davey and Quick Mike, as Little Bill had done in an earlier scene of his brutal beating of another killer out for the reward, English Bob (Richard Harris). Interestingly, in the exchange between Ned and Munny at Greely's, Logan sometimes seems to call him "Bill," solidifying the connection between Will and Little Bill that reaffirms other qualities of character that make them comparable. As a sign of Munny's mental state and identification with guilt and death, when Little Bill asks Will for his name, Munny replies with the name of the man he killed, "William . . . Hendershot."

Then, beaten and kicked senseless by Daggett, the helplessly sick and fever-ridden Will crawls on the floor of Greely's out into the rain and onto the soaked and muddy street. Ned and the Kid retrieve him. As Ned sews up the deep cuts on Will's face by candlelight, Will relates his most terrifying vision of guilt and fear. Will says he has seen the dead Claudia. Will says, "She was all covered with worms. Oh, Ned, I'm scared of dying." He pleads with Ned not to tell anyone about his crimes. He says, "I've seen him, Ned. I've seen the angel of death. He's got snake-eyes . . . I'm scared of dying. . . . I'm scared. I'm tired. Don't tell nobody. Don't tell my kids none of the things I did."

Claudia, death, conscience, and terror merge in Will's horrible vision.

The Body, the Sacred, and the Face

Will Munny's relations with women and his attitude toward sex dramatize the meaning of the hold of repression and sublimation on him. As Kristeva insists, in "representing and symbolizing" the subject's "functioning and activities" with other people, "sexuality" constitutes "the hinge of this metaphysical dualism" between the biological body and meaning (*HF*: 209). In *Unforgiven*, sexuality and sexual attitudes become a significant register between, on the one hand, deadly, life-destroying repression and, on the other, the striving for love that intimates the ethical and sacred. The sustained tension between the two forms of sexual expression – repression and stultification as opposed to love and the sacred – makes Munny into an unstoppable sick prisoner of death in the film.

The crisis of sexuality for Munny expresses itself in a memorable exchange between Munny and Logan during the first phase of the journey. Still getting reacquainted as they ride together toward Wyoming, Ned, who has been aware of Claudia's death and Will's lonely, even morbid isolation, asks, "Hey, Will, you ever go into town?" Will answers, "On occasion, to sell a hog or pick up supplies."

This tracking shot of the two men riding and talking on open prairie recalls John Ford's Westerns. Like Ford, Eastwood repeatedly breaks the 180-degree rule by having the horseriders change direction on screen, a technique that highlights each man. The counter-intuitive movement reinforces the surprise that comes in the conversation. Eastwood in this and other scenes brilliantly establishes a rhythm and grace of the relationship between rider and horse and between the riders and the landscape.

Ned again asks Munny about going into town, saying, "No, I mean to get yourself a woman or something." Stoic Will answers emotionlessly, "No. I never go into town for that. A man like me . . . the only woman a man like me could get is one he would have to pay for and that ain't right . . . buyin' flesh." Will touchingly adds, "Claudia, rest her soul, would never want me to do something like that . . . me being a father and all."

The simple honesty of Will's answer powerfully contrasts with the values of commercialization and domination of Greely's whorehouse, and of Big Whiskey itself. His words establish a significant ethical difference with what has preceded this moment in the film, involving Delilah, Strawberry Alice, and all the events surrounding them. The statement proffers an important structuring of moral and ethical values for *Unforgiven*.

On another level of meaning, however, Will's statement suggests a deep problem of ethical character for Will in that his words indicate a source for his ethics in the psychology of his dependence upon Claudia. The ethical discussion in *Unforgiven* becomes more problematic with Munny's repeated attribution to Claudia for providing the basis and authority for his reform, as opposed to his own internalized set of values and beliefs. Will's claim continues the ambiguity of the strength of his moral and ethical character.

Ned then shocks Will with his next question. He asks, "You just use your hand?" The expression on Logan's face demonstrates his genuine curiosity about the issue, as though he cannot comprehend such extended self-denial involving sex. In contrast, Munny's look of shocked horror constitutes one of Eastwood's most expressive moments of great self-mockery for the macho actor and public figure. Looking off, Will suggests the depth of his despondency and detachment. He says, "I don't miss it all that much."

In a later scene with Delilah, Eastwood transforms Will's sexually repressive adherence to Claudia's project for his personal reform into a moment of ethical transcendence. The moment takes *Unforgiven* to a new level of artistic power and ethical meaning. In the scene, the torn and scarred flesh of Will's and Delilah's faces becomes the basis for a transformational ethical encounter. The bodies of a prostitute and killer present the possibility for the renewal of the flesh through the ethical relationship with the other. They share in a new time of dispossession of their own egoistic being to put a priority on the other. Eastwood probably comes closer here than at any previous time in his directing to portraying what Kristeva terms "our need for the sacred" as a conjoining with "the need for the survival of our species." Appropriately for this scene, she writes, "Women are positioned at the intersection of these two demands" (*HF*: 12).

The scene transpires in a shed where Logan and the Kid have taken Will, fever-ridden and critically ill after his beating from Little Bill. In the manger-like scene, Will has been near death and unconscious for a religiously significant three days. Covered in a blanket evoking, as Stephanie Page Hoskins notes, Jesus's shroud, Will awakens to Delilah's cut-up face. His face looks just as brutalized and torn with gashes and cuts from Little Bill's beating and Logan's desperate stitching of his wounds. He says, "I thought you was an angel," reminiscent of his vision of the angel of death; but this angel could be a sign of resurrection. Surprised, she says, "You ain't dead."

The brief encounter between Will and Delilah that follows epitomizes Levinas's argument of the holiness and humanity of the face and of Kristeva's notion of spiritual beauty. Will and Delilah envision, as Levinas says, "death in the face of the other" as they reach out to the other.

In the confines of the shed that accentuate their intimacy as wounded outsiders with lasting external and internal scars, Will obviously feels Delilah's tempting feminine presence and her sexuality, softened by her lovely eyes that express her painful vulnerability. He realizes, "You gotta be the one cowboys cut up." Will says, "I must look kinda like you now." She answers, "You don't look nothin' like me, mister."

Eastwood then cuts sharply to the outside of the shed. It seems like a simple act that allows Will to enjoy the view of the mountains that have become covered in snow. Also, eating food that Delilah brought him, as though celebrating life through a food ritual, Will comments that before his near-death experience, he would not have noticed the "high country" scenery. He obviously has undergone an awakening.

In spite of its apparent simplicity, the sudden cut takes the sequence of interior to exterior shed scenes to a new

*Will Munny mistakes the cut-face whore Delilah (Anna Thomson) for the "angel of death." (*Unforgiven, *1992, Warner Bros, Malpaso Production, dir. Clint Eastwood.)*

temporal and religious dimension of meaning. The sequence dramatically transitions from one temporal realm of ordinary, daily human engagement to a very different one of achieving ethical subjectivity and transcendence.

The interior shed scene fits into a traditional narrative pattern that organizes time synchronically according to the linearity of clock time. The interior scene occurs in a conventional narrative order of a journey with Munny's partners, Ned and the Kid, who took him to the shed in the hope that he would survive his fever, his beating, and his nightmares of his own death and Claudia's decomposing face in death. The religious elements of the interior scene of Munny's burial cloth or blanket and the manger-like setting function symbolically as part of the *mise en scène* that includes Will and Delilah as brutalized souls bearing signs of persecution on their flesh and seeking redemption.

The sudden shift from the interior to the exterior of the shed disrupts orderly, regular clock time, setting up the new temporal regime in the transition. Special notice of a significant time change occurs when Munny expresses regret to Delilah for saying "the other day" that they "look kinda like" each other with their wounds. In fact, the sharp cut to Will, eating outside after being unconscious and not eating for three days, clearly suggests the move outdoors occurs on the same day as his awakening inside the shed.

The misstatement of time projects the exterior scene into a different temporal order. Also, the time of the snowfall seems somewhat indefinite. An exterior establishing shot indicates the snow had fallen during Will's state of unconsciousness. The cut moves Munny and Delilah physically outside but also outside of regular clock time.

Thus, the shift from the interior to the exterior entails a transition from a specific moment in linear time as part of a conventional narrative order to a domain of disjunctive, disruptive diachronic time. The diachronic time of the exterior setting dramatizes what Levinas postulates as the disjointed time that compels dislodging and displacing the subject from ordinary time to confront the ethical and transcendent time of the other. For Levinas, diachronic time constitutes the time of the infinite and transcendence, thereby making the relationship of the subject to the infinite and transcendent possible. Levinas argues that the genuinely ethical occurs in diachronic time that enables the transcendent and infinite.[12]

Eastwood's startling and dramatic cut to the exterior scene places Munny and Delilah in such a diachronic temporality for a relationship that goes beyond the ordinary and mundane to a sense of the transcendent. Eastwood directs the exterior scene to have Munny and Delilah interact visually and verbally so as to engender a time of diachronic transcendence between them, a time that places the priority on the other before the self. As opposed to simply asserting such transcendence through dialogue, rhetoric, or the narrative, Eastwood's art sustains the move into diachronicity by constructing the scene to dramatically visualize the transcendence of the other in the scene's artistic structure, particularly in its treatment of Delilah's face.

Mentioning at one point in their conversation how Logan and the Kid have been getting "free ones" from Alice and a prostitute named Silky, Delilah seems to offer herself to Will. She asks, "You want . . . a free one?," but then looks stunned by Will's awkward rejection, not knowing about Will's abstinence since Claudia's death. Looking off as though hiding her face from Will, she says with conviction, "I didn't mean with me. Alice and Silky, they'll give you a free one . . . if you want."

Filmed in this and other scenes to reveal thinning hair and other signs of age and vulnerability, Will responds to Delilah with humanity and generosity. Clearly, Delilah has touched Munny in a significant, altering way that can be felt and read as temporarily softening the crippling hold on him of the repressive power of Claudia's overly aggressive conscience. Still not able to free himself completely, Munny in this situation transcends his limitations to evidence considerable sensitivity in caring for another.

In a careful, thoroughly convincing voice and manner, Munny talks softly to Delilah, gently restoring her sense of dignity and worth. He explains to her that he did not mean that he was rejecting sex with her because of her face. The camera focuses on him while also stressing his reassuring, healing impact on Delilah. He then refers to his comment of "the other day." Will says, "What I said the other day about you looking like me . . . that wasn't true. You ain't ugly like me. It's just that we both got scars. But you're a beautiful woman, and if I was to want a free one, I'd want it with you, I guess, more than them other two. It's just that I can't on account of my wife."

A falsehood about Will's wife "back in Kansas . . . watching over my young ones" soothes Delilah's feelings, but Munny's voice and gestures indicate Delilah's effect on him. Her face moves him. Will uses the departed Claudia in caring for Delilah. With bright exterior light on Delilah's face, she embodies Kristeva's assertion that "Beauty is the soul made fully visible, like a flower in summer light" (*HF*: 57). Her soulful beauty accounts in part for the inspiration that impels Will to such sensitivity and care. In this moving scene with Delilah, Munny, as Steven Shankman writes in another Levinasian context, "experiences a transcendence of his own ego in the direction of ethics."[13]

At this moment of interaction between Delilah and Munny, when her scarred face radiates the quality of beauty that Kristeva describes, Delilah also epitomizes "the

*A face-to-face encounter awakens a new time of ethical consciousness and transcendence for Munny. (*Unforgiven, *1992, Warner Bros, Malpaso Productions, dir. Clint Eastwood.)*

transcendence of the face" that plays such a key role in Levinas's thought. Levinas contrasts the "nudity" of the face with "the work of language" which "is entirely different." The nudity of the face appears "by itself and not by reference to a system," so that the intimacy and immediacy of the "face to face" establishes "a relation between me and the other beyond rhetoric."[14] Levinas thinks the transcendence of the face cannot be reduced or confined to language or even systematically thought.

Eastwood uses Munny in the shed scene with Delilah to convey such transcendent meaning to her face, withholding any patronizing overt pity over her wounds so as to suggest that she remains sacred and with dignity in her humanity. As Eastwood directs the shed scene, Munny's transforming response and relationship to Delilah call out the power of her face as the expression of transcendent beauty. In seeing and articulating the significance of the silence, openness, and vulnerability of Delilah's face, Will also makes the distinction that Levinas articulates between the "nakedness of the body" and "the nakedness of the face." For Levinas, the naked face "is at the same time its absence from this world" in that the face signifies the relation of the human to the infinite and transcendent.[15] In denying himself the opportunity for a "free one" with Delilah, Munny maintains the difference he envisions between the transcendence of her face and the presence of her body.

Eastwood recognizes the indispensable work of what Levinas terms the "gaze" for proffering the meaning of the face. For Levinas, "this gaze is precisely the epiphany of the face as a face."[16] Munny's gaze that instigates the "epiphany of the face" imbues meaning into the diachronic time of the shed scene, fulfilling the promise of transcendence for the scene's special temporal regime. The epiphany of the face intimates for Delilah the transformation of her wounded flesh into a transcendence with the hope for renewal, a potential that dims for her when Eastwood later injects a note of disheartening realism into his story of the struggle for redemption. Still, the epiphany of the face impregnates the special temporal dimension of the shed scene with purpose.

Interesting, at this moment of ethical transcendence toward the other, Munny also can be seen as coming closest to identifying with the feminine. His claim of not looking like Delilah constitutes another small lie for a bigger purpose of making her feel better. The greater lie may be one of denial to himself, what Freud calls *Verleugnung*, disavowing the meaning and symbolic significance of those cuts on his face. The deep cuts and gashes on each face could be read as evocative of female sexuality. For Delilah and Will, the cuts fetishize sublimated and abjected female sexuality, emphasizing continued ambiguity regarding the body. Earlier, when Munny described to Ned the horrible violations the cowboys did to Delilah, he could not resist saying the cowboys "done everything but cut up her cunny" in order to further arouse Ned's interest, suggesting a fetishized preoccupation.

Eastwood's interest in occupying and sharing the feminine goes back to his first film, *Play Misty for Me*, and evolves through several of his other films.

In *Unforgiven*, when Munny tells Delilah that "we both got scars," Eastwood creates a moment of special ethical meaning with a low-angle shot that positions Delilah in the foreground and Munny behind her in the background, both facing toward the camera. The positioning and organization of the scene structure the ethical engagement between them and imbue the moment with meaning beyond their words. Turning to face each other, they fulfill the ethical encounter in a visual image of a new ethical moment.

For Will, his brutal beating by Little Bill as a kind of rape accentuates his lack or emasculation. The wounded psyche of the scarred body processes abjection for reconfiguring subjectivity under the serious trauma of lack and loss. For Will, the repression of the abject, as Kristeva's theory would have it, undergoes crucial modification in this special situation with Delilah. Delilah nurtures a change in the usual direction and meaning of death-dealing forces of repression. The intervention of the face of the other, meaning Delilah as an angelic vision, mitigates repression. In the scene, the Levinasian epiphany of the face occurs or, as Kristeva puts it, "abjection . . . cracks when the permanent watchman repression eases up" (*HF*: 187).

Will's experience of the feminine constitutes a form of ultimate demarcation and working of borders in the construction of the subject. In the shed scene, repression and sublimation take a momentary holiday as abjection suggests the "sublime" (*HF*: 188) in the light of Delilah's face. While Delilah finally loses to Claudia in Will's ultimate inability at the time to love freely and completely and break the bonds of repression, *Unforgiven* insinuates the initiation of a process of radical subjective reinvention for him.

The ethical journey in *Unforgiven* suggests a slow process of renewal for the three men who undertake it, Will, the Kid, and Ned. The Kid escapes, discovering himself as anything but a real killer after seeing death once. He meets the face of death in an outhouse and cannot stand the smell and look. Ned becomes a sacrificial figure for the importance of seeing the human as sacred. In contrast, Will initially takes the path of regeneration through violence in response to Ned's death at Little Bill's hand. The film's final inscription suggests he eventually stopped fighting death with death. In the shed scene with Delilah, he starts.

Sublimation, Filthy Lucre, and an Outhouse Killing

The shed scene between Munny and Delilah effectuates a new moral economy and exchange in *Unforgiven*, involving the soul in the transformation of the flesh. The scene represents a gesture toward the sacred in a moment of ethical transcendence in which love, sacrifice, and renewal temporarily triumph. This shed scene provides a moral and ethical challenge and alternative to the murder and death that follow, turning the ethical catastrophe of the killings that Munny inflicts into a possibility for potential change. The shed scene informs the final scenes and meaning of the film and elucidates the moral and ethical purpose of *Unforgiven*. The forgiveness and understanding that Delilah and Munny share with each other counter the nihilism and death of *Unforgiven* with an ethical argument that proposes the possibility of a different way and outcome for human relationships that revision and rethink the meaning of death.

Thus, the moral economy between Delilah and Munny contrasts sharply with the fundamental economic motivation behind Munny's journey with the Kid – money. The bloody concluding portion of the film puts the obsession and need for money in a crucial psychoanalytical and ethical context of the body. The Delilah–Munny sequence indicates the need and the path for going beyond the destruction of the body that the film's conclusion enacts and represents. A key to the conclusion of *Unforgiven* involves what Kristeva calls "the first productions of our body – excrement" that relates to sublimation and repression (*HF*: 204).

Following the shed scene, the three killers finally find Davey working with other cowboys in a box canyon. In a thoroughly unglamorized and unromanticized setting and situation, Munny kills Davey but only after Ned finds it impossible to do the killing himself. Visibly shaken, frightened, and confused, Ned cannot force himself to finish Davey, leaving Munny to do it. Meanwhile, the Kid remains useless as a sniper and killer because of his poor eyesight and nervousness and simply becomes a nuisance. Davey dies slowly and painfully from a bullet wound to the stomach. "You murdering bastards, you killed our Davey boy," one of the cowboys shouts. Davey's pony also gets hit and goes over in a fierce somersault that traps Davey until the wounded cowboy manages to free himself to crawl to his death. So Munny has returned to the abuse of animals as well as humans.

With Ned leaving almost in silence to return to Kansas, only Munny and the Kid look for and find Quick Mike to finish the killing. They catch him by himself in the outhouse while several other cowboys and a deputy rest and talk in the nearby bunkhouse. At first seeming to be a gratuitous gesture designed merely to disturb and even shock the sensibilities of the audience, the events and language of the outhouse prove crucial to understanding the meaning of the film. The outhouse also provides an important symbolic contrast with the shed scene.

Before the killing, as the Kid and Munny wait for Mike to emerge from the bunkhouse to use the outhouse, the Kid says, "Sure is ripe," and Munny, no doubt thinking about death retorts, "Gonna get a lot riper." Nervous and excited, the Kid plans to do the killing of Quick Mike at close range by the outhouse. As they wait for Mike, the Kid complains, "He's holdin' on to his shit like it was money." In a while, however, inside the bunkhouse, Mike prepares to use the outhouse and talk of defecation dominates the conversation. Mike announces he will go by himself without protection from the others to "Take a shit" and then rebuffs the offer of a cowboy to go with him to guard against the possible appearance of the killers. Mike says, "You could wipe my ass."

In spite of Munny's coaxing and urging, the Kid out of nervousness, fear, and inexperience fails to shoot Mike on his approach to the outhouse. Then when Mike goes to the outhouse, the deputy emerges from the bunkhouse, forcing Munny to fire at him and the bunkhouse. The Kid finally goes to kill Mike on the seat in the outhouse. Both men look frozen until the Kid pumps three shots into him while mayhem breaks out with the bunkhouse cowboys trying to respond.

Will and the Kid escape to an open field and wait for their money. The Kid says, "Shit, I thought they was gonna get us." Still nervous and excited and drinking big gulps from a whiskey bottle, he says, "I shot that fucker three times. He was takin' a shit and he went for his gun . . . an' I blazed away." He describes the shooting and grows increasingly nervous and agitated. The Kid repeats, "Three shots . . . he was takin' a shit . . ."

This obsession with the function and language of the outhouse warrants critical attention to gain additional insight into the meaning of *Unforgiven*. Remembering Kristeva's study of abjection and the fluidity of the body in relation to subjectivity and culture, it will be helpful to turn to a pre-Kristevan scholar of the psychoanalysis of religion, culture, and history, Norman O. Brown, who analyzes the multiple connections of excrement to money, sublimation, and culture. His study sheds important light on the meaning of *Unforgiven*, especially the aspect of the film that dramatizes what Brown terms "'the excremental vision.'"[17]

Like Kristeva, Brown begins with Freudian and psychoanalytical readings of literature and culture, focusing on "the conflict between our animal body, appropriately epitomized in the anal function, and our pretentious sublimations." He argues that "Freud pursues the thought that the deepest cause of sexual repression is an organic factor, a disbalance in the human organism between higher and lower functions" (*LD*: 186, 187). While repression, Brown says, instigates sublimation, both processes of sublimation and repression redirect the power of sexuality toward anality, anal retention, and anal eroticism. Sexual repression relates to repression and control of other bodily operations.

From this perspective of Brown's theory of psychoanalysis, the anality of the outhouse murder of Quick Mike emphasizes the importance in *Unforgiven* of sublimation and repression in promoting violence. The language and focus on anality speak to the repression that characterizes Munny's sexuality. Thus, Will willfully holds his sexuality in the same way that Quick Mike, according to the Kid, held his bowels.

The historic equation of money with anality also suggests that in a sense Will Munny's quest for money operates on an unconscious level of anality, sublimation, and repression. Money and its function in the film externalize the operation of repression on the body and psyche. Brown says, "The category of property is not simply transferred from feces to money; on the contrary, money is feces, because the anal eroticism continues in the unconscious" (*LD*: 191).

Developing this theme in literature and theory, Brown describes money as "the dream of sublimated anality" (*LD:* 257).

Brown further argues that money in this sense of anality means the denial of the body. He says, "All sublimation as such presupposes the repudiation (negation) of the body" (*LD:* 293). For Brown, the denied body becomes an object in itself. He says, "The ever increasing denial of the body is, in the form of a negation, an ever increasing affirmation of the denied body. . . . The more the life of the body passes into things, the less life there is in the body" (*LD:* 297).

Unforgiven uncannily implements Brown's theory of the importance of excrement in the relationship of repression and sublimation to sex, love, social organization, and culture. The film especially develops the importance of the connection of excrement to money. Munny himself makes the most blatant statement connecting money to excrement. This occurs when Munny overrides the Kid's objections and promises to give Ned his share of the reward even after Ned decides to abandon the project. Munny says, "Don't pay no attention to what the Kid said about your money and all. I'll bring your share." And then in a close-up, he says, "It's full of shit!"

Also, when Munny goes to Greely's to avenge the death of Ned, he asks, "Who's the fellow who owns this shit hole?," associating money and the corruption and vice of Greely's with excrement. Little Bill implies a connection of the feminine to filth and money when he dubs the reward "whores' gold" that could attract killers throughout the West to Big Whiskey. He also uses the term while kicking and nearly beating the life out of English Bob.

In addition, Brown's theory of money, excrement, and sublimation also enlightens the contrast between Delilah and Munny's shed scene and the outhouse murder. The scenes dramatize what Brown calls "the money complex" versus the "religion complex." Brown says, "The money complex is the demonic, and the demonic is God's ape; the money complex is therefore heir to and substitute for the religious complex, an attempt to find God in things" (*LD*: 240).

Accordingly, engaged in a money complex, Munny's quest coheres with a form of religion that supports Claudia's repressive hold on him. Claudia propounds a religion of repression that dictates the denial of the body and bodily impulses as opposed to the kind of religion complex of non-repressive love that the scene with Delilah proffers.

The Dominion of Death

In the end, two death camps consume *Unforgiven*. Munny fulfills his past to be an emissary, figure, and embodiment of death. The force and energy of compacted repression and sublimation explodes in his massacre of Little Bill and others at Greely's. In that scene, he epitomizes death-in-life, the slaughter of people as meat without symbolic value, meaning or the sacred. He destroys the flesh. In contrast, Little Bill incorporates in his body, voice, and language the violence and brutality of the state. He personifies the sadism of sublimated, eroticized pain and violence as expressed in a totalitarian personality.

In the build up to the slaughter at Greely's, Eastwood brilliantly intertwines two story sequences, a pattern of storytelling and filming he has followed through much of *Unforgiven*. The murder of Davey Boy along with the outhouse murder constitute one storyline. The second story sequence involves Little Bill, the agent of torture and brutality. Intertwining the two stories establishes an equivalence between the two forces of death. Both Munny and Little Bill operate on their own and endow themselves with the authority to do what they want – to impose their own idea of justice – and to kill.

In Munny's case, his story enables the individual ethical choice of his partners, Ned, who leaves without any money, and the Kid, who understands that he will never kill again. Realizing his limitations and identity, the Kid says, "I ain't like you, Will." The Kid, who has been nearly blind through much of the film, finally achieves a degree of insight about himself somewhat like Munny's awakening in the shed with Delilah.

The Kid finds himself unable to stop thinking about the murder he has committed. Munny tells him, "You sure killed the hell out of that fellow, today." Munny then articulates his own insight about killing. He says, "It's a helluva thing, killing a man. You take away all he's got and all he's ever gonna have." In the face of such finality, when the Kid tries to justify the murders by reiterating the mutilation of Delilah by the cowboys, Munny says simply, "We all have it coming."

Coming after the cowboy killings and in anticipation of the Greely's whorehouse massacre, Munny's words prove ominous. They constitute a stark contrast with the idea of the sacred and love in the shed scene. They indicate that Munny's quest for reform flies in the face of an opposing set of beliefs that would subvert redemption. Munny says that death takes everything from a person with no meaning beyond the physical and existential. His words depreciate the worth of striving for the transcendent in human relationships and narrow the meaning of the ethical. To this grim belief, he adds the similarly dark view of inherent, universal guilt. He suggests destructive nihilism accompanies ethical and moral uncertainty and helplessness. Munny's words indicate his other words of reform have been in opposition to a deeper inner core of belief in the impossibility of love to overcome death in relation to the other. The outhouse becomes the temple for the value of life as measurable only in terms of money and power.

Waiting with the Kid in a field to collect their bounty, Munny learns that Ned was caught on his way to Kansas and brought back to town to Little Bill. Munny grows dumbfounded as he hears that Ned was tortured, died, and then put on display in a coffin that he later sees also bears a crudely written sign with the words, "This is what happens to assassins around here." Munny's speech pattern of dumbly repeating as a question everything the young prostitute, Little Sue, tells him dramatizes the depth of his disbelief. The close-up of Munny's face portends doom. Its significance grows through the reaction it creates in the Kid, who only wishes to leave with his life and his money.

In the intercuts between the outhouse killing and the events in Big Whiskey, Eastwood exposes the undiluted sadism beneath Little Bill's insistence on being the sole arbiter and enforcer of justice in Big Whiskey. Thinking Ned knows where to find Munny and the Kid, Little Bill takes special pleasure and pride in setting up Ned for a whipping to extract information from him. He sadistically tells Ned that he will compare Ned's information about Munny and the Kid with the stories of the prostitutes, assuring Ned that he will not hurt a woman but only whip and punish him more severely to extract the truth.

The scene exhibits the puritanical streak in Little Bill that helps him to justify his violence. Little Bill dedicates himself to purifying his town of characters he deems unworthy, thereby reflecting the abjection, purification, and repression that also characterize Munny. This drive for purity in Little Bill manifests itself in the pathological violence of his brutal beating of English Bob (Richard Harris), the first killer to arrive in Big Whiskey to answer the call of the prostitutes.

Before beating the fever-ridden Munny at Greely's and calling him the kind of "trash" that should be kept from contaminating Big Whiskey, Little Bill made a lesson of English Bob to dissuade other killers from coming to his town. The presence of a writer at the scene promises help in the dissemination of the sheriff's message to stay away from Big Whiskey. Accompanying English Bob to write of his exploits and life for the penny press, W. W. Beauchamp (Saul Rubinek) acts as witness and chorus, signifying the perverse power of publicity and the media. Little Bill soon educates Beauchamp, who switches his loyalty from English Bob to the sheriff, about his own exploits and ideas of the West.

In the scene with the captured Ned Logan, the camera tightens on Ned's face and upper body. Ned stands with outstretched arms tied to prison bars and awaits the brutal whipping like a sacrifice on the cross. Little Bill speaks softly, sexually, in Ned's ear, intimating the current of eroticism in his pleasure at anticipating his infliction of the biting pain of the fetishized whip. Little Bill says, "I'm gonna hurt you, not gentle like before." Throughout *Unforgiven*, the development of Little Bill becomes a major triumph for both Hackman and his director and co-star. Hackman gives a command performance, a triumph of film-acting in presenting the complex character of Little Bill.

Hackman makes Little Bill into a kind of genius, a verbal and physical powerhouse of intimidation and force. The film brilliantly exploits the irony that while English Bob pretends to personify genuine cultural and linguistic authority as an Englishman, Little Bill with his basic native American intelligence, gift of language, wit, and supreme confidence in his own judgment and character clearly represents the stronger man, even as a figure of uninhibited violence.

While scenes with Little Bill sadistically beating and brutalizing his victims provide a great example of Hackman's outstanding physical acting and skill, his most impressive performance centers around his portrayal of Little Bill's explosive powers of mind and speech as a charismatic public figure. Hackman convincingly conveys Little Bill as a leader always on stage to persuade, bully, inspire, and control those around him. This aspect of his character compounds his complexity as a man who also spends much of his time building a house, a monument to himself. The number of leaks in the roof signifies Little Bill's inadequacy as a builder, lawman, and person.

Thus, an extraordinary scene occurs in Little Bill's jailhouse after his beating of English Bob. With English Bob behind bars, bloodied and bruised, and lying barely conscious on the cot in his cell, Little Bill reads Beauchamp's writings about Bob's brave exploits. Among other things, Beauchamp's role shows that Eastwood shares with other directors a fascination with the refashioning of Western history into myth. Bill mocks both men by purposely misreading and mispronouncing the title of one of the books about Bob to be the "Duck of Death." After author's vanity gives Beauchamp the false courage to correct Bill that the title should read "Duke of Death," he finally gets Bill's message of his own humiliation.

Hackman then proceeds to deliver a true tour de force as an actor by re-enacting the events in Beauchamp's book to tell them based on his personal experience, as opposed to the self-serving renditions that English Bob had provided Beauchamp. Hackman renders a brilliant double performance, not only revisiting the past of the stories to expose English Bob as a cowardly killer of helpless men but also using the moment to further intimidate and dominate both men. Fully exercising his verbal and emotional powers, Little Bill turns over a revolver to Beauchamp that could be used by Bob to escape from the jailhouse, thereby creating a pregnant moment of danger and uncertainty that ends with Bob's failure of nerve, a final humiliating proof of his cowardice. This scene also makes the crucial point that an effective method of telling a story, as Mark Twain avowed, joins in making the truth as opposed to merely reflecting a fixed reality.

After Little Bill deposits English Bob on a stagecoach out of town, a low-angle shot shows the prostitutes and their pimp watching from the Greely's porch. Framed together, the women stand in serial isolation in a kind of visual distribution of power and status, from the foreground with Alice the madame in the front to the background with Skinny near the top as the master. The women's faces reveal anguish. The cut face of Delilah projects despair. The camera remains steady on the scene of hopelessness and helplessness as the condition of the women. Watching Bob disappear, Alice says, "Nobody's gonna come!" Skinny compounds the despair by disparaging Delilah, telling her to clean the tables and to start wearing a veil. He says by wearing a veil "maybe somebody would hump yuh."

Eastwood changes to a precisely timed montage of intense close-ups of the women, especially Delilah and Alice, to emphasize their desperate abandonment. Forlorn and alone in sadness and misery like the other prostitutes, Alice notes the coming rain and stares into the emptiness, unaware of the three men on horseback already caught in the thunderous rain on their way to change things in Big Whiskey.

Such scenes set up the climactic tension of the final confrontation between Munny and Daggett at Greely's. Munny arrives in pouring rain and in the darkness of the night to avenge the torture, death, and public exhibition of Ned Logan. Shot in the kind of interior darkness and shadow that has attracted and intrigued Eastwood at least since *Pale Rider*, the scene with all of its excessive melodrama still proves compelling in its evocation of the transcendent figure of

Eastwood's earlier movies, an invincible hero with incredibly unique power for killing. In *Unforgiven*, the hero becomes the personification of inescapable death. He fulfills and culminates the image of death in Revelations that *Pale Rider* dramatizes. In the end, Munny, like death itself, cannot be stopped. It surprises even Munny himself, with the stupefying death of his partner, Logan. The intimation of possibilities for dealing with death differently in the shed scene with Delilah gets lost in Munny's need to play out the battle with Little Bill.

Undetected by the self-absorbed and excited cowboys crowding the barroom as they prepare to go out to find him, Munny appears out of the shadows. After killing the unarmed Skinny for decorating the saloon "with the body of my friend," he prepares to kill Little Bill. Little Bill says, "You be William Munny out of Missouri who killed women and children." In contrast to the last time they met at Greely's, Munny unapologetically acknowledges his identity, saying he now will kill Bill for what he did to Ned. Indeed, at the end of the slaughter at Greely's, Beauchamp reports to Munny that he has killed five men, proving Little Bill's earlier argument that in killing, calmness of nerve, patience, and poise count for more than speed and numbers.

After Munny shoots Little Bill and the others at Greely's, Little Bill lies wounded on the floor. He reaches for his gun in one last failing effort to get Munny. Munny stops him and takes aim for the execution. Bleeding and dying, Little Bill says, "I don't deserve to die like this. I was building a house." Munny answers, "Deserve's got nothing to do with it." Little Bill snarls back, "I'll see you in hell, Will Munny," and dies stoically.

Eastwood's use of the word "deserve" reinforces the view of both men about existential guilt and responsibility. When Munny and Little Bill say "deserve," they echo what Little

Bill said earlier after being told by Alice that in beating Munny in his first encounter with him at Greely's, he beat "an innocent man." Little Bill answers, "Innocent? Innocent of what?" Bill's question compares to Munny's remark to the Kid regarding death and guilt that "We all have it coming." The two men, Munny and Little Bill, embody and project guilt with meager possibilities for redemption. Little Bill lives according to his own code of manliness, honor, and the law. He personifies the imperious self, a manly citadel of power and self-worth immune from the weaknesses of others. He lives in a world of universal guilt in which he operates and pontificates as ultimate authority and judge. Love and the feminine suggest infirmity and weakness to him, a boundary of identity and relationships to be avoided. Love does not figure in his moral economy. His vision fails to go beyond the opportunity he sees for himself for retiring some day to the porch of his unfinished house to drink his coffee and watch the sun set over the mountains.

For Will Munny, life has meant death in the form of the existential struggle with fear, guilt, and conscience. Even his battle for others finds its energy and motivation in fear and guilt. Guilt transforms love for him into torturous obligation. Nevertheless, on his search to change his boundaries and free himself, Munny unwittingly becomes an agent in the awakening of others, Ned, the Kid, and Delilah.

Munny's own awakening to the face of Delilah marks only a tentative beginning for him of a search for meaning in relationships to others. At the same time, in avenging the torture and death of Ned with murder, Munny even as a killer still honors another man and sees a responsibility beyond his own fears and the needs of his immediate family. Also, seeing the beauty of the "high country" with Delilah becomes a metaphor for envisioning a higher realm of ethics and love. Conceivably, the sacrifice of Ned and the awakening with Delilah provide guidance to a new path toward a new life.

To his credit, Eastwood in *Unforgiven* refuses to minimize or trivialize the challenge of such a path to a love and life greater than the boundaries of fear and guilt. He even complicates the meaning of Munny's relationship to Delilah by having her learn from Alice that Munny has no living wife watching over his children in Kansas. Delilah's painfully stony reaction to the news keeps its impact upon her ambiguous. Interestingly, other prostitutes go as messengers to the killers. Delilah apparently stays away to live with the uncertainty of what she meant to Will Munny in the shed, in a moment that has been drained of its sentimentality for her but perhaps not of its ultimate meaning.

The destruction and death at Greely's signal at least a temporary triumph of a culture of death and the death instinct, making a mockery of editor Horace Greeley's famous call to the young men of the nineteenth century to go West to seek their destiny on a new frontier of opportunity in a time of self-reliance, initiative, and enterprise. Munny stands and remains unforgiven and unredeemed at Greely's for past and current sins. The prominence of a contemporary American flag, waving behind Munny as he berates the hiding townspeople at the end of the film, insinuates a message to a nation that also must seek redemption for its sins of the past by living up to its ideals of justice and ethics.

The sublimation and repression that dominate civilization in *Unforgiven* also can be found in perverse forms throughout modern culture. In response to such forces, Norman O. Brown asserts that "current psychoanalysis has no utopia" (*LD*: 233). Certainly, the end of *Unforgiven* can be seen as sustaining such pessimism concerning the possibility for modern culture to find the means to renew life and hope. At the same time, contemporary work in psychoanalysis and ethics by such thinkers as Kristeva and Levinas proposes if not a utopia then an alternative vision for renewal and hope, one that seeks to revivify the life of the soul and the priority of the other over the self.

Munny seems to arrive at such a momentary shelter for renewal in the shed scene with Delilah before continuing on his errand as the messenger of death for all those who see and know him. Also, the symbolic sacrifice of Ned, the change in the Kid, and the death of Daggett create a context for the crawler at the end of *Unforgiven* for believing that Will Munny at last may have found his way for himself and his family to a life of greater value and meaning somewhere around San Francisco, coincidentally the area Eastwood personally finds hospitable. The crawler suggests Munny at the end found the answer to the call that propelled him to search for a way greater than a limited life in the service of meaningless death with no higher ethical purpose than the self.

In contrast, Little Bill's ethical downfall starts and continues from the opening moments of *Unforgiven* when he looks at the face of Delilah, a bleeding, helpless, and infinitely sad prostitute, and sees nothing.

3

MO CUISHLE: A NEW RELIGION IN
MILLION DOLLAR BABY

The Fight: Tough Enough

"You got a fight I don't know about?"

Morgan Freeman speaks those words to Clint Eastwood toward the end of *Million Dollar Baby*. In one of the strongest performances of his long career, Freeman plays "Scrap" or Eddie-Scrap-Iron Dupris, a half-blind former prizefighter who lives as a janitor in the Hit Pit, a rundown boxing gym in the Skid Row area of Los Angeles that he keeps clean and orderly for its owner and his best friend, Frankie Dunn, a cut man and trainer, played to near perfection by Eastwood. The rhetorical question from Scrap initiates what apparently will be the last conversation and encounter between him and Frankie. It takes place in the shadows of the locker room of the Hit Pit. The shot directs minimal but precise light on Scrap in the darkness, reinforcing the somber mood of the scene and the film. Scrap, the former boxer, speaks softly but with the power and compassion he has expressed from the beginning as the film's narrative voice. He also functions as a vision of moral consciousness for the film. Throughout *Million Dollar Baby*, Scrap's close-ups and look invariably evoke the moral meaning of a scene. His gaze conveys a sense of moral consciousness and omniscience.

Scrap's statement to Frankie relates to the condition of Maggie Fitzgerald, a crippled professional prizefighter played by Hilary Swank in her Academy Award performance. She has been trained and managed by Frankie. When first approached by Maggie to train her, Frankie gruffly snaps, "I don't train girls." In the pugnacious way she adopts with him, Maggie answers, "People see me fight, say I'm pretty tough." Frankie mistakenly thinks he can settle the matter then and there, in the underground passageway of a boxing arena. He rudely tells her, "Girlie, tough ain't enough," echoing the words on a sign that decorates his gym.

After months of watching her workout aggressively by herself with only bits of informal and occasional guidance from Scrap, Frankie finally relents to her pleas and Scrap's example. Taking her on, Frankie manages her boxing and her life to the point of getting her a fight for the welterweight championship of the world in Las Vegas against the reigning champion, Billy "The Blue Bear" Astrakhov (Lucia Rijker), a notoriously dirty fighter.

At the bell to end the fifth round of the championship fight, Maggie correctly holds back from throwing a left hook to Blue Bear's jaw but in turn receives an unfair, illegal right hand from the champion that not only makes Maggie wobbly and puts her down on the canvas, but also lands her with all of her weight concentrated at her neck on her ring stool before Frankie can reach in and pull it back from her corner. In the original story "Million $$$ Baby" that provides the core for the film, Gerald Boyd under the pseudonym of F. X. Toole writes that "the back of her neck came down full force on the metal band of the ring stool, her neck breaking at the first and second vertebrae, the sound of it like a boot squashing a snail."[1]

The boxing stories in the film come from Boyd's collection entitled *Rope Burns: Stories from the Corner*. Boyd, according to Robert Sklar, became interested enough in boxing to begin his own career in middle age as a cut man, the person who works on a fighter's cuts.[2] About Maggie's condition after she had "stopped breathing" in the ring, following that sneak right from Blue Bear in the fifth round, Toole writes:

> She'd been nine days in a coma. They'd kept her doped-up to keep her head immobile for two weeks after that. Because of her MRI and other tests, her neurologists determined that she was a permanent, vent-dependent quadriplegic unable to breathe without a respirator. As a C-1 and C-2, she was injured at the first and second cervical vertebrae, which meant she could talk and slightly move her head, but that was all. She had lost the ability to breathe on her own, to move her limbs. She could not control her bladder or her bowel movements. She'd be frozen the rest of her life. (*RB*: 85)

In the story, Maggie tells Frankie from her hospital bed, " 'I'm a C-1 and C-2 complete, boss.' " Toole continues, "She was gaunt and sallow and the spunk in her was gone. The flesh around her sunken eyes was dark and lifeless. 'That means my spinal cord's so bad they can never fix me' " (*RB*: 85).

In the locker-room scene between Frankie and Scrap toward the end of the film, Scrap intuits that Frankie faces a fateful decision regarding Maggie. Scrap's word "fight" resonates on many levels. Agonizing over Maggie's appeal to him to end her misery and take her life, Frankie must consider and contend with the forces arrayed against such an action

– the law and civil society, the church, social norms. His own internal stone-cold code of ethics and morality and his religious devotion as a practicing and churchgoing Catholic render such an action inconceivable to him. Maggie's failed attempts to take her own life aggravate her horrible condition, thereby making her appeal for relief through death even more compelling for Frankie who has come to love her like his own estranged daughter, Katy. At the Tribeca Film Festival with Darren Aronofsky, Eastwood in Richard Schickel's *Eastwood Directs: The Untold Story* (2012) calls the film "a father–daughter love story."

As Scrap enters the scene in the Hit Pit locker room, Frankie has already gathered the syringe and adrenaline for the deadly procedure. In Toole's story, he describes how Frankie gathers "a fresh, one-ounce bottle of adrenaline chloride solution 1:1000" and a "syringe and detachable needle" (*RB*: 98). All of the culminating tensions that the film has steadily developed become concentrated toward these dark moments of final decision-making in the locker room.

Eastwood beautifully shoots the scene with an exquisite balance of light, shadow, and darkness. The light on Freeman's sad countenance in the dark makes Scrap seem like a disembodied figure, matching the soulful smoothness of his disembodied voice-over that has held the film together from the beginning. His intuitive sensitivity to this special fight for Frankie testifies to the depth of his affection and loyalty to Frankie.

Scrap also observes the actual mercy killing. Scrap stands, apparently without Frankie's certain awareness of his presence in the shadows at Maggie's hospital, as a silent witness while Frankie puts Maggie to her final rest. As Sara Anson Vaux notes, Eastwood describes the composition and meaning of Scrap's part and place in this scene as "'a deliberately abstract space.'"[3] Scrap's gaze upon the mercy killing suggests a form of unspoken sanction. Both men know the act of euthanasia takes Frankie into a realm where normal speech and conventional belief no longer apply. Overruling all of his basic impulses to save and preserve life, Frankie realizes he goes alone to a place where the approval or condemnation of others necessarily grows irrelevant before the enormity of his decision to take the life of a woman he loves more than himself.

If Frankie's pain in *Million Dollar Baby* inoculates him against caring about others' opinions, a portion of the public as well as critics at the time of the film's release felt the theme of euthanasia required discussion. For example, the film prompted a *New York Times* story with the headline "Groups Criticize 'Baby' For Message on Suicide," which focused on concerns of individuals and advocacy groups that the film suggested suicide and death as preferable alternatives to life with disabilities. Liberal writer Frank Rich, also in *The New York Times*, relished the agony of Eastwood's former conservative fans such as radio hosts Rush Limbaugh, who called *Million Dollar Baby* " 'liberal propaganda,' " and Michael Medved, who said " 'hate is not too strong a word' " for his feelings about the film.[4] In contrast, the film critic A. O. Scott of *The New York Times* called *Million Dollar Baby* Eastwood's "new masterpiece," while David Denby of *The New Yorker* said the film "joins the honor list of great fight films" and "has a beautifully modulated sadness that's almost musical" with the "smoothly melancholic tones of Coleman Hawkins at his greatest."[5]

In response to criticism of the film's treatment of the euthanasia issue, Eastwood told Sharon Waxman of *The New York Times*, " 'The film is supposed to make you think about the precariousness of life and how we handle it. How the character handles it is certainly different than how I might handle it if I were in that position in real life.' " Eastwood further explained that the film closely follows Toole in the original story. Of Toole, the Maggie character, and the issue of euthanasia, Eastwood said, "'That's one person's feeling. He wrote that as her desires. Probably no quadriplegic has ever not asked himself that question, or ever broached that subject. It's the ultimate trauma a person could suffer, short of losing all bodily control.'" Eastwood emphasized the difference between himself and the story. He said, "'You don't have to like incest to watch Hamlet. But it's in the story.'"[6]

As Eastwood suggests, *Million Dollar Baby* does not attempt to justify mercy killing. It does not make a general case for euthanasia under particular circumstances. Such readings misrecognize the ethical and moral achievement of the film. *Million Dollar Baby* makes an important case for the power of film art to dramatize complex ethical engagement.

In the original short story, Toole describes Frankie's last contact with Maggie. He writes, "Frankie closed the eye with the tip of his finger, made sure Maggie's pulse was still with his thumb. With his shoes in his hand but without his soul, he moved silently down the rear stairs and was gone, his eyes as dry as a burning leaf" (*RB*: 101). Frankie in this story leaves Maggie and the hospital with the suggestion that with the closing of Maggie's eye, the case of Frankie's soul also has been closed.

In contrast, the case for closure does not apply so readily in Eastwood's *Million Dollar Baby*. The structure, composition, organization, pacing, and momentum of *Million Dollar Baby* make the continuing moral and ethical drama of Frankie's soul the real story of the film. All the elements of the narrative – Maggie's rise and fall; her relationship with Frankie as her surrogate father; the partnership between Frankie and Scrap; the nature of Maggie's death; and Frankie's internal and external battles – ultimately feed into and develop the question of Frankie's search for redemption.

Million Dollar Baby takes the "moral economy" argument of *Unforgiven* to a new dimension of difficulty and complexity involving the basic issue of moral choice over impossible options of life and death. Eastwood's film in its entirety takes the drama into the moral and ethical realm of the unknowable and ineffable. The battle over Frankie's soul in the film continues into an ethical time outside of the ordinary, linear, mundane time of boxing matches and ordinary daily life experience.

Until her crippling defeat, Maggie justifiably believed that she had realized her dreams under Frankie's tutelage. With Frankie's training, guidance, and love, Maggie found her destiny. She owned the world. Under the spotlights of the boxing ring, she could rightly claim for herself Emmanuel Levinas's famous quote from Blaise Pascal, the seventeenth-century French philosopher of faith and science: "'That is my place in the sun.' That is how the usurpation of the whole world began" (*Pensées*: 112).[7]

In stark contrast, Frankie discovers in his relationship to Maggie that he has surrendered himself to the responsibility for the other. While Maggie's condition enables her to claim the right to die, Frankie has gone beyond the priority of his own being. Frankie must live with the disjunction between the immanence of his selfhood and identity and the transcendent responsibility outside of his own being that puts the priority on Maggie's time as opposed to his own. Frankie experiences what Steve Shankman terms "the transcending of the subject's own ego."[8]

Frankie's assumption of responsibility for Maggie as the other deeply immerses him in a realm of uncertainty and the unknowable. He can know what he feels and believes to be right for himself. To be responsible for the other, however, without suspending or compromising that responsibility by conforming to conventional rules and codes becomes the torture for him of ethical transcendence. Not finding comfort or guidance that he can use in this critical time from traditional religious, social, or cultural auspices, Frankie stands alone in a situation of what Levinas terms "passivity" or being infinitely accessible to, as J. Aaron Simmons says, "the call to responsibility."[9] Concerning Maggie, Frankie faces, as Levinas says, "a responsibility that cannot be declined," one that offers him no escape.[10]

Levinas's ethics of the other complements in his disciplined philosophical sphere a more mundane philosophy closer to the daily grit and language of the Hit Pit, namely, what could be called Frankie's body of thought on boxing as related by Scrap. Boxing, as Scrap says, goes "backwards" for Frankie. Scrap's narrative voice-over says, "Frankie liked to say that boxing is an unnatural act . . . That everything in boxing is backwards." With Maggie, boxing eventually moves Frankie away from his position of defensive selfhood to the other. In surrendering himself to Maggie, to the other, he adopts a Levinasian way that also proves his theory of boxing as "an unnatural act." The reverse direction of his life from himself to Maggie, from the immanence of autonomous selfhood to the transcendence of the ethical relationship and responsibility for the other, proves Frankie's precepts about boxing as going against the obvious.

Thus, Scrap's voice-over says, "Sometimes best way to deliver a punch is to step back . . . But step back too far, you ain't fighting at all." Later Scrap's voice-over says, "Boxing is an unnatural act . . . You want to move to the left, you don't step left . . . you push on the right toe . . . To move right, you use the left toe . . . Instead of running from the pain like a sane person would do, you step into it. Everything in boxing is backwards."

Beneath the cover of Scrap's soft voice-over, the film dramatizes how both boxing and life work backwards for

Frankie. Frankie helps and trains Big Willie Little (Mike Colter), but gets hurt when the fighter leaves him for another manager with "connections" for a championship fight. While Frankie sits home alone without any reward or recognition for his fighter's success, Big Willie wins, delivering the overhand right that Frankie had taught him to use. Even the name of this big fighter, whom Frankie worked to protect, expresses contradiction and opposition.

Mostly, Frankie moves backwards with Maggie, going against all he believes, and ends her life to save her. Smothering his instinct for self-preservation, he loses the person he loves most by accepting responsibility for an ethical challenge of ultimate meaning.

Witnessing

Levinas's idea of "witnessing" proffers a frame of reference and terminology for addressing the challenge of ethical transcendence and intersubjectivity confronting Frankie. Witnessing for Levinas means an ethical experience that exceeds insistence on what is and what exists in consciousness and language and what can be known with certainty. Scrap dramatizes in his person, identity, sympathies, and actions the witnessing aspect of ethical transcendence in *Million Dollar Baby*.

Thus, Scrap through his gaze and his presence suggests the transcendence of the ethical encounter. In dramatizing the importance and centrality of such witnessing to his ethical philosophy, Levinas returns to the Bible, great literature, and major thinkers. Thinking of such influential ethical sources, Levinas develops the phrase that has become so closely identified with his philosophy of witnessing and ethical transcendence: *"me voici"* or "Here I am." In sentences that could speak to Scrap's importance to the meaning of the film for articulating his awareness and understanding of Frankie's experience, Levinas writes:

> "Here I am" as a witness of the Infinite, but a witness that does not thematize what it bears witness of, and whose truth is not the truth of representation, is not evidence. There is witness, a unique structure, an exception to the rule of being, irreducible to representation, only of the Infinite.[11]

What better or more meaningful words could Frankie speak to Maggie or Scrap to Frankie than "*me voici*" – "Here I am"?

As the force and personification of witnessing, Scrap becomes the gaze and the eyes, the voice and the language in *Million Dollar Baby* of ethical awareness. Scrap remains ineluctably connected to Frankie and Maggie on many levels throughout the film. Scrap envisages the condition for the relationship that develops between Frankie and Maggie. His witnessing allows for the possibility in the film for the transformation of the meaning of Frankie's ethical journey in his relationship with Maggie.

Frankie, Maggie, and Scrap: Cinetext and Performance Text

Maggie begins with nothing and builds up. Frankie starts as a tower of austere and autonomous detachment. She slowly drains the blood from him, breaking him down and redirecting the blood and new life back to him, transforming him into a person who shatters the boundaries of his being and ethical subjectivity. The transformation steadily emerges and manifests itself in the looks and expressions on Eastwood's face, the movements of his body, and in the sounds of his voice. Freeman's Scrap works in between them, a facilitator for the transfusion of love and responsibility.

Million Dollar Baby matches *Unforgiven* in the brilliance of
its execution of what can be called cinetext, namely, the elements that comprise film-shooting, editing, *mise en scène*,
pacing, cinematography, photography, montage, camera
movement, narrative, and framing. As in *Unforgiven*, Eastwood directed *Million Dollar Baby* with great attention to
detail. Each frame, scene, and image comes through as a
careful artistic construction of creative efforts, primarily by
Eastwood as director but in collaboration with the writer,
Paul Haggis, the editor Joel Cox, who also worked on *Unforgiven*, and the cinematographer Tom Stern, among many
others. The timing and pace of the film establish an exquisite,
sensitive, and sustaining rhythm that reinforces its meaning,
complexity, and beauty. As Vaux indicates, "deliberate pacing,
unrushed exchanges between characters, and refusal to glam-
orize boxing" make up the film.[12]

Special attention, however, should be given to performance text in *Million Dollar Baby*, meaning the semiotics, rhetoric, and work of performance, especially by Eastwood
himself. *Million Dollar Baby* provides a case study of how
cinetext and performance text depend upon and sustain each
other. The success of appearance, gestures, voice, presence,
movement, character, and charisma rely upon the effective
work of cinetext. In *Million Dollar Baby*, performance, filming,
and editing become an organic whole. For this film, Hilary
Swank and Morgan Freeman won Academy Awards in their
respective categories, Best Actress and Best Supporting Actor.
Eastwood won Academy Awards for Best Picture and Best
Director, missing out on best actor to Jamie Foxx in *Ray*, an
ironic development for arguably the best performance of
Eastwood's career.

The great boxing films of the past, such as Robert Rossen's
Body and Soul (1947) with John Garfield, Mark Robson's
Champion (1949) with Kirk Douglas, John Huston's *Fat City*

(1972) with Stacy Keach, Martin Scorsese's *Raging Bull* (1980) with Robert De Niro, and perhaps even Michael Mann's biopic *Ali* (2001) with Will Smith, tend to concentrate on the external physical battle of the fighter in the middle of the ring as a visual enactment of the greater internal struggle of moral character involved in the fighter's rise to fame and glory. The real measure of the fighter comes not from statistics about wins and losses or money. Instead, the films emphasize the fighter's rise and fall and rise again as a flawed moral and ethical being who must confront the temptations and vices of great success and overcome them.

Perhaps seeing that he could exploit an unusual situation for film with a female lead in a women's boxing film, Eastwood breaks from this boxing-film history and pattern of concentrating so sharply on the fighter and shares the leading role spotlight with Swank's Maggie. Following Frankie's dictum that boxing invariably works backwards, *Million Dollar Baby* focuses on the redemption of the trainer, Frankie Dunn, as much as it dramatizes Maggie's struggle. The film places a special burden and challenge upon Eastwood's shoulders as an actor. He triumphs.

Robert Sklar brilliantly delineates the significance of Eastwood's performance to *Million Dollar Baby*. Sklar puts Eastwood's performance in *Million Dollar Baby* in the context of the vexing nature of performance for many film critics and scholars. He notes how difficult it has proven to be for many to give performance the attention other aspects of film art often receive. While general audiences and the public at large tend to describe a film as a vehicle for star performance and identify a film with the actors in it, critics and scholars often neglect performance and find acting to be an inconvenient distraction from complex theories of analysis and interpretation, ranging from the philosophical and psychoanalytical models that we often use to semiotic, feminist,

and ideological modes of analysis. Historically, brilliant performances that not only inform and enlighten but in fact
determine the meaning of a film get smothered under our
proclivity toward theoretical jargon and the hermeneutics of
interpretation. Equally significant, the importance of actors'
public personalities and images to the roles they play in a
film also often gets overlooked. As scholars such as James
Naremore and others emphasize, film performance in a
particular role on the screen, public image in the media,
and documentary analysis of a particular star and performance all ineluctably interact to shape meaning in a film.[13] As
Sklar notes in his essay on *Million Dollar Baby*, "Performance
is one aspect of movies that critics have the most difficulty
in writing about – particularly those of an academic bent.
Many seem to regard films as akin to words on a page, except
that actors speak the words."[14] Sklar moves fluidly and persuasively through performance and public personality and
biography in explaining how these elements work together
to infuse a film performance and a film with significance and
meaning.[15]

   In analyzing the importance of Eastwood's performance to
Million Dollar Baby, Sklar insightfully emphasizes the significance of Eastwood's own aging body to his performance.
Sklar also notes that Eastwood's body as part of his performance does not operate in isolation. It clearly helps the success
of Eastwood's physical performance that he works so well
with Swank and Freeman. As Sklar says, "*Million Dollar Baby*
is overwhelmingly a triumph not only of performance but
also of actors displaying their lived bodies (and voices) on
screen. Eastwood, Freeman, Swank's images in this film likely
will be remembered long after Frankie, Scrap, and Maggie's
names have been forgotten."[16] Although Sklar's view of the
longevity of the film itself as a work of film art and a cultural
product can be questioned, it seems quite obvious that the

performances of all three stars and the use of their bodies in their screen performances prove extremely important to the film's overall success. The effectiveness of the performances helps to make *Million Dollar Baby* a classic of lasting significance.

Accordingly, the synthesis of the elements of cinetext and performance text in a coherent and organized progressive movement constitutes a crucial aspect of *Million Dollar Baby*'s artistic triumph. For Eastwood, he proves himself as an actor in a serious character role, not only using his body to effect in an older role, which he had been doing for some years, but primarily to demonstrate and portray internal change and meaning. Eastwood in *Million Dollar Baby* embodies his character in a way that he had not achieved so completely before. In his role as Frankie Dunn, he acquires a new maturity as an actor becoming the character he plays, thereby even exceeding his acting success in *Unforgiven* a dozen years earlier. His star identity as Eastwood adds depth and history to his role as the trainer but does not prove indispensable for the success of his work and acting, a situation, as Sklar notes, that occurs so often in star performances in film. This acting achievement in *Million Dollar Baby*, therefore, differs from many of Eastwood's previous film performances in which being the star personality proves crucial to the identity of the character. In *Million Dollar Baby*, Eastwood acts.

Eastwood constructed the success of his performance in *Million Dollar Baby* upon a foundation of years of acting and directing experience. Two films in which he directed himself after *Unforgiven* seem instrumental in advancing Eastwood to his work in *Million Dollar Baby*. The star and public personality aspects of Eastwood's history and identity contribute to his success in both roles. In *A Perfect World* (1993) with Kevin Costner (Butch Haynes), Eastwood plays Red Garnett, a Texas Ranger in charge of recapturing Haynes after his escape from prison. Throughout the film, Eastwood exhibits his macho charisma, standing with ramrod strength and discipline as the embodiment and personification of police and military authority.

At the end, however, it becomes clear that Garnett's unforgiving treatment of Haynes as a youthful offender contributed to Haynes's life of delinquency and crime. Learning finally that Haynes has a core of decency and a loving nature that never developed because of abuse and imprisonment, Garnett expresses regret and uncertainty over his earlier actions toward him that at least verbally undermine the Ranger's rock-solid pose of masculine confidence. He says, "I don't know nothing. I don't know a damn thing." The admission by Ranger Garnett involves more than accepting responsibility for a mistake in years past, for it also suggests a new degree of uncertainty about his own values and capabilities. Even so basic a gesture as Eastwood's words of regret and self-doubt in *A Perfect World* seem significant in the development of Eastwood's acting and directing. Such a recognition of vulnerability follows the signs of serious maturation in *Unforgiven* just the year before.

Two years later, after many shots of an extremely fit and handsome Eastwood, one scene in particular in *The Bridges of Madison County* (1995), with Meryl Streep, especially suggests his growing confidence as both a director and performer. Standing soaking wet in the rain with his head uncovered, his thinning hair a straggly mess over his wet high forehead, his face a picture of yearning and weakness, Eastwood as Robert Kincaid, the peripatetic photographer, hopes that Francesca Johnson (Streep) will leave her husband and children and their Iowa farm to start her life over with him. Eastwood in this film, as Streep has told Richard Schickel, evidences a "feminine sensibility" that suggests depth and intensity of character.

When Eastwood has shown himself vulnerable and at risk before, he has often conveyed a hidden dynamic of potentially explosive resilience and power, as in *Unforgiven*, that goes a long way toward countering any actual diminution of his masculinity and strength. Unmitigated masculinity usually obtains for Eastwood's adventure-style popular films. In contrast, in the rain-soaked scene in *Bridges of Madison County*, an initial long shot of Eastwood in the downpour decreases his size and potential threat, while the close-up of his longing expression of need for Francesca leaves no doubt about his sense of abandonment.

While both *A Perfect World* and *Bridges of Madison County* evidence Eastwood's growth that took him to his masterful performance in *Million Dollar Baby*, his return to working with Morgan Freeman in *Million Dollar Baby* after their extraordinary success together in *Unforgiven* also helps account for the success of the boxing movie.

In their roles in *Million Dollar Baby*, Eastwood and Freeman operate with each other in combative compatibility, a cranky, crotchety old-man competitiveness that masks deep layers of sentiment and affection. The two men engage each other in a kind of Hemingway hard-boiled style of interaction that sometimes borders on verbal abuse that could be mistaken for genuine antagonism. Hemingway sometimes referred to this style of language and life as managing "to show a little irony and pity."[17] Frankie and Scrap growl at each other over the cost and brand of bleach for cleaning, the holes in Scrap's socks, the continued presence in the Hit Pit of "Danger" (Jay Baruchel), the mentally challenged young man Scrap tries to nurture and protect over Frankie's vociferous objections.

In one argument between them over Frankie's failure to keep Big Willie as a boxer, Scrap says ironically but with a touch of bitterness as well, "Right, you're the smart one . . .

You're the one learnin' Greek." With palpable petulance, Frankie sneers, "It ain't Greek . . . It's Gaelic."

In fact, one of the signs of Frankie's isolation involves his immersion in the study of Gaelic as well as the poetry of William Butler Yeats.[18] He studies a language that guarantees an inability to communicate with most other people. In spite of the allusion to Frankie's dedicated intelligence and independent learning, Scrap gets the better of him in this argument over Big Willie with a smart rejoinder that again speaks to the excellence of Haggis's screenplay. Scrap says, "Well, you just protected yourself out of a championship fight. How do you say that in Gaelic?"

Ultimately, the relationship between the two men achieves a new degree of intimacy through their connection to Maggie. Frankie's history of trying to protect Scrap on matters of race and of failing to protect him as a cut man in the ring, so that Scrap was blinded in one eye, and Scrap's consistent loyalty as the secondary partner in the relationship merge in the displacement of their energy onto Maggie. They become like doting parents. In this development, Scrap leads the way.

In one scene, Scrap stops shutting the lights of the gym for the night when he hears Maggie by herself pounding the heavy body bag. The scene pictures Maggie in her own light, signifying her single-mindedness and lonely determination. She looks up at Scrap as he goes toward her. He tells her to think of the heavy bag as though it were a man, how to hit when the bag moves away so that it doesn't knock her back, how to hold her shoulder in anticipation of throwing a punch, and how to balance herself. At the end of the brief lesson, he tells her to just close the gym door when she finishes her workout, but he also lets her satisfy her curiosity and peek into his room in the gym and then laughs with pleasure over her innocence and inexperience when she enthusiastically says, "It's nice!" – a charming moment in the film, providing a perfect rendering of how such a neatly kept and apparently secure place, no matter how meager and modest, can look so comfortable and cozy as to make Maggie smile with appreciation.

A subsequent scene puts Scrap, Frankie, and Maggie together when Frankie looks disapprovingly at Maggie's struggles with the speed bag. Scrap had told her that after working the heavy bag, she could start on the speed bag. Once, as Frankie passes, she says, "Working the bag, boss," and he responds without stopping, "I'm not your boss and that bag is working you." Also watching her on the speed bag, Scrap says to Frankie, "She might just be a natural . . . Looks like she's got something." Unconvinced, Frankie answers, "She's got my speed bag, that's what she's got."

The successful outcome for Maggie over her struggle with Frankie for the speed bag anticipates her greater triumph over boxing in their relationship. Finally succumbing to her out of a mocking fear that she will cry, he barks, "Here . . . keep the God damn thing," but asks her just not to lose it.

Mo Cuishle: My Darling, My Blood

In a kind of rough poetry of boxing, Scrap's voice-over says what it will take to make Maggie into a real fighter, a champion. It occurs after Frankie takes her on. As a montage of images shows Frankie working with Maggie, jabbing and stabbing at her, going on his knees to position her legs, instructing her on how to move and balance, Scrap says, "To make a fighter, you gotta strip 'em down to bare wood." Throughout that voice-over, the montage shows Maggie getting stronger and stronger as she slugs away at Frankie and his punch mitts. She goes through other exercises and actions, steadily demonstrating increasing power and skill.

Scrap's voice-over also details Maggie's background story to indicate how far she will have to rise to achieve her goals. Early into the movie, Scrap relates how Maggie grew up in poverty in the Ozarks. The montage with this voice-over shows Maggie working in a restaurant, scraping dishes, cleaning tables, and grabbing food half-eaten by patrons for herself. Scrap says, "She grew up knowing one thing: she was trash."

The sign of a momentous change in Frankie occurs in a pivotal scene when he decides to help Maggie. It occurs in the Hit Pit after Frankie and Scrap have commiserated with each other following Big Willie's championship bout earlier that evening. Scrap has just commented on how Frankie's conscience compelled him years before to help Scrap in a jam over race in Tupelo, Mississippi. Conscience calls again, this time in the sound of Maggie hitting the speed bag, as usual by herself in the gym with everyone somewhere else. Scrap does not need to think about the source of the sound and activity. He simply says, "It's her birthday."

Frankie with his jacket on his arm leaves Scrap behind on his cot, eating his gift of a cheeseburger, and walks into the darkened Hit Pit. Over the months, he has watched her from his office window working and getting stronger. In a long shot in the dark gym, shadow covers the top part of Frankie's body as he walks into the light and observes Maggie in her own shaft of light, surrounded by shadow, trying to catch her breath after hitting the speed bag. In the gruff growl that Eastwood carefully cultivated for Frankie's voice and speech patterns, he says, "You're not breathing right, that's why you're panting." He moves a little closer. "So it's your birthday, huh? How old does that make yuh?"

As Frankie moves into her light, Maggie answers with one of her longest single speeches of the film. Eastwood shoots, lights, and paces the scene with care, making a sequence of great simplicity, honesty, and beauty. Light bathes and reflects off of the white brick of the wall by the hit bag. Key light and shadow show Eastwood with his military-style close haircut and the intense expression of a Marine sergeant. He wears a simple T-shirt in a kind of military green fatigues color that shows how he remains in good physical shape. In the background a red light such as an exit sign over a door and another light give the scene dimension and depth. A reverse shot cuts to Maggie with her hands on her hips. She stands half in shadow with the reflected light on the wall much brighter and sharper than in the previous shot. The hit bag hangs between them. They face each other squarely, his height giving him a bit of an edge over her.

She says, "I'm thirty-two, Mr. Dunn. And I'm here celebrating the fact that I've spent another year scraping dishes and waitressing, which is what I've been doing since I was thirteen, and according to you I will be thirty-seven before I can throw a decent punch." Maggie stops and in frustration strikes the bag and adds, "which after hitting this speed bag for a month and gettin' nowhere, I now realize may be God's simple truth."

As Maggie continues to speak, her voice gets more intense, breaking a bit and wavering with emotion. The camera stays on her, moving closer, but also cutting to show Eastwood intently listening and observing, though without any obvious emotion. She says, "Other truth is, my brother's in prison, my sister cheats on welfare by pretendin' one of her babies is still alive, my daddy's dead and my momma weighs 312 pounds. And if I was thinking straight, I'd go back home, find a used trailer, buy a deep fryer and some Oreos." Without interruption or even a significant facial gesture from Frankie,

she ends with a summary of the meaning of her life to that
point. She says, "Problem is this is the only thing I ever felt
good doin'. If I'm too old for this, then I got nothing else.
That nuff truth to suit you?"

As she starts hitting the speed bag again, Frankie in frustration over her words and her poor timing and awkward
motion with the bag stops her, gesturing to make a serious
concession. He growls, "Hold it! Hold it! I'll show you a few
things and then we'll get you a trainer." From over his shoulder the camera cuts to her face. Without any pause, she says,
"No, sorry!"

The camera cuts back to an astounded Frankie. The look
on his face and his voice signal that this birthday for Maggie
will mark a new beginning for both of them and for *Million
Dollar Baby*. Her words of rejection have struck right at him.
The shock of it awakens him to a moment of recognition and
revelation. His expression shows that he suddenly comes
closer to seeing her. He sees her face. She suddenly stops
being just an annoyance, an intrusion into his comfort zone,
a pathetic and lonely alien figure. He no longer needs to fight
the demand to feel sorry for her. Eastwood's response to
Maggie's rejection turns the scene and the film.

Tilting his head just a bit in wonder, Frankie in a voice
that has lost some of its growl, becoming almost a gasp, says
to her, "You're in a position to negotiate?"

Frankie starts to realize that he has walked into her light
in the gym with his guard down and she has won. She changes
the terms and language of negotiation, already making their
connection a parental relationship where he exercises control
but she holds the power. Maggie says in answer to his question, "Yes, sir, because I know if you train me right, I'm going
to be a champ." She then turns the weight of the situation
back on him like a smart counter-puncher. She says, "I seen
you looking at me."

Dumbfounded, Frankie Dunn (Eastwood) asks Maggie Fitzgerald (Hilary Swank), "You're in a position to negotiate?" when he offers to help her. (Million Dollar Baby, 2004, Warner Bros, Lakeshore Entertainment, Malpaso Productions, Albert S. Ruddy Productions, Epsilon Motion Pictures, dir. Clint Eastwood.)

His automatic response lacks fire and conviction, reflecting a habit of speech and emotion that works with Scrap and others to deflect the painful and uncomfortable. He says, "Yeah, outa pity," but she immediately rejects and overcomes the sarcasm with the power of pure and honest emotion. Her voice rises and changes pitch and tone in anger as she even outstares him. She says, "Don't you say that! Don't you say that if it ain't true."

While Scrap watches from the shadows in his usual secondary position, she returns to the bag. Frankie shouts for her to stop and throws his jacket down. "What the hell are you doing?" He starts the new relationship with the words, "Okay, if I'm going to take you on?," but she interrupts him a couple of times like a happy child, and he moans, "God, this is already a mistake," an appeal that will grow in significance.

An emotional and artistic purity suffuses the scene in the gym. It relies on the interaction between the actors and the power of language, timing, and setting. The scene remains honest as she accedes to his insistence that he will agree only to "teach you to fight" and then will leave her with a real manager.

As he talks to her and tries to set the terms for their relationship, Frankie's speech becomes a kind of monologue filled with anger at himself over this new turn in his life. The more he mutters and growls, the more she smiles, her face ultimately glowing in the heat of his emotion, like a teenager with her father.

The scene then changes to a different tone and becomes charming as Frankie immediately starts his instruction but with a sudden awkwardness and self-consciousness that his growl only accentuates, as Maggie smiles and beams like a daughter. Frankie tells her about balancing her feet and shifting her weight. He tells her to "Bend your knees a little bit . . . Get in an athletic position . . . Look like you're gonna hit something." He says "how" you hit means more than hitting "hard." He works the bag himself to show her, using an ice-pick example to describe the backhanded motion, and tells her to count to contrive a punching rhythm with the bag. As he makes his own rhythm with the bag, restrained non-diegetic music starts, signaling a transition but more importantly a transformation in both characters.

Frankie's promise to himself and to Maggie to stay with her only to teach her, and then for both of them to move on, contains its own undoing. Their relationship will change the meaning of "teach" for Frankie. Levinas writes, "The presence of the Other is a presence that teaches." For Levinas, such teaching "wrenches experience away from its esthetic self-sufficiency, from its *here*."[19] The rest of *Million Dollar Baby* dramatizes the wrenching of experience to take it away from the immediate and the present to another realm of connection.

Maggie becomes a living illustration of training to fight as a metaphor for the existential challenge of finding and being one's self. This learning process hits a bump and then restarts when Maggie makes the innocent mistake of asking Frankie about his family. From the beginning, the film has created ambiguity about Frankie's history with Katy, the absent daughter, who returns his weekly letters to her with the words "Return to Sender" written across the envelopes. Upset about his daughter, Frankie turns Maggie over to another trainer.[20]

The film and Frankie redeem themselves quickly, however, when Frankie and Scrap soon reappear to attend Maggie's first fight under the new trainer-manager. They watch Maggie regularly drop her left so that she gets hammered persistently by her opponent. Seeing the opponent go over Maggie's left again and again, Frankie shouts "Jesus!" and finally moves out of the shadows to the ring to help Maggie. When both the new manager and the referee demand to know why Frankie now acts like Maggie's manager, Frankie growls, "Yeah, this is my fighter," and the life returns to Maggie's face as Frankie then instructs Maggie to lower her left as she has been doing to the benefit of her opponent, but to step to the side when the opponent cocks her right shoulder to throw her punch. He tells Maggie to then unleash her own "good night hook." The cuts to Frankie's and Scrap's faces as Maggie knocks out her opponent show beautiful approval and joy in typical fight-film fashion.

In the dressing room as Frankie cuts off the tape on Maggie's hands, she says, "You gave me away. How was that protecting me?" She asks, "You gonna leave me again?" A close-up of Frankie, who had moved to the door, shows him moving back from the shadows to the light and to her. He promises what will remain true for the rest of the film and Maggie's life, "Never!" Looking to create a ritual to celebrate the significance and permanence of their new relationship, Frankie asks Maggie where they can find some genuine lemon pie.

When Frankie moves Maggie up in class and her nose gets broken in a fight so the match could be called, close-ups put the emphasis on the anguish, panic, and determination on Frankie's face as he mends her, rather than on the pain that Maggie feels. After Maggie knocks out her opponent, Frankie for the first time says to her from the ringside, "*Mo Cuishle,*" his words in Gaelic of utter affection and admiration. He and Scrap then take her to the hospital. At the hospital, Scrap teases about Frankie's passion for the poetry of Yeats. Scrap says, "Talk a little Yeats to her. Show her what a treat that is." Eastwood proves brilliant in close-ups of various facial expressions of serious parental concern about Maggie. With his reading glasses halfway down his nose and in a half-sleeve green casual golf shirt, he becomes the most devoted and committed of parents.

In the second part of the film, Frankie and Maggie fill space together like a family after so many previous scenes of their separated, isolated lives. In her apartment to tell her about an upcoming fight in England, he sneaks a look at her checkbook like a concerned parent, to check on her finances, and advises her like her real father.

In England, before a fight that could lead to a championship bout, Frankie gives her an audacious and expensive Kelly-green robe with the words in Gaelic on it, *Mo Cuishle.* Montage and voice-over continue to propel the story as Maggie wins the fight in England against her Jamaican opponent and becomes a boxing sensation, first in Europe and then in America, with the words *Mo Cuishle* becoming a clarion call for her cheering and riotous fans. After fighting in Paris, Edinburgh, Amsterdam, and other European cities, Maggie returns to the States, as Scrap says, "in a whole new league."

While Frankie arranges Maggie's life with a fight that will end her career and lead to her death, the introduction into the film of Maggie's actual family cements the relationship between Frankie and Maggie. Frankie keeps his distance when he accompanies Maggie to visit her family so she can make a present of a house she bought for her mother. The unappreciative mother and family act out in a few minutes what Maggie had said about them regarding obesity, selfishness, and slovenliness, increasing Frankie's felt responsibility for her. The encounter with her family also speaks to issues of class and poverty as part of Maggie's background and personal triumph.[21]

After seeing a little girl with her pet dog at a gas station, Maggie tells Frankie on the drive back from visiting her family about how much she loved her deceased father. She elicits a sympathetic response from him with her story about her father's love for a dog named Axel. She says her father eventually had to put Axel to sleep.

With those memories and the day's events in mind, Maggie tells Frankie in the darkness of the car driving through the night, "I got nobody but you, Frankie." He whispers, "Well, you've got me."

In another beautiful scene of simplicity, immediacy, and emotional honesty, Eastwood's softly sensitive guitar music accompanies lights from passing cars that flash on Frankie's and Maggie's faces; the rhythm of the lights and shadows makes its own kind of music. Following the story about her father and the day's experience with her family, the close-ups in light and darkness contribute to the rhythms of care and love. Frankie puts a smile on his face over his comment about Maggie always having him. He teases, "At least, that is, until we find you a good manager." His broad grin and strong face belie the proven uncertainty in a promise of permanence, of always being there.

The scene ends with their new ritual of celebrating their relationship with real lemon pie, this time at a special roadside diner where Maggie used to go with her father. Replacing Maggie's deceased biological father, Frankie's relationship with her takes on a new dimension of meaning about love, care, and responsibility. After the ritual of eating real lemon pie together, he declares his readiness for heaven. His worst time on earth, however, has yet to come.

Mo Cuishle and *Akedah:* Frankie and the Priest

At a crucial point in the film, a clash of egos between Frankie and Scrap over hurt feelings, pride, and responsibility for Maggie manifests deeper tensions about the body, masculinity, gender, and race. In the scene, excitement over good news instigates the opening of old wounds and attitudes. The pungent exchange of insults starts when Frankie's report of a deal for Maggie's championship fight with Blue Bear inspires Scrap to depart from his usually reserved demeanor to follow after Frankie with his mop in his hands and express his enthusiastic approval; but Scrap then offends Frankie by declining his offer to take him to Las Vegas as his "second." Feeling the tension, Scrap peevishly tells Frankie to get "somebody there in Vegas . . . somebody with young hands" to be his second in the corner. Frankie mockingly responds, "You're not gonna cry now, are you? I've already got one girl." Wishing to tease Scrap out of any hurt feelings, Frankie unfortunately wins their exchange with sentiments that echo his previous sexist language and views.

Frankie's words foreshadow his own tears at the end of the film. Scrap's someone with "young hands" to work in Maggie's corner foreshadows the fateful placement in the ring by a stranger's hands of the stool that cripples Maggie.

Frankie's remark compels further elaboration given its various implications. His tease about girls and tears equates Scrap's and Maggie's bodies. His words feminize Scrap, picking up on Freeman's wifely nurturing role in *Unforgiven*, while patronizing and diminishing Maggie. The tease uncovers currents of racism and sexism in Frankie's attitudes that contradict his better nature. Given their past histories with Frankie, both Maggie and Scrap overcome any hurt feelings.

Frankie's wisecrack, "I've already got one girl," in fact speaks more directly to Frankie's own way of being in the world. The joke distances and therefore protects him from the very people and the situations he cares most about, while at the same time indirectly recognizing their importance to him. Still going backward, doing and saying one thing but meaning another, Frankie's teasing about changing gender and sexuality dissimulates his respect for Maggie and his own self-satisfaction over her achievement in proving him wrong about training girls by transmogrifying her flesh into the armor of a fierce fighter, a great first million-dollar women's champion.

The focus remains on Eastwood as he instructs his fighter how to win. (Million Dollar Baby, *2004,* Warner Bros, Lakeshore Entertainment, *Malpaso Productions, Albert S. Ruddy Productions, Epsilon Motion Pictures, dir. Clint Eastwood.)*

Most important, psychologically Frankie's tease acknowledges that Maggie embodies the words inscribed on her robe, *Mo Cuishle*, my darling, my blood, the promise of their paternal relationship. The words signify a transformation of her life and flesh into a new being with a new identity related to him, Frankie the father. He teases in part to gain control of his emotional investment in Maggie and his relationship with her.

For Frankie, who loves and reads poetry and studies Yeats, *Mo Cuishle* becomes a simple two-word poem that takes on religious significance to give life new meaning for Maggie and him. Their blood bond clearly signifies a kind of religious transformation. The word becomes flesh for both Maggie and Frankie. The words make Maggie his own flesh and blood, substituting her for his absent daughter, Katy. Frankie's refusal to tell Maggie the meaning of the words *Mo Cuishle* deepens the mystery and power for her of these words. Their mystery suggests more than just a kind of father and daughter game. She esteems the religious aura of the words as part of the ritual of transformation. She must learn their meaning only from her new spiritual father at the appropriate time of his choosing. Through his words and actions, he gives, and she happily and hungrily takes in his own body and blood.

The movie implies the crowds at Maggie's matches help create the atmosphere of a religious ritual. They sense in Maggie and her victories the triumph of something new. They become part of the religious ceremony, believing in the transforming power for themselves of the drama of the match and the mystery of the name in a foreign tongue. As Scrap says, no matter the city or country, they all want to be Irish.

Frankie's use of *Mo Cuishle* also follows what Richard Kearney terms a "sacramental aesthetic." Kearney says in such writers as Proust and Joyce, "the work of metaphor" becomes a force to suggest "figures of resurrection and transubstantiation." He argues that "the textual deployment of metaphor as sacramental act articulates an artistic imagination" that has survived the challenges of atheism and agnosticism, what the German sociologist Max Weber, says Kearney, famously calls the "'disenchantment of modernity.'"[22] For Frankie, the words *Mo Cuishle* enable him to imbue Maggie and himself with, in Kearney's phrase, "a refigured existence." Kearney writes, "The double trope of metaphor-metonymy is what we have been calling transubstantiation. The reversible translation of word into flesh and flesh into word" (*RK*: 117, 118).

Kearney goes on to develop his argument on substantiation, transformation, and metaphor in his discussion of Kristeva's work on language, psychoanalysis, and philosophy. Kearney says Kristeva also sees an "aesthetic of transubstantiation" in such writers as Proust and Joyce. He writes, "In both writing and healing, the reversible transubstantiation of word and flesh expresses itself as catharsis" (*RK*: 98). He says that Kristeva wants us "to think flesh more phenomenologically," to reconsider how to view and think about the flesh, so that it becomes possible to achieve the transcendent in the immanent, to go beyond the immediacy of the physical, empirical body to another form of experience that includes both the body and what she calls the soul or psychic life (*RK*: 97, 99). He says "Kristeva takes the miracle of the carnal" as a basic model for "therapeutic healing" as well as for "reading literary texts" (*RK*: 97–8).

Kristeva in turn relates her writing in the novel *Murder in Byzantium* (2006) to other forms of discourse, saying "every event of discourse" inevitably "is inseparable from the passion of a living body: from its flesh, its perceptions, its familial, social, and historical bindings and unbindings." Kristeva continues, "There is no event that is not somehow word and flesh, and the event itself is nothing other than the copresence of word and flesh."[23]

Kristeva argues that the inescapable connection between the word and flesh becomes especially important in "the Orthodox faith." She says that "the Word is made Flesh in an Orthodox Church, no doubt about it."[24]

Kristeva, as previously discussed, also insists that throughout history in religious practice and belief the ritual of sacrifice fuels and structures the interconnection between the body and language. She says, "The Bible offers the best description of this transformation of sacrifice into language, this displacement of murder into a system of meanings."[25]

The relationship Kristeva proffers between the transformational power of literature and the regenerative violence of sacrifice connects immediately and powerfully to the story of Frankie and Maggie in *Million Dollar Baby*. Enacting his metaphors and symbols, Frankie oversees and Maggie lovingly participates in boxing as a ritual of sacrifice to motivate and revivify the imagination, the body, and the soul for transformation. The interaction between the flesh and the word for the desired transformation compels a ritual of a sacrifice to infuse special meaning and significance into the body–word relationship, one that boxing uniquely provides. As Sara Anson Vaux says, "the possible parallel between boxing and religious ritual" exists in *Million Dollar Baby* so that the boxing in the film "resembles human sacrifice."[26]

Maggie's sacrifice contrasts with a bleeding Jake La Motta (Robert De Niro) in *Raging Bull*, in his struggle for a purely personal redemption in his last fight with Sugar Ray Robinson. More like Charlie Davis in *Body and Soul*, Maggie fights and sacrifices to be part of something greater in her relationship with Frankie and Scrap. She fights to achieve a new life and identity.[27]

Mo Cuishle also fulfills on both psychoanalytical and ethical levels of meaning probably the deepest and most profound desires for both Maggie and Frankie, the desire for the parental relationship of infinite love, care, and responsibility. Frankie enacts and performs a term Kristeva repeats from Freud that also was important in other Eastwood movies such as *Pale Rider*. Frankie becomes the " 'Father in personal prehistory.' " Kristeva writes, "Freud characterized this particular Father, who is necessary for the Ego-ideal, as a support for 'primary identification.' He referred to him as the 'Father in personal prehistory' (*Vater der personlichen Vorzeit*)." She maintains "Freud postulated that apprehension of this father is 'direct and immediate' (*direkte und unmittelbarre*), and emphasized that he internalizes both parents and genders."[28]

The duality of this figure of the *Vater* that Kristeva and Freud emphasize as both father and mother informs the relationship between Frankie and Maggie. As Kristeva says, "The immediacy of this absolute, which the young child of a Mother-Father in personal prehistory brings back to a mysterious and direct grasp, guarantees his ability to idealize."[29]

Frankie becomes that father in personal pre-history for Maggie, an idealized figure who replaces her dead father and uncaring mother. Following Freud, in Maggie's mind Frankie even takes on something of a transcendent aspect, somewhat like other figures in previous Eastwood films.

In the first part of the film's narrative, scene after scene propels *Million Dollar Baby* to the terrifying moment of Maggie's horrific injury. The strengths and details of *Million Dollar Baby* up to the Blue Bear championship fight, including all aspects of cinetext and performance text, enable the film to transition artfully to the challenges of filming Maggie's new condition of total immobility and incapacitation. With Maggie literally imprisoned in her own immobile body and the trappings of life-preserving devices, the camera tends toward even greater concentration upon Frankie and how he deals with the new situation. Swank has the difficult task of performing while unable to move; she also has to speak and work with a tube projecting from her neck and other devices attached to her body. Under Eastwood's careful direction, the montages of Maggie training, working, struggling, and fighting in the first part of the film fade into a new, slower, mournful rhythm of trauma, shock, and grief.

Eastwood brilliantly signals the change in mood, tone, and feel of *Million Dollar Baby* from the seconds that Maggie crashes to the canvas of the boxing ring and smashes her head against the stool that has been put there for her by an unfamiliar corner man. The overhead spotlights that made Maggie the fighter the center of attention swirl around in a shot from Maggie's position on the canvas as bodies encircle her and faces look down on her with anxiety and horror, most importantly Frankie's anguished face and look.

With what deserves to be called film-making brilliance, Eastwood uses the technique of the fade to black to articulate the sudden nothingness that becomes Maggie's new existence. The blackness opens to Maggie in her hospital bed. The sounds of the respirator that will persist through the rest of the movie help establish the new tempo of the distance, separation, and isolation of Maggie's condition. The camera closes in on her bruised and battered face. A tube passes into her neck through an opening in a harsh yellow neck brace that holds her head up. Her eyes show the confusion of a caged animal. She makes a gurgling sound that dramatizes the impossibility of speech and of words to convey her loss. The camera fades to black again, leaving Maggie in darkness and separation.

In the cut to Frankie at Maggie's bedside, the sound and tone of his voice and the simplicity of his words incorporate a new rhythm into the film. The shot shows half of Frankie's face in strong light with the other half in complete darkness. His face and bearing suggest a difficult mixture of a strong presence and calming influence with a complex sense of the incomprehensible as he looks at Maggie. The cuts to darkness insinuate in black Maggie's condition of mental and physical despair and nothingness.

At her bedside in the hospital in Las Vegas, he simply says as she opens her eyes, "How you feelin', darlin'?" and looks into the emptiness in her eyes. Even then, they manage to engage each other without pity. She comments on his stubble of beard. He clearly has been visiting her over several days without shaving, waiting for her to wake from the coma. She says, "You growin' a beard, boss?" He answers, "I thought it might help me with the ladies," and she says before closing her eyes, "Can't say it does."

As Maggie drifts off, Frankie reaches out to touch her. He lovingly, even caressingly like a mother, wipes her forehead and strokes her head, gestures of love and care that illustrate the evolution of his relationship with Maggie.

Just as Maggie tries to understand by blaming herself, Frankie displaces the frustration and guilt he feels over his role in her injury by directing it toward Maggie's doctors. Instead of the usual argument with Scrap, he argues ironically and sarcastically with himself about the doctors. In the Las Vegas hospital, Frankie growls, "I'm gonna get you outa here . . . These doctors around here don't know squat . . . Why else would they be living out here in the desert?" He says, "I'm gonna find some place where they actually studied medicine."

With the aid of the somber tone and beat of Scrap's voice-over, *Million Dollar Baby* assiduously details Frankie's deepening role as Maggie's nurse and caretaker. As the film progresses, Maggie's unspeakably sad condition actually

worsens and grows increasingly dire. The more she deteriorates, the more Frankie gives of himself to her in love
and care.

Still in her Las Vegas hospital room, Frankie sponges her,
carefully holding up her arms and tenderly washing them.
His face registers and the voice-over reports that her immobility causes skin ulcers. Frankie sees them with helpless
concern and pain. As he washes her, she says, "They got
nurses for that, you know!" He answers, "Yeah, but they're
amateurs." Frankie now makes a profession of being Maggie's
nurse and caretaker. He has changed his work to a profession
of caring and loving. Key light on his face shows his concentration on her. As shadow soon covers both their faces, she
whispers in close-up, "Thank you," and the camera then stays
on Frankie's face to show absolute, hopeless sorrow. To the
accompaniment of Eastwood's ever so soft music, the camera
holds on his face long enough to make the sadness almost
unbearable. He turns and looks off to his left. The shot
accentuates a scar over his right eye that extends from above
his eyebrow to his upper cheek. Other close-ups later show
steadily deepening teary lines like thin channels cut into
his face.

In the Serenity Glen Rehabilitation Center that Frankie
finds for Maggie in California, he remains in constant attend-
ance at her side, often with his glasses down his nose as he
reads his book. When she says he can go, he says how much
he enjoys being there. She responds with a smile when he
jokes, "In fact, if you weren't here, I'd come here anyway to
read my books." Holding his book in front of her face, he
soon stops her feeble attempt at reading Gaelic, but then
reads from the Yeats poem himself to her in English.

Some scholars, as previously noted, find the idea of Yeats
writing and even knowing Gaelic problematic. Yet the
meaning of the poem, as Wes Davis says, "expresses a

*As Frankie nurses and cares for the crippled Maggie, Eastwood's face reveals depths of pain, anguish, and helplessness over her condition and his inability to change it. (*Million Dollar Baby, *2004, Warner Bros, Lakeshore Entertainment, Malpaso Productions, Albert S. Ruddy Productions, Epsilon Motion Pictures, dir. Clint Eastwood.)*

*After reading the poetry of William Butler Yeats to Maggie, Frankie tenderly tutors her. (*Million Dollar Baby, *2004, Warner Bros, Lakeshore Entertainment, Malpaso Productions, Albert S. Ruddy Productions, Epsilon Motion Pictures, dir. Clint Eastwood.)*

yearning for escape that fits perfectly with the movie's hope that it may be possible to build a new life." Richard Ellmann similarly maintains that Yeats "filled his poems and stories with dim, pale things, and longed to return to an island like

Innisfree, where his 'old care will cease' because an island was neither mainland nor water but something of both."[30] Reading from "The Lake Isle of Innisfree," Frankie says, "I will arise and go now, and go to Innisfree,/ And a small cabin build there, of clay and wattles made." Skipping some lines, Frankie continues, "And I shall have some peace there, for peace comes dropping slow,/ Dropping from the veils of morning to where the cricket sings." Frankie walks around her, holding the book in his hand and says, "Not bad, huh?" In response to her comment, he says he never will find such peace from boxing. He says, "I'll never quit, I like the stink too much, I guess."

Somewhat like his use of poetry in *Play Misty for Me* to make connections and signal meanings, Eastwood in the scene with Maggie finds in the poem a means to deepen the bond between Frankie and Maggie, as the poem presents the false hope that the two of them could find refuge for themselves in their own small cabin somewhere. The idyllic poetic images of peace and cabins for escape, refuge, and love contrast powerfully with the "stink" of Frankie's actual work and Maggie's condition, but also with the contrary picture of violent, disorderly, and ugly home life that Maggie's biological family reinserts into the film.

With the arrival of Maggie's ungrateful and greedy family for their final scene at the Serenity center, Maggie realizes she belongs only with Frankie as family. The story explains the break with her family as the result of their disastrous visit during which they attempt to gain control of her money and benefits. Frankie with great self-restraint watchfully keeps his distance amidst the family turmoil, maintaining his readiness to help Maggie if necessary. It becomes her decision to place her life and loyalty solely in a new family consisting of Frankie and herself, one that goes beyond biological origins and relies upon a transformation of the flesh for a new vision of her life, a vision something akin to the search for peace in Innisfree.

Interestingly, in the original short story for *Million Dollar Baby*, Toole seems to take pleasure in describing in considerable detail how Frankie through a series of punches and body moves takes out Maggie's brother and even hits her mother and sister. In the conclusion of his account of the parking lot encounter, Toole writes, "Frankie put everything into a right hand and a hook that were designed to rupture J. D.'s left kidney. J. D. screamed and rolled into a gasping ball on the asphalt. Frankie took two quick steps to the mother and daughter and slapped both of them full force in the face. The sister sat flat down, and Earline yelled at J. D. for not protecting her" (*RB*: 89–90). While the film remains true to the story's depiction of the selfishness and crudity of the family, it significantly alters Frankie's behavior by emphasizing his self-control with Maggie's family. In this portion of Toole's story, the Mickey Spillane/Mike Hammer tough-guy prose and violence contrast with Frankie's position in the film of watchful protection of Maggie. In fact, the film puts in a somewhat similar scene of protective and retributive fighting for Scrap as "Old School" against bullies in defense of Danger, the mentally challenged young man at the Hit Pit, perhaps in part to expand Freeman's role.

Frankie's selflessness compared to her family's selfishness cannot stop the steady deterioration of Maggie's body. As Frankie sits in a chair in the background, a doctor tells Maggie that a horrible, bloody scar on her left calf means she probably will have to lose her leg. She closes her eyes and the close-up on Frankie repeats the expression of desperation that has become his look during this portion of the film. In the cut to the next scene, Frankie finds another returned letter from his daughter, Katy, on the floor as he enters his bungalow at night after visiting Maggie. The low-angle close-up of his face conveys an even greater sense of endless loss and emptiness. The scar over his right eye in this close-up now seems to extend to new scars and rivulets of pain down his cheek.

Eastwood creates compelling imagery of time as loss in the next cut as Frankie stands in Maggie's room, looking out the window at the bright California sunlight. Empty space in the middle of the frame indicates the absence of Maggie and her bed. Then overlapping images put her back in the room, but after the surgery that removes her leg. Frankie turns from the window as she awakens. He leans down to her. She says, "They took my leg, boss." He gets closer to her and whispers back, "It's gonna be alright, you hear?" And she answers through her drowsiness, "I always hear your voice, boss," as though Frankie the higher authority has become a transcendent presence and voice to sustain her.

Frankie then leans his body over her to bury his face on her forehead and cheek. He caresses her. He turns his face

In one of Eastwood's most touching moments of emotional expression of love and sympathy, Frankie attends to Maggie after scars compel doctors to remove her leg. He whispers, "It's gonna be alright, you hear." (Million Dollar Baby, 2004, Warner Bros, Lakeshore Entertainment, Malpaso Productions, Albert S. Ruddy Productions, Epsilon Motion Pictures, dir. Clint Eastwood.)

more deeply into hers with kisses. As he raises his head, a cut to his right profile above her shows him in a gesture of bowing his head as though in prayer, his eyes closed above the plastic brace on her neck. The camera pulls back as Frankie rises and turns to sit on the bed with her.

The shot from the corner of the room, of Frankie's back tilting slightly to the right in silent but clear pain and exhaustion, pictures the great tension between endless love and endless impossibility. This may be the single most physically and emotionally compassionate sequence in all of Eastwood's films. It would be hard to find another in his films as actor and director up to this point where he shows greater compassion, love, and tenderness through physical, spiritual, and emotional bonding. Eastwood's restraint adds to the emotional authenticity and power of this hospital scene.

An overlap dissolve shows darkness outside the window and Frankie with his spectacles reading by her bedside by the light from over her headboard, a perfectly evocative and familiar hospital scene. As she awakens again and he asks her if she needs anything, she says, "Need to know what *Mo Cuishle* means." He answers, "Well, you didn't win, I don't have to tell yuh." She smiles in appreciation for his caring tease and says, "You're the meanest man I ever met. No wonder no one loves you." She adds, "You remind me of my daddy." They manage to smile some more about how her daddy "musta been a very intelligent and handsome man," and noticing the large-sized catalogue in his hands, she appeals, "You ain't gonna make me talk no more Yeats, are you?"

He explains that he has been looking at courses for her at City College and thinking about getting her a wheelchair with controls on it that would enable her to attend classes. She can blow into a straw to manipulate the chair. The whispering, teasing banter between them, and the expression of

Frankie's plans for her future and school work like timed beats to set up for the shock of her next request. The close-up of her face indicates no reaction to his idea about going to school, but she says she has a favor to ask. A reverse shot from Maggie's angle in bed shows him lowering his glasses as he says, "Sure," in eager anticipation over doing something to please her. He takes his glasses off, turns to her, and says, "Anything you want."

Her statement puts a totally different expression on Frankie's face. She says, "Remember what my daddy did for Axel?," reminding him of her father's dog that he put to sleep. In quick cuts, the camera moves closer to Frankie's face. He says, "Don't even think about that."

The movement of the camera, the pulsating respirator, and Eastwood's sensitive non-diegetic music all work together to indicate the unreality and impossibility for Frankie of Maggie's request. Maggie appeals to him with her own dignity about how she had achieved great heights as a boxer because of him. She says, "People chanted my name. Well, not my name, some damn name you gave me." Having fought at birth to get into the world as a two pound, one and a half ounces baby, she says her father said she also would have to fight her way out. She says with calm determination that she has received all she needs from life and now feels prepared to go without having to lose more of herself in such painful increments of helpless dependence.

Frankie listens to her in quiet intensity. His face shows unbearable strain. He grits his teeth and moves his face ever so slightly. He whispers precisely, "I can't. Please. Please, don't ask me." She says, "I'm asking," and he begs, "I can't," and looks down in silence.

The immediacy of the issue for Frankie sharpens when Maggie twice tries to take her life by biting her tongue so hard that she would bleed to death. In her first attempt,

Frankie gets to the hospital in the middle of the night for the horrible sight of Maggie's face soaked in blood. Pushing an attendant aside, he yells and pleads with Maggie, "Stop! Stop! Look at me! Look at me!" Scrap's voice-over describes how after stitching her up the second time, the doctors padded her mouth to prevent her from trying it again.

Everything in the film has been geared to this point of Frankie's ultimate ethical battle. In carefully constructing Frankie's relationship with Maggie as trainer and then just as carefully reconstructing their relationship with Frankie as nurse and caregiver, the film reaches this moment of absolute ethical and moral crisis.

Maggie's appeal and then her failed attempts at suicide turn the metaphor and idea of sacrifice into an immediate choice for Frankie. The issue of Maggie's life and death becomes the crisis of Frankie's soul. Moreover, Eastwood's performance and direction painstakingly show how Maggie has become Frankie's own lifeline in that his care for her has given him new life in the form of love and meaning. Killing her, he also would take part of his own new life.

From the beginning of *Million Dollar Baby*, Frankie has been a man on an existential, ethical, and emotional search for meaning. In a sense, he also has been looking along with Maggie for his own father in personal pre-history. His search can be considered religious but not just because of his Catholic faith and practice. As a practicing Catholic, Frankie not only attends Mass every day; he also regularly prays, including a prayer at the beginning of the film imploring God to watch over his estranged daughter Katy and someone named Anne, who remains a mystery. In addition to such practices, his search throughout the film for meaning greater than himself makes his quest a religious one.

Maggie's request brings Frankie to the ethical and moral breaking point. He must choose. Like Abraham on Mount

Moriah with Isaac at the moment of the *Akedah* or "the binding of Isaac," Frankie stands ready to end the life of the one he loves. In developing Frankie's character and his relationships to others so well, *Million Dollar Baby* positions him to engage and dramatize the many dimensions of the ethical crisis over Maggie with credible intelligence and passion.

Frankie's search for meaning at the beginning of the film takes its most obvious form in his penchant for pestering and badgering his priest, Father Horvak (Brian O'Byrne). Frankie tests the Father's patience and tolerance by continually asking him questions the Father believes any child could answer through the concept of faith. Close-ups of Frankie show a kind of juvenile smirk of pleasure over tormenting the priest with questions about the Holy Trinity and the Immaculate Conception. Frankie manages to goad the Father into cursing him as a "pagan." The Father gets back at him by checking if Frankie continues to write to Katy every week. In spite of Frankie's antics that compare to his verbal jousting with Scrap, the priest recognizes Frankie to be a man on a quest, one that the priest really cannot quite understand but that he knows demands attention.

Frankie, therefore, goes to the priest in his hour of need. He appears in a long shot moving toward the camera and looking lost, in a daze on an empty city street in the early morning hours. He has become the sleepless man of the night who can find no rest from the torment of his conflicting values and demands. Out in the night, he waits for the break of dawn to find help.

A high-angle establishing shot from the rear of the church shows Frankie and Father Horvak seated in the first row to the right of the altar. Frankie has prayed before for Maggie by himself with his head bowed at this church. The Father's voice takes the long shot to a reverse shot from the front of the church to focus in a medium shot on the two men together, with Frankie hunched over a bit. Sitting sternly next to him with his hands clasped on his lap, Father Horvak says, "You can't do it. You know that."

In this scene with the priest after Maggie's failed suicide attempts, Eastwood once again in *Million Dollar Baby* goes to an unprecedented extreme for him as an actor in displaying emotion and succumbing to his character's fears and vulnerabilities. With the priest, Frankie drops all pretense of control over the situation. He ultimately becomes unhinged, especially for an Eastwood portrayal.

Frankie's low gruff voice, barely above a whisper, resonates in the empty church. He says, "I do, Father. You don't know how thick she is . . . how hard it was to train her . . . Other fighters would do exactly what you'd say to them and she'd ask why this and why that and then do it her own way anyway . . . How she fought for the title . . . It wasn't by anything . . . it wasn't by listening to me."

As Frankie speaks, the camera remains in a two-shot of the two men, cutting from the left to the right and back. The camera movement envelopes them together as they speak and engage each other. The camera then moves a good bit closer, shooting from an angle from the left of the frame. The Father looks intently at Frankie, whose face goes into shadow as he looks up to the altar and Christ on the crucifix. The Father turns sharply to look also and the camera cuts to their left and the right side of the frame. From this angle, lines cover the left side of Frankie's face. His eyes strain on the brink of tears. The camera moves in closer, and he can barely speak as his face draws tighter and tighter. He says, "But now she wants to die, and I want to keep her with me." A quick close-up shows Father Horvak completely immersed in Frankie's words and emotion.

Looking down and fighting back tears, Frankie says, "I swear to God, Father, it's committing a sin by doing it . . .

By keeping her alive, I'm killing her." At this point, as his facial movements follow his softly spoken words, Frankie starts to break, almost crying. Frankie puts his chin down and chest back, horrified by the impossible situation his words describe. He appeals to the priest, "You know what I mean?"

Frankie describes two opposing, contradictory sinful acts for him – to kill Maggie outright or to kill her by keeping her alive so that she dies painfully every minute of every day. He confesses to what he sees as his great guilt over wanting to keep her alive for himself, so that she therefore would die just a little bit with each passing minute. For Frankie, believing that keeping her alive constitutes a sin at least as bad and perhaps even worse than killing her puts him on a road by himself, condemning him either way he goes. He says to the priest, "How do I get around that?"

Still sitting next to Frankie, with a cold look and with calm resolution and certitude, Father Horvak says, "You don't. You step aside, Frankie. You leave her with God." In response, Frankie's voice and face express a hideous, unresolvable tension between total hysteria and self-destructive control. Inexpressible anger and the torture of unbearable guilt come through in his face and words. Near to tears of impotent moral and emotional outrage, Frankie turns to the priest. He growls, "She's not asking for God's help. She's asking for mine!"

Father Horvak speaks with force. His careful pauses and breathing accentuate his seriousness. He says, "Frankie, I've seen you at Mass almost every day for 23 years. The only person comes to church that much is the kind who can't forgive himself for something. Whatever sins you're carrying, they're nothing compared to this. Forget about God or heaven and hell." As he speaks, the Father looks from Frankie's face to the cross and back again. He says, "If you do this thing . . . you'll be lost . . . somewhere so deep, you'll never find yourself again."

Listening to the Father's words and looking at him, Frankie's lower lip starts to quiver uncontrollably. His face cracks into entrenched lines of pain and torture. He lowers his head and neck and shoulders, and breaks into unrestrained sobbing.

For at least the second time in this film, Eastwood performs and films himself in a scene that constitutes a climax for his entire career of emotional intensity and vulnerability. Both scenes, one in the hospital with Maggie after her amputation and the second with the priest in the church, center on feelings of desperate weakness before extreme challenges of love and responsibility.

Frankie's honest expression and moral insight into his emotional self-interest in keeping Maggie alive so that he can love and care for her speak to the depth of his character and the brilliance of the film's moral complexity. Going backwards again, Frankie surrenders himself for another. Paradoxically, to give up Maggie means giving up himself to gain

Frankie breaks into uncontrollable tears over the multiplicity of impossible ethical and personal demands placed upon him by Maggie's request for him to take her life. (Million Dollar Baby, 2004, Warner Bros, Lakeshore Entertainment, Malpaso Productions, Albert S. Ruddy Productions, Epsilon Motion Pictures, dir. Clint Eastwood.)

himself in the struggle. Feeling compelled and responsible for deciding for her, Frankie refocuses his moral and ethical vision. Rightly or wrongly, he cannot step aside. Instead of leaving the issue to God, he engages God and his own ethical responsibility to Maggie in determining his moral position and action.

Frankie's position with regard to Maggie and God comes as the culmination of his journey from the beginning of the film, which includes his religious practice and observation as well as his accumulated experiences with others. The founding and structure of his belief do not rely upon an oppositional encounter with his priest and church. He grounds his conscience, beliefs, and actions in felt experience and his thinking and reading about experience, as opposed to abstractions, dogma or orthodoxy. He tests his belief and faith in practice as well as in books. Frankie's special relationship with Maggie places him in an inescapable confrontation with ultimate questions.

Relying in his search for meaning on his innate intellectual propensities and native intelligence, Frankie resists reducing the idea of God the father to a Freudian level of what Kearney calls "infantile dependency" as opposed to viewing the father as a source for psychological structure and philosophical insight. Kearney's project for a rethinking of the relationship to God involves the building of a foundation of belief that can survive childish wishes for the immediate gratification of needs and for the satisfactory resolution of fears and doubts, especially in times of challenge and trauma, precisely the kind of crisis of belief and action that Frankie faces with Maggie. Kearney asks, "When we pray In the Name of the Father do we regress to the primitive rites of infantile dependency and projection (as Freud suggests)? Or is there more to it than that? Something beyond childish superstition and fetishism?" (*RK*: 57).

Similarly, Levinas in "Loving the Torah More than God" also insists on distinguishing between a kind of infantile belief in God and adult religious belief. He argues that a system of belief that reduces people to children inevitably will produce frustrations and disappointments that ultimately open the path to atheism and cynicism. He asks, "What can this suffering of the innocents mean?" He argues that for those who believe that a "fairly primary sort of God had dished out prizes, inflicted punishment or pardoned sins – a God who, in His goodness, treated men like children," for such people with that sort of belief, then innocent suffering eventually could prove the existence of "a world without God, where only man measures Good and Evil."[31]

Levinas argues instead for a different conception of God and the relationship of God to suffering, one that compels an adult response to ultimate questions about meaning. He writes, "The path that leads to the one God must be walked in part without God. True monotheism is duty bound to answer the legitimate demands of atheism. The adult's God is revealed precisely through the void of the child's heaven. This is the moment when God retires from the world and hides His face" (*DF*: 143).

Levinas therefore insists that if at times God seems especially distant and hard to find for answers or comfort, then it becomes incumbent to act like an "adult" by continuing the search alone if necessary but still with absolute responsibility for others. Both Levinas and Kearney affirm the basis of the relationship to God in human relations and the social experience. In other words, individual and social responsibility inhere in religious commitment and the relationship to God. Levinas says, "Man can have confidence in an absent God and also be an adult who can judge his own sense of weakness. The heroic situation in which he places himself gives the world value and equally puts it in danger" (*DF*: 145).

Certainly Frankie experiences for himself the situation
Levinas describes of "the void of the child's heaven" (*DF*:
143) and must walk alone with all of his weaknesses to find
his answer for what to do about Maggie. In his treatment of
Maggie after the injury, Frankie in his unfailing daily acts of
love for her satisfies the demand that Levinas asserts for
"daily fidelity" to the care of others. In "A Religion for
Adults," Levinas says, "The law is effort. The daily fidelity
to the ritual gesture demands a courage that is calmer, nobler
and greater than that of the warrior" (*DF*: 19).

Maggie's wish to die, however, forces Frankie into another
ethical and moral dimension than daily effort and care, one
that he feels he cannot leave only to God. Frankie remains
unable to deny his own individual responsibility to Maggie.
Even facing ultimate ethical and moral questions, he feels
compelled in dealing with that dimension of meaning to go
through the existential person rather than circumvent the felt
and immediate responsibility to the other, to the human. As
Levinas says, "The fact that the relationship with the Divine
crosses the relationship with men and coincides with social
justice is therefore what epitomizes the entire spirit of the
Jewish Bible" (*DF*: 19).

Still on his journey for meaning, Frankie finds himself
chosen, not literally or personally by God but existentially by
Maggie, to consider the Abrahamic dilemma of human sacrifice. For Frankie, Maggie's plea to die constitutes what
Levinas terms "an election, the promotion to a privileged
place on which all that is not me depends."[32] Maggie puts
Frankie in such a "privileged place" when she appeals to him
for a ritual sacrifice of her to conclude the rituals that have
given her life special meaning with him.

In the biblical story of the *Akedah*, God commands
Abraham (Genesis 22:1–19) to sacrifice his son Isaac on
Mount Moriah as an act of faith. Ready to strike with the

knife in his hand, Abraham must choose between one angel who tells him to slay his son and the second who chooses life. Fortunately for Isaac, Abraham chooses not to kill his son. The *Akedah* as studied by a thinker like Levinas can enlighten the meaning of another story of human sacrifice as seen in the case of Maggie and Frankie.

Levinas significantly concentrates much of his analysis of the binding of Isaac by Abraham on perhaps the most famous discussion of it in modern ethical philosophy by Søren Kierkegaard.[33] He writes, "Kierkegaard has a predilection for the biblical story of the sacrificing of Isaac. Thus, he describes the encounter with God as a subjectivity rising to the religious level: God above the ethical order!" (*PN*: 74). Levinas questions what he considers to be Kierkegaard's misplaced emphasis in the story that subsumes ethical subjectivity and intersubjectivity below religion. He says:

> In his evocation of Abraham, he describes the encounter with God at the point where subjectivity rises to the level of the religious, that is to say, above ethics. But one could think the opposite: Abraham's attentiveness to the voice that led him back to the ethical order, in forbidding him to perform a human sacrifice, is the highest point in the drama. That he obeyed the first voice is astonishing: that he had sufficient distance with respect to that obedience to hear the second voice – that is the essential. (*PN*: 77)

Levinas also alludes twice to what he sees as Kierkegaard's major oversight in that "Kierkegaard never speaks of the situation in which Abraham enters into dialogue with God to intercede in favor of Sodom and Gomorrah, in the name of the just who may be present there" (*PN*: 74, 77).

Levinas also worries over the potential violence that he believes Kierkegaard promotes with his priorities of the religious over the social and the intersubjective. He says, "Violence emerges in Kierkegaard at the precise moment when, moving beyond the esthetic stage, existence can no longer limit itself to what it takes to be an ethical stage and enters the religious one, the domain of belief" (*PN*: 72).

Levinas argues that Kierkegaard's problem goes back to an historic concentration in Western philosophy, including from Spinoza to Heidegger, that Kierkegaard assumes with his emphasis on being and the self. Levinas terms this "egotism." He finds "that same tension on oneself that still defines Kierkegaardian subjectivity" (*PN*: 70, 71).

Levinas insinuates his understanding of ethical subjectivity and transcendent responsibility for the other in his response to the challenge to belief and action that the *Akedah* drama-tizes so powerfully. Regarding the story of the *Akedah*, Levinas impugns Kierkegaard's interpretation by refocusing on the responsibility of the subject for the other to the point of making subjectivity dependent on the ethical relationship to the other. He poses the "question" that "signifies the responsibility of the *I* for the Other." He says, "Subjectivity *is* in that responsibility and only irreducible subjectivity can assume a responsibility. That is what constitutes the ethical" (*PN*: 73).

The importance of Levinas's interpretation of the *Akedah* to the situation of sacrifice in Eastwood's film concerns the relation Levinas proposes of the transcendence of the ego to love and responsibility in the ethical movement to the other. With all of the profound differences between the biblical story and the film, including those of sources, outcome, reli-gious meaning, and historical implications, the biblical nar-rative still can be read to elucidate the ethical crisis and encounter in *Million Dollar Baby*.

Accordingly, what Levinas's post-Kierkegaardian interpre-tation of Abraham and Isaac says about subjectivity and ethics also applies to Eastwood's movie. In his argument with Kierkegaard about the *Akedah*, Levinas sees the ethical and religious, the human and the divine, as inexorably sealed as a mandate for responsibility and transcendence. Frankie could say with Levinas in any language of his choice, "To be myself means, then, to be unable to escape responsibility" (*PN*: 73).

J. Aaron Simmons in his study of contemporary phenomenology and religion gives a sense of the enormous background of study not only on the long history of readings and interpretations of the *Akedah*, but also on the extensive heated philosophical and scholarly debate over the similarities and conflicts between Levinas and Kierkegaard on that subject in particular and on modern ethics. In his discussion of Levinas's reading of the *Akedah*, Simmons insightfully notes that "For Levinas, the relationship to God cannot be separated from the relationship to the other person; to love God is to love the engagement with others that occurs in study; to love Torah is, then, also to love the dialogical exchange between those who love it."[34] In the same vein of multiple responsibilities, Frankie too tries to deal with his obligations to God while also living up to his responsibilities to the other. Simmons also notes how Levinas's ethical position on alterity and the other contrasts sharply, as suggested earlier in this study, with Pascal's image of selfhood as " 'my place in the sun.' "[35]

Ironically, in his refusal to surrender responsibility, Frankie, after a lifetime of trying to protect himself and teaching others about self-protection, capitulates to the other in the transcendence of his own ego toward the other. As Levinas says, "The putting in question of the *I* in the face of the Other is a new tension in the *I*, a tension that is not a tensing on oneself. Instead of destroying the *I*, the putting in question binds it to the Other in an incomparable, unique manner" (*PN*: 73). Thus, the gesture that Maggie signals to

Frankie at the end to take her life frees her from the prison of her own injured body and life, but leaves Frankie in a situation of infinite responsibility.

The path Frankie takes in his relationship and responsibility to Maggie does not allow him to step aside as the priest counsels and as his own self-protective instincts would take him. Nor does it quite lead him into the "existentialist turmoil" of Kierkegaard that Simmons describes.[36] Instead, Frankie starts on a path toward what both Kearney and Simmons term "kenosis" or a "self-emptying." Following Levinas, kenosis would take Frankie, as Simmons says, toward "the emptying relation of my self to each and every other with whom I share the world."[37]

Kearney elaborates on kenosis as part of a greater project of rethinking God and the relationship between God and human society in a postmodern, post-Nietzschean world after Auschwitz that imagines God as less of a sovereign, all-powerful God and more in terms of a "divine self-emptying" as proposed by such thinkers as Gianni Vattimo of Italy and Stanislas Breton of France. Imagining a "recovery of the divine within the flesh, a kenotic emptying out of transcendence into the heart of the world's body," Kearney envisions "a sacredness beyond sacrifice" that especially incorporates "the poor and oppressed." He wishes for "a recognition that the infinite is to be found at the core of each finite now, that the divine word inhabits the flesh of the world, in suffering and action" (*RK*: 91, 133, 136, 137).

Kearney, of course, in his philosophy of *Anatheism*, a rethinking about God in a world after God, goes far beyond a simple *Mo Cuishle* in proffering the reversible transformations of the word into the flesh and the flesh into the word for a project on God, religion, and atheism. Eastwood settles for focusing on the relationship of one cut man and his surrogate daughter in a context of the search for transcendence, redemption, and meaning. In the film, Eastwood, as Maurice Yacowar says, makes "an argument for love, not for euthanasia."[38] The moral and ethical questions *Million Dollar Baby* raises in regard to euthanasia, however, help provide the structure for elaborating upon profound issues of belief and the search for meaning, issues of prominence in Eastwood's works from the beginning. As Drucilla Cornell says of his major films, "Eastwood gives us no easy answers to the ethical questions that he raises." Thus, Cornell also examines Maggie and Frankie's relationship from a Levinasian ethical and religious perspective in explaining Frankie's response to Maggie's call to him to take her life. Cornell says, "Yet in Levinas's terms, we never confront God directly. Rather we are powerfully confronted by the ethical demand put on us by the face of the Other who calls out to us for help."[39]

Frankie returns to see Maggie after she has been sedated to prevent her from trying once again to kill herself. Under the influence of the drug, her eyes roll back, indicating her grogginess, until they slowly open on Frankie staring intently back at her. The camera holds tightly on Frankie in deep thought until it cuts back to a close-up of Maggie. Her eyes, the slight opening of her lips, and the angle of her face search him with the question if he will do what she asked of him and end her life. The close-up of his well-lit face in turn shows a thoughtful, calm resolve to be there for her to do what she wants.

He returns once again at night, in silence, to a darkened hallway and her room. He sits at the side of her bed, his face again divided with the left side in pale light and the right side in total shadow. He briefly explains to her how he will put her to sleep. He then leans closer. He whispers, "*Mo Cuishle* means 'my darling, my blood'," and kisses her softly on the cheek with palpable tenderness, warmth, and love. Her face and eyes have been in shadow, but when he raises his head

after kissing her, her eyes look at him with love and appreciation. Her lips manage a smile. A tear trickles down her cheek
as she closes her eyes.

As the father figure Maggie chose and loved, Frankie
helped give her a new name with a new identity and life. He
then takes it all from her. He completes the sacrifice. He
confronts and answers an ultimate demand that was placed
upon him. He assumes on his own the responsibility to act.
With one last kiss to Maggie's face, he walks off alone without
any certain sign in the film if he goes as a murderer who has
sacrificed his soul and being for another, as the priest and
even Toole in his story suggest, or if he has performed
a sacrifice as an act of redemption for a love that revivifies
the soul and overcomes death by giving life new meaning
through love.

At the conclusion of *Million Dollar Baby*, Scrap's voice-over
reveals that Frankie has disappeared and that Scrap's words
have been his letter to Katy, Frankie's daughter. Scrap says,
"No matter where he is . . . I thought you should know what
kind of man your father really was." The statement suggests
approval for Frankie's actions and admiration for him in
finding the courage to act. Throughout the film Katy and
her returned letters have worked as a kind of idea or abstraction, never quite making her a living, concrete reality. Rather
than suffering demonization or vilification in the film for her
absence and her refusal to respond to her father, she evokes
a condition of guilt, loss, and the unknown, a remnant of the
idea in *Unforgiven* and other Eastwood films about life and
the world as unfair in felt existential experience and as the
abyss and the void in meaning.

Such a world and situation, the film suggests, require adult
belief and action. As Levinas says, "This condition reveals a
God Who renounces all aids to manifestation, and appeals
instead to the full maturity of the responsible man. But this

God Who hides His face and abandons the just man to a justice that has no sense of triumph, this distant God, comes from within" (*DF*: 143). Eastwood's film presents such a man of responsibility in Frankie Dunn.

For years, Eastwood's heroes often possessed transcendent or superhuman powers or evidenced pathological proclivities. In *Million Dollar Baby*, however, Eastwood submerges Frankie Dunn in his own humanity. Frankie continues his solitary search for meaning greater than himself in a context of responsibilities that have been thrust upon him as a man and father figure. Called or elected into that position of the ideal father of the Freudian paradigm but also as a man without divine assurance and certainty, Frankie struggles on alone, to paraphrase Levinas, beneath "the void" of an empty sky of pain and uncertainty. Frankie finds his ethical direction in the face of the other that demands an inconceivable and unforgivable fatal act from him, an act that compels the surrender of his own priorities and self in submission to an absolute responsibility to another. In the face of the other, he also finds and confronts the emptiness of that void with "the full maturity of the responsible man."

In the end, Frankie Dunn becomes Eastwood's fullest expression in an individual character of the infinite ethical possibility and the inherent experiential limitations of the human condition. In portraying Frankie so convincingly in a film of such carefully detailed and distinguished direction, Eastwood comes closer than in any of his other movies to imagining the possibility of transcendence in the ethical and human responsibility to the other.

4

CRIES FROM MYSTIC RIVER:
GOD, TRANSCENDENCE, AND A
TROUBLED HUMANITY

God and the Mystic River: A Lost People

Clint Eastwood places God in *Mystic River* with an aerial shot of the Mystic River and South Boston before any of the actors appear in the film. The repetition of aerial and skyward shots at crucial moments in the film along with a powerful musical theme of Eastwood's composition confirms the intended identification of the shot with a godlike world view. Throughout *Mystic River*, references and allusions to God and religion in vital dramatic, intellectual, and spiritual contexts reinforce the importance of what Sara Anson Vaux calls the "God's-eye camera sweeps" in the film.[1]

As the director of the film, Eastwood ironically calls the shots, so to speak, regarding the frequency and meaning of God's aerial shots. The art and manner of Eastwood's direction and inclusion of God in *Mystic River* reflect an ongoing search in his major films for a perspective from which to look for ethical and moral meaning, including the Deity's role in human events. Since aerial shots open and close the film, thereby enveloping the characters, anything that occurs within that context also happens within God's purview and authority. God becomes a player in the drama just as God operates as part of the story under the direction of Frank Capra in *It's a Wonderful Life* (1946). The omnipresent view from heaven creates a religious mood and tone for *Mystic River*. This heavenly envelope of opening and closing shots places *Mystic River* within an ineluctable ethical and moral dimension of meaning. The structure of *Mystic River* makes ethical, moral, and religious discussion a crucial part of the story.

The question then becomes for Eastwood and *Mystic River* a matter of how well the film holds up under this heavenly pressure. In brief, *Mystic River* constitutes another triumph for Eastwood of both art and idea, this time in a film in which he does not appear. The art form infuses, structures, and becomes part of the ethical and moral project. The work of the aesthetic imagination in *Mystic River* informs the discussion of the questions the film raises about ethics and relationships.

Thus, Eastwood's success in *Mystic River* in sustaining and advancing the implications of the opening shot comes in part from the integrity of the film's conceptualization and dramatization of its idea of God. Significantly, Eastwood assiduously avoids any anthropomorphic rendering of God. Eastwood never tries to show or suggest the face of God. He never conjures up the voice of God. No figure appears as a manifestation of God, and no one tries to act as a representative and voice of God.

Eastwood's camera insinuates an unnamable, ineffable God. Eastwood suggests a God of moral and ethical awareness and vision. This aerial camera-eye idea of God

constitutes an ethical and moral canopy for the film that
extends the vision of *Mystic River* to a horizon of infinite
ethical responsibility.

The characters in *Mystic River* operate in a world of inevitable ethical encounter. Ethics and morality form the condition for the existential self and for social and cultural life in
the film. The view from above assures such encounter. The
nature of each character's ethical engagement in *Mystic River*
helps define that character's place in the human condition.
Eastwood structures the development of the film with the
suggestion of a narrative progression that commingles ethics,
morality, psychology, social place, and philosophy.

Mystic River begins with a prologue of the kidnapping and
rape of one of three boys playing on a Boston street. Identifying themselves as police and religious authorities, perverts
take the boy. *Mystic River* then jumps forward 25 years to the
boys as adults in a detective story of tragic dimensions filled
with murder, betrayal, and suffering.

The three main characters in *Mystic River* suggest different
ways of being in the world. They each form a self-identity in
social and ethical contexts and construct ethical subjectivity
through time in relation to others. They face challenges
individually as adults at first, but ultimately their separate
stories merge tragically. Eastwood positions each of them
in life-and-death encounters that get to their inner core as
ethical human beings.

In this story of ethics, identity, and redemption, Eastwood's way of positioning and invoking the Deity with his
camera converts abstractions of ethical subjectivity into
accessible narrative experience. The meaning of Eastwood's
cinematically expressive melding of art and idea in *Mystic
River* can be compared to what Emmanuel Levinas articulates
as "witnessing," "the saying," and "the face." Eastwood's
camera in *Mystic River* envisions and enacts what Levinas in

his ethical philosophy proposes for the opening to the infinity of transcendence.

For Levinas, witnessing, the saying, and the face mean breaking from the self's ordinary time to another temporal sphere that points to the infinite importance and responsibility for the other. The time of witnessing and the saying entails challenging fixed and totalized meaning that cuts off the possibility of the infinite and transcendence. Levinas writes that "the Infinite passes in saying" so that "saying is witness." Because the ethical for Levinas requires placing priority on the time of the other, it opens the possibility of the infinite in the responsibility for the other. He writes that the infinite "is what makes the plot of ethics primary." He says that "the ethical is the field outlined by the paradox of an Infinite in relationship with the finite."[2]

Rhapsody in View: Cinematic Rhythms

Mystic River continues a quest that Eastwood began decades earlier for a form of redemption and renewal in a historic age of profound ethical and moral confusion. His journey involves a search for a dimension of meaning in human relationships and understanding that goes beyond the narcissism of the self and the same to a time of responsibility and love for others. The search for moral and ethical meaning in *Mystic River* manifests itself in part in Eastwood's continued engagement in the film with religious matters, an engagement that goes back to his earliest films such as *Pale Rider* and persists through such works as *True Crime* (1999) and such classics as *Unforgiven* and *Million Dollar Baby*.

The dramatic debate over ethics and relationships in *Mystic River* ultimately also extends to a conflict over the politics of transcendence and the autonomous subject. The roots for this political aspect of the ethical debate in the film go back to claims by some that violent authoritarianism or even incipient fascism constitutes an important element in the role of the transcendent hero in Eastwood's early films.

In addition, overarching symbols in *Mystic River* help to define the parameters of meaning and debate in the film as fluid and open-ended. The symbolization in the structuring of the ethical debate in *Mystic River* conveys an ongoing process for meaning and for conceptual clarity. The river and sky, the bridge and urban landscape, night and day, assume classic symbolic significance for invigorating and expanding the discussion of ethics and transcendence and for establishing priorities in human relationships.

Mystic River defies simple reduction to easily accessible meanings and interpretations. It challenges categorization by any one of its many themes: good versus evil, redemption, history, child abuse and pedophilia, psychological trauma, ethnicity, tribalism, social codes, primitivism versus modernity, the dysfunctional family, unconscious psychological demons that appear like wolves in the night, religion, determinism, injustice, the law, the criminal justice system, and the urban environment.

With all of these themes to develop and assimilate into a coherent whole, *Mystic River* refuses definition by a single genre or sub-genre as a detective story, a psychological study or a revenge drama. David Denby in *The New Yorker* compared the film to a Greek tragedy that eclipses even the efforts of a figure as renowned as Arthur Miller. Denby writes, "*Mystic River* is as close as we are likely to come on the screen to the spirit of Greek tragedy (and closer, I think, than Arthur Miller has come on the stage)." Similarly, A. O. Scott says, "*Mystic River* is the rare American movie that aspires to – and achieves – the full weight and darkness of tragedy."[3]

Eastwood's musical composition in *Mystic River* displays his maturation as a director with the capacity to aestheticize experience according to the beat and sensitivity of his own inner light. Established critics maintain that most especially in *Mystic River*, Eastwood does much more than simply augment or lubricate his story with a vibrant soundtrack.

Rather, Eastwood intelligently and sensitively makes his musical composition part of the film's storyline and character development, fluidly integrating the thematic motifs and phrases of the music with the other elements of *Mystic River*, giving the film in its entirety the effect of a continuous and coherent visual and musical rhapsody in sound and image. As conducted and orchestrated by Leonard Niehaus with the Boston Symphony Orchestra and the Tanglewood Festival Chorus, the music suffuses the film with mystery and sadness.

Moreover, as part of his growth as an artist, Eastwood's use of his music in *Mystic River* inspires a rethinking for some of how to describe his overall achievement as a director. Thus, after noting the importance of music to other Eastwood films, Geoffrey O'Brien in *The New York Review of Books*, emphasizes how *Mystic River* demonstrates "the musical character of his approach to direction." He writes, "After the superb solos and duos of many of his previous films, he has here realized a stunning work for ensemble. The rhythmic sureness instills from the outset a sense of dread."[4]

O'Brien hears the music in *Mystic River* as consistent with Eastwood's ability to sustain his creative power and energy in all aspects of the film. He writes, "What is most impressive about *Mystic River* is the equal importance assumed by each scene and character in turn, even those that might for a moment seem digressive or incidental."[5] Interestingly, in Richard Schickel's documentary, *Eastwood Directs: The Untold Story* (2012), several figures such as Steven Spielberg note the profound influence of music that "personalizes" meaning in Eastwood's work.

Eastwood was involved in eight films between *Unforgiven* and *Mystic River*. He starred in *In the Line of Fire* (1993), which Wolfgang Petersen directed, and Eastwood directed but did not appear in *Midnight in the Garden of Good and Evil* (1997), which was based on John Berendt's non-fiction novelistic account with the same title as the film (1994) of a scandal and killing in Savannah, Georgia. Positioned in the midst of the six other films he directed and starred in during this period, the film does not anticipate the breakthrough of *Mystic River* as a new mode or stage of Eastwood's work as a director of films in which he does not act. As Richard Schickel writes, "*Midnight* is the most languid film Clint ever made, lacking the try-anything liveliness of even his least aspiring genre efforts. It feels, much of the time, conscientious but sprawling, with none of its characters achieving wayward life. They don't seem to grow naturally out of the Savannah scene; rather, they seem to be pasted into it."[6]

Of the six other films that Eastwood directed and in which he starred during this period between cinematic masterpieces, conceivably the crime, police, and detective features of *A Perfect World* (1993), *Absolute Power* (1997), *True Crime* (1999), and *Blood Work* (2002) may anticipate the importance of detective work in *Mystic River*. All of the films he directed in this period, including *The Bridges of Madison County* (1995) and *Space Cowboys* (1995), exhibit his professionalism and technical expertise but not necessarily the artistic achievement or visionary prescience of ethical, cultural, and historic issues of *Mystic River* and some other later work.

In *Mystic River*, Brian Helgeland, who also wrote the screenplay for *Blood Work*, gave Eastwood a screenplay of special efficiency, economy, and intensity. Writing under the demands of condensing a novel of about 560 pages into a film of about 137 minutes, Helgeland's screenplay, as Scott, O'Brien, and Denby all note, encapsulates with emotional intensity and precise psychological and social detail the social milieu, character studies, and themes of Dennis Lehane's novel. Described by the critics and the public as excellent detective or crime fiction, Lehane's *Mystic River* (2001) resonates with classic works in American literature of urban and ethnic realism, in some ways suggesting for the working-class Irish of Boston the feel and flavor of James T. Farrell's influential naturalistic Studs Lonigan novels of the 1930s about the Chicago Irish.

Eastwood takes this solid foundation and framework for his film and makes his version of *Mystic River* into an original filmic art form of audio-visual rhythms. His camera takes the solid written text of Helgeland's screenplay and invests new life into it with his artful direction.

The Prologue: A Visual Poetics of Narrative and the Aporetics of Time

The philosopher Paul Ricoeur sees "narrative as a guardian of time" and maintains that "there can be no thought about time without narrated time." Given this inescapable binding for Ricoeur of narrative to any thought of time, he relates the "poetics of narrative" or the structures of narrated events and "emplotment" to the "aporetics of time," meaning the ineluctable paradoxes of time that have frustrated thinkers throughout history. Ricoeur explains "this initial great aporia, the aporia of a double perspective in speculation on time" as the contrast between a consciousness or phenomenology of individual time and universal time.[7] Ricoeur thereby distinguishes "phenomenological time" or the "time of individual consciousness" from the universality of Kantian "cosmological time" that entails the "presupposition of every

empirical change" (R: 244). Adding to the aporetical or paradoxical nature of time, Ricoeur also notes the tendency to
consider time as a "collective singular" or "oneness" while
recognizing what he terms the "three ecstasies of time – the
future, the past, and the present" (R: 251, 250).

As I discussed elsewhere, the structures and strategies of
narrative that refigure time for Ricoeur also apply to narrative in film.[8] A visual poetics of narrative in cinema includes
the movement of visual images and the varieties of sound in
the construction of a narrative. Such a visual poetics of narrative proves crucial in helping to guide or organize time in
film. Thus, a visual poetics of narrative in film facilitates the
refiguring of time in film by working through the multiple
aporias or paradoxes that inhere in time.

The visual poetics of the opening sequence or prologue
of Mystic River starts with, as noted earlier, a "God's-eye"
aerial shot of a south Boston neighborhood and Eastwood's
somber and soulful music. The shot focuses on a working-
middle-class neighborhood of clean streets, neat backyards,
comfortable multilevel porches, and frame houses that have
managed to survive decades of rough New England weather.
The music blends with, as A. O. Scott says, "the shadows that
flicker in the hard, washed-out New England light" to suggest
an air of ominous danger and foreboding.[9]

The camera centers on the young boys playing hockey
together on Gannon Street in Boston's East Buckingham
neighborhood. City kids, they use an orange-colored street-
hockey ball that gets lost down the opening to a gutter drain.
The conversation of two male beer-drinking parental figures
on a second-floor porch indicates the time to be the 1975
baseball season when Luis Tiant of Cuba was a star fastball
pitcher for the Boston Red Sox.

After losing the ball, the boys turn their attention to
writing their names on some wet cement on the sidewalk.

Young Jimmy Markum (Jason Kelly) and Young Sean Devine
(Conor Paolo) scratch their names on the sidewalk, but
Young Dave Boyle (Cameron Bowen) stops writing his name
with just the crooked capital letters DA when he gets inter-
rupted by the honk of a horn from a car that has stopped in
the middle of the street. Dave's inability to finish writing his
name proves prophetic as a sign of the stoppage of time for
him at that moment. He will never be able to get past what
happens to him on that day and the days that immediately
follow.

A man, the driver (John Doman), emerges from the car,
exhibiting what looks like a police badge. Responding to his
ugly bullying, supposedly for writing in the cement, each of
the three boys quickly demonstrates qualities of character
that will continue with them into manhood. Young Sean
Devine, the future detective, appears confident and thoughtful but aware of the seriousness of the situation; Young Dave
Boyle shows signs of his lifelong insecurity and fears;
Young Jimmy Markum stands out as a combative leader and
tough street kid whom the driver calls "the hard case of the
group." In classic literary and dramatic tradition, the last
names of the boys carry symbolic significance for their individual characters and personalities. Dave Boyle always seems
caught in a kind of seething inner state of uncertainty
and confusion. Sean Devine looks for meaning in events
outside of his immediate realm of experience. Interestingly,
Jimmy's name in the novel of Marcus changes in the film to
signify and emphasize his status as marked by the law and by
destiny.

The driver, somewhat cautiously eyeing the street and the
windows of the houses, chooses frightened Dave as the easiest
victim and the most vulnerable one who says he lives on
nearby Rester Street, and so is outside of the immediate
purview of his own family and neighbors. With Dave's home

and family on another street, the driver will have more time
to get away. The driver's eyes and look indicate his conjecture
that people on Gannon Street, the block on which he has
stopped the boys, might not immediately go to the aid of
someone else's child in an encounter with a person pretend-
ing to be a policeman. The film's unspoken suggestion of
such a moral and ethical lapse demonstrates the subtlety of
Eastwood's direction in proposing the absence of a strong
and deeply embedded ethical foundation in the community,
and even a failure in understanding the meaning of community for most of the characters in the film. (The scene of a
neighborhood's blindness to profound evil in its midst eerily
anticipates the discovery in Cleveland, Ohio, in early May
2013, of three women and a child who had been held captive
and brutalized for years by a man known throughout the
community.)

As Jimmy and Sean watch in nervous uncertainty, Dave
gets pushed into the back of the car that has trash on the
floor while an old man on the passenger seat turns to smile
at Dave, holding his hand out with a ring on one finger. The
ring has a cross on it, indicating an official Church connection for him. After the car drives off, an accelerated montage
of Dave's entrapment in a basement suggests that he was
repeatedly raped by the men until he manages somehow to
escape, racing wildly through woods as sounds and visions of
imaginary wolves echo and reverberate through his discon-
nected and terrified mind. The fear of wolves becomes the
sign for Dave of lifelong psychological trauma that results
from his experience.

The wounds from rape traumatize Dave most especially, of
course, but all three boys will suffer from lifelong issues such
as the fear of castration and of women that they will struggle
to overcome, as Drucilla Cornell suggests, with varying
degrees of success.[10] Upon Dave's return home, one of the

parental figures who appears in the opening sequence can be heard in the crowd calling Dave "damaged goods," an epithet that obviously feminizes him, while later in the film adult Jimmy (Sean Penn) says that if he had been the one kidnapped that could have kept him from having the manhood and courage to pursue the queenly and intimidating woman who became his first wife, Marita. At the very end of the film, adult Sean (Kevin Bacon) says that sometimes he thinks all three boys got in that car with the perverts and never got away.

As a moment of lost innocence for all three boys, the crime signifies a crucial change for each of them. In a sense, time for each boy changes in the prologue. They begin to mature without ever completely escaping from their introduction to evil on that day. As pre-teens on the cusp of adolescence and puberty, the images of a mysterious black car, the intimidating facial expressions and body gestures of a fake policeman, and the unnerving stare on the weak face of a grotesquely malevolent old man will shade subsequent experiences for them.

This focus on the boys in the beginning of *Mystic River* maintains a persistent theme over several decades in Eastwood's work on the care and protection of children as a form of register of the ethical and moral viability and value of an individual and society.

Mystic River Murders and Narrative Identity: Time, Subjectivity, and Ethics

The refiguration of time, especially in the development of ethical subjectivity, proves crucial to the work of telling the stories in *Mystic River* of the three men who open the film as boys. Indeed, Eastwood solders their temporality, their relationships to time, to their emerging narrative identities and manhood. Time as organized by the construction of their narrative identities helps to fashion their self-images, to define them as individual men, and to position them in their relationships to others and to society. The visual poetics of narrative in *Mystic River* dramatizes these complex sets of temporal and ethical relationships in the articulation of subjectivity and identity.

Each of the three men in *Mystic River* relates to a specific temporality of past, present, and future. Dave Boyle (Tim Robbins) remains mentally in the past; Jimmy Markum (Sean Penn) epitomizes a deep-seated emphasis on presence and power; and Sean Devine (Kevin Bacon) stands as the only one of the three with a vision of the future to take him out of the community that spawned all three of them. This foundational identity in time for each helps to define their very way of being and their thought and behavior throughout the film.

As filmed by Eastwood, *Mystic River* becomes a complex narrative of the challenge to achieve selfhood and ethical subjectivity in a social and cultural domain of self-enclosed ethical and temporal horizons. For Jimmy and Dave, limited visions of both existential and ethical possibility collapse the horizon of renewal and change back onto them. They remain caught and smothered in a temporal regime that inculcates a psychology and ethics of the same.

Thus, when Jimmy and Dave look for answers to questions about the meaning and value of their lives and the direction they should take in considering how to live their lives, they necessarily only see themselves in a circularity that closes off opportunity for spiritual and existential renewal. They live within the boundaries of a spatial time zone of limited change and renewal that stifles moral imagination and life. In spite of their hopes for themselves and their best intentions regarding their loved ones, such limitations of vision for Jimmy and

Dave make them part of what Christopher Lasch called a "culture of narcissism."[11]

Interestingly, after decades of making films filled with killing and murder and violence, Eastwood in *Mystic River* makes a masterpiece about murder in which murder occurs at the level of metaphysics and ethics as well as in the physical realm of the destruction of life. The temporal boundaries of narrative identity for Jimmy and Dave in *Mystic River* constitute an enclosed ethical context in the film for the multiple murders that advance the plot. Their stories articulate the dilemma of achieving ethical and responsible manhood in a society of self-centered egoism. With only their own will and moral character to stop them, men in such a society, according to Levinas, bequeath to the next generation a legacy and inheritance of murder. In *Mystic River*, Jimmy and Dave and children commit the murders.

For Levinas, murder entails a violation of a greater time related to the transcendent and infinite. Levinas argues that only such an understanding of time can put murder in its proper sphere and perspective. He describes it as: "This infinity, stronger than murder, already resists us in his face, is his face, is the primordial *expression*, is the first word: 'you shall not commit murder.'" Levinas writes, "The infinite paralyses power by its infinite resistance to murder, which, firm and insurmountable, gleams in the face of the Other, in the total nudity of his defenceless eyes, in the nudity of the absolute openness of the Transcendent."[12]

From the opening aerial shot of Boston in *Mystic River*, the wonder and the search regarding such a transcendent dimension of the infinite occurs as an important concern in the film. The film suggests that the absence of a perspective or position from this transcendent ethical domain reduces murder to an act that involves only human power, control, and aggression, whether it be murder out of revenge as in

Jimmy's double murders, murder as an emotional release as in Dave's case, or murder as a trivialization of human life as occurs in the senseless killing of a teenager by children. In *Mystic River*, it falls upon Sean the detective to look for, in Levinas's words, an "infinity stronger than murder" in order to develop a resistance to murder by looking in the face of the helpless other.

Three Tales of Manhood: Dave, Jimmy, and Sean

Following the prologue, the three tracks of narrative in *Mystic River* move sequentially and alternately from track to track in pulsating movements until coalescing into an ever-tightening constriction of fear, anger, and grief that finally erupts in terrible loss and tragedy. Each narrative line tells the story of one of the three men in the prologue. The stories move in spurts, catching up with each other until merging. The narratives of the three men, Dave, Jimmy, and Sean, grow out of their common origins in the Boston neighborhood and their shared background in the abduction and rape of Dave. The marriages and family situations of the three parallel each other in developing their characters and identities.

It could be argued that Eastwood learned how to cry as a man in *Million Dollar Baby* from directing and observing the performances of Sean Penn and Tim Robbins in *Mystic River*. As many critics have noted, the performances of not just Penn and Robbins, but Kevin Bacon as well, make the film a case study of an absolutely brilliant diversity of acting styles and techniques to create an ensemble of profoundly moving and truly affective characters. A supporting cast also measures up to the remarkable standard for performance of the three male leads.

After the account of the kidnapping and rape at the beginning of the film, *Mystic River* reintroduces Dave, Jimmy, and Sean into the story as adults. The first of the three-track narratives to come online, so to speak, presents Dave's story.[13]

Dave's story assumes a lethargic tempo and rhythm that reflects his character as it developed since the kidnapping and rape. It soon becomes clear, however, that the second storyline about Jimmy will establish the dominant thrust and movement of the film. The rhythm and tempo of Jimmy's scenes and the power of his interactions with others make him the dramatic center of the film as a charismatic leader. Jimmy's emotional drive and intensity provide a crucial focus of the film. The third storyline with Sean moves quickly and aggressively. He operates with a veneer of clean professionalism, precision, and accuracy that signifies his awareness of evil in the world and covers his sensitivity to the pain and suffering of others. Sean recognizes the moral and ethical complexity of experience that makes the path forward, toward ethical subjectivity, painful and difficult.

Dave: Lost in the Past

The structure and design of the scene of Dave's re-entry as a grown man into *Mystic River* visually dramatizes his relationship to time in the construction of his narrative identity. The scene establishes a tension between external space and internal movement that replicates and illustrates temporal tensions. The background space of the scene stretches outward to a potential for freedom, while internal movement presses inward toward enclosure. A long establishing shot opens the scene. The Tobin Bridge in the distance supports the background of the shot that exhibits Gannon Street, the street on which Dave had been abducted. The bridge goes over the Mystic River, its steel beams and suspension projecting a sense of movement and transition.

In contrast with the thrust of the bridge that points outward toward change and escape, Dave and his young son appear in the scene and walk in the opposite direction from the bridge toward the frame's foreground, returning Dave into the internal confines of the street and neighborhood. They walk back into geographic and mental enclosure. The conversation between father and son also repeats the past. Responding to eight-year-old Michael's (Cayden Boyd) concern about not being a good enough hitter and ball player, Dave argues that as his son Michael would have to follow in Dave's footsteps to become the kind of outstanding shortstop Dave was at Trinity High School.

Emphasizing the scene's sad focus on the dead past, Dave looks to the gutter drain that 25 years earlier ate up the orange hockey ball to end his game with Jimmy and Sean. Dave also then glimpses the sidewalk with his unfinished crooked initials still intact below the larger and straighter lettering of Jimmy's and Sean's names. A sharp flashback recalls the horrible scene of abduction. Dave once again hears the sound of the driver pounding his hand on the car for emphasis and remembers the man shouting at him to get into the vehicle. As young Michael expresses interest in exploring the gutter drain for the years of lost balls there, Dave's face makes it clear that at least psychologically, much of his life has been something of an underground existence since the rape and kidnapping.

Throughout the brief scene, Tim Robbins's visual and sound representation of Dave's mental state through his posture, walking, and voice conveys his character's lost bearings and insecurity. Wearing a Boston Red Sox baseball cap, Dave looks like an overgrown kid in spite of being in his late thirties. Stooped shoulders, a disheveled appearance, a gawky childlike look, all suggest a man of little power, presence, and confidence. As he walks off the scene with his son next to him, the slope of Dave's stooped shoulders and his posture indicate a frightened, unhappy, displaced man still in hiding from the world. Throughout the film, Dave retains this posture and physical bearing of loss, including in powerful scenes that occur between him and Jimmy. Even when he triumphs with imagination and intelligence over police interrogators about a murder, Dave, as played with brilliant sensitivity by Robbins, maintains his look of desperate dislocation.

Jimmy: Power, Possession, and the Moment

A cut to a small business "Cottage Market" in the bright sunlight on a neighborhood corner reintroduces Jimmy Markum as a middle-aged man. The following interior shot of the neighborhood market intensifies the sense of self-protective enclosure that began with the psychology and movement of Dave in the preceding Gannon Street scene, with the important difference that in contrast to Dave's profound isolation and alienation, Jimmy's interior, secure space quickly reveals itself as a tight center of business, community, and family affairs.

The considerable amount of detail in this tightly congested inner space provides a semiotic rendering of the signs of Jimmy's environment, psyche, and philosophy of life. He sits as though entombed in this office by things for the store as well as other business and personal items, including altogether soda, cigarettes, cereal, a radio, a clipboard, coffee maker, file cabinet, shelved books, and tapes. Jimmy appears self-consumed by commodities and a bottomless clutter of fetishized objects of needs and desires that indicate more than mere store items, but also the inner impulses of his ego for incorporation, possession, and saturation.

Within this inner sanctum, Sean Penn immediately conveys the compressed power and incipient danger of Jimmy, even just by simply sitting lost in his own thoughts and studying his business sheets of stock and orders. Penn from these opening seconds of his appearance as Jimmy becomes the character he plays, demonstrating the charisma and dynamism of Penn the actor. Just looking over his glasses at a store clerk named Pete (Jonathan Togo), Jimmy gives the young man a piercing look of annoyance that suggests an emotional undercurrent of threat and temper. This dark, diminutive businessman, a grocery man, appears even in this mundane setting capable of exploding violently at any moment.

The development of this scene into a longer sequence of significance again testifies to the brilliance of both Penn and Eastwood. As Jimmy goes back to his books, a straight medium shot shows the entry through parted curtains of a young woman, his daughter from his first marriage, nineteen-year-old Katie Markum (Emmy Rossum). Rossum's youthful energy, natural beauty, and vivacious charm animate and charge the scene. This carefully designed moment captures Katie's character in her relationship to Jimmy. In the novel *Mystic River*, Dennis Lehane presents Jimmy's view of Katie. He writes:

> Nineteen years old and so, so beautiful, all her hormones on red alert, surging. But lately he'd noticed an air of grace settling in his daughter. He wasn't sure where it had come from – some girls grew into womanhood gracefully, others remained girls their whole lives – but it was there in Katie all of a sudden, a peacefulness, a serenity even.[14]

Fulfilling this description in the film, Katie makes a perfect dramatic entrance into Jimmy's inner office and pokes him from behind saying, "Hey, you!"

The affection and joy on Jimmy's face immediately convey a history of loving this young woman, his daughter. Their comfort and ease with each other fills the space with love and care. She hugs him closely, draping her arms around his neck. Planting an affectionate kiss on his cheek, she informs him that she will be going out that night with her two girlfriends, and he approves with an important caveat that she needs to be home early because of "your sister's first Communion, tomorrow," a reminder of the place of religion in this film. As they speak with her arms still wrapped around him from behind, their physicality provides a strong demonstration of their love and ease with each other.

Still behind him, Katie makes a sweeping, womanly movement from Jimmy's right shoulder and cheek to go to his left side. As she does so, she keeps her hands on his shoulders and neck, as he happily turns his head and face to follow her motion when she warmly kisses him on the cheek, both of them smiling all the time but with Katie in confident control of him. The physical intimacy and playfulness indicate the depth of their bond and affection and also provide the basis for the distance and nervous concern Jimmy's second wife, Annabeth (Laura Linney), soon will suggest about her own feelings toward this stepdaughter.

The physical and emotional energy between Jimmy and Katie as seen by a competing second mother, Annabeth, indicates from her outside perspective the inward turning spiral of Jimmy's psychology and way of loving and being in the world. As part of his defensive narcissism, Jimmy seems somewhat less than prescient in apparently not fully appreciating Katie as a figure of displacement for her deceased mother. Still in prison years before for robbery during his first wife's illness and death, Jimmy's guilt over his failure to be with his wife and their baby daughter feeds into the emotional depth and power of his feelings for Katie.

Having gotten the foreordained approval she wanted from her father to go out that evening with her friends, Katie starts to head out of her father's inner office, but then she stops, turns, and lingers, while father and daughter flash smiles and looks at each other, almost like parting lovers. Still pausing, she moves her shoulders ever so slightly and says, "Later," and he responds with a smirk of fatherly pride and approval. Something in her hesitation suggests a thoughtful wish to savor the moment with her father. Indeed, later, Jimmy will recall that scene of their last parting, remembering her look and hesitation as portentous omens of the dreadful events to come.

This powerful and realistic scene with Jimmy grows in significance when juxtaposed with the following scene between Katie and her boyfriend, Brendan Harris (Tom Guiry). The intensity and intimacy of the two scenes together evoke for Eastwood as a film director suggestive resonances with aspects of Shakespeare and Verdi, as excessive as such comparisons at first may seem. In light of the striking intensity of the father–daughter scene in the grocery and Katie's subsequent encounter with Brendan, Eastwood makes the beautiful and charming Katie much like a vibrant Juliet or a passionate Gilda in *Rigoletto* (1851). Each of the three romantic young women suffers and dies over transgressions with their lovers against loving fathers.

Katie's actions demonstrate that the intensity of Jimmy's love for her plants the seed for the daughter's freedom and independence that will lead to her deception of him. The intimacy and physical freedom that Katie experiences with her father clearly transfers in her confidence with the ardent and boyish Brendan.

Significantly, on the night that Katie and her girlfriends go out together, which also will be the night of Katie's murder, she and her friends dance with youthful exuberance and pride on the bar of a neighborhood establishment. Dave sits at the bar with other patrons, drinking his beer and observing the girls, noting the uninhibited presence of his childhood friend's daughter on the bar. The public exhibitionism of the dancing girls indicates Katie's spontaneous nature that originated at least in part in the intensity of her father's love and affection. Katie uses her body to gain attention and affection as she has done with her father.

At the same time, the youthful lovers give their brief scene a Romeo and Juliet quality of energy and joy that Eastwood and the actors magnificently convey. The charm of youthful infatuation pervades the scene. In the young lovers' scene, Brendan hides in Katie's car behind the passenger seat to surprise and frighten her. A shot from inside the car shows Katie in all her youthful beauty leave the store and walk to the driver's side. She still radiates joy and happiness over her previous encounter with her father. After entering the car and starting the engine, she screams when Brendan surprises her and pokes her as she had just jabbed her father. They obviously relish teasing and playing with each other. She says somewhat crudely, "Brendan, you scared the shit out of me."

It then becomes revealed that Brendan had another reason for hiding in Katie's car other than the wish to surprise her. He says, "Sorry. But I didn't want your dad to see me waiting." She laughs over his fear of her father. She says, "He sees you sneaking into my car, he'll shoot you." After the couple kiss, Brendan asks what her father would do if he saw them kiss. She turns the question into a joke. She teases, "Shoot you . . . then kill you." The joking about his fear suggests that, at some level, Katie actually understands the reality of her father's nature and history and, therefore, his willingness to be as violent as he deems necessary to protect and advance his interests.

Brendan's next comment encapsulates the tender emotion of youthful infatuation. He confesses, "It's been six hours. I had to see you." Then, in a brilliant touch, the sound of footsteps sends a truly frightened Brendan ducking once again behind the car seat in fear that it could be her father. His action causes her to laugh happily. Additionally, the couple's balcony-scene enthusiasm dissembles the hidden intention of the scene. Not only do they meet in secret as a transgression of the father's demands and rule; they also plan to leave the next day for Las Vegas to marry. As one of Katie's friends later explains to the police, she desperately hoped to escape from the neighborhood and her life.

Thus, the car scene between the young lovers ultimately directly reflects the father–daughter relationship as a verification of Jimmy's limitations. His adoration of his daughter evolves into her deception and efforts to escape. His blindness about his daughter, her plans, her boyfriend, and her dreams dramatizes his profound lack of vision to see anything beyond the encirclement of his own enclosed world view.

Sean: Vision and Meaning

The reintroduction of Sean (Kevin Bacon) as an adult and Massachusetts state trooper into *Mystic River* occurs with a profound camera movement and filming strategy. The design, thrust, and direction of the movement distinguish Sean from Jimmy and Dave in terms of his identity as a man and his understanding of his place and future in relation to others. In Sean's case, the visual poetics of narrative become more complex, varied, and dramatic compared to the Gannon

Street scene with Dave and the grocery and car scenes involving Jimmy.

To bring Sean as an adult into *Mystic River*, the camera starts with Katie's car. As Brendan hides behind the passenger seat in her car, he tells her to drive away and drop him off round the corner, so he can get out of the car without the possibility of Jimmy seeing him. The camera watches Katie's car as it moves and then turns right into the interior neighborhood.

In somewhat unusual continuous filming for Eastwood, the camera arches up and to the left, becoming aerial as it had been in the very opening for the prologue to the film. The sounds of seagulls emphasize the new aerial dimension of the scene and the filming.

Eastwood then creates a provocatively original image and frame. As the camera rises above the reddish-brick and gray frames of the East Buckingham houses and the green leaves of treetops, Eastwood presents the Tobin Bridge in a bleached, whitish-gray above the city. The contrast in colors visually presents two different zones of meaning, time, and reality. The camera starts with a city street and skyline in color and then dramatically and self-consciously shifts into a creative image of a bridge in a bleached whitish color, constructing and proposing a mental bridge. The bridge in such grayish-white becomes a specter of a bridge, a ghost bridge in a very different temporality than the previous street scenes. The image of the ghostly white bridge climaxes the self-conscious trajectory of the camera from street level to the rooftops and skyline and to the aerial suspension of the bridge.

This arch and sweep of the camera and the metaphoric mental bridge propose more than an aerial shot for information. Movement and metaphor suggest a reaching for a transcendent dimension through the visual imaging of an elevating transcendent gesture by the camera. The aesthetic

Eastwood's camera arches over city rooftops to an aerial shot that creates a grayish white specter of a bridge of transcendent meaning. (Mystic River, 2003, Warner Bros, Village Roadshow Pictures, NPV Entertainment, Malpaso Productions, dir. Clint Eastwood.)

bridge stretches toward a metaphoric destination. The camera clearly intends to propose the effort to rise above the ordinary mundane existence of the Boston neighborhood to reach another realm of meaning. Moreover, in a film that consistently injects religion into its story, it can be conjectured that one bridge in *Mystic River* serves man in the human city of ordinary affairs while the Augustinian mental bridge extends toward serving a force and power beyond the vicissitudes of everyday life. Thus, before showing the photographic detail of the physical, worldly bridge, Eastwood creates an imaginary bridge over troubled Mystic River waters to signal another kind of meaning and experience with a different temporality that compels another view of the world, reality, and relationships.

As the camera lands on the Tobin Bridge to record a deadly criminal incident, Eastwood makes a self-reflexive point about the philosophy of his filming, again in just a matter of seconds. Like a documentary or news cameraman, he records a road-rage killing on the bridge. Eastwood's facile

fluctuation between documentation and transcendence constitutes a statement about the aesthetic and ethical capabilities of his camera and filming. Capable of recording events
in documentary fashion with reportorial precision, his camera
and filming also can create a mystic bridge as suggestive of a
world that transcends empirical observation, the transpar-
ency of representation, and rigid systematization.

On the Tobin Bridge, state trooper-detective Sean Devine
attends to the road-rage killing. Devine's presence on the
bridge at this point associates him with both the ghost bridge
of the ethical imagination and the physical bridge of daily
police work. The gesture toward transcendence of the camera
positions Sean to enact the camera's purpose of ethical exploration and discussion as consistent with the development of
his narrative identity in the film. Sean establishes a metonymical connection with both bridges. So his individual narrative identity and transcendent purpose and motivation
cohere.

On the bridge, Sean turns from the car incident and death
to go to the edge of the bridge to look off in the distance at
his old East Buckingham neighborhood. The obvious symbolism of his search from the bridge establishes his distance
from the past, which distinguishes him from his old friends.
The shot makes Sean a visionary trying to bridge the transcendence of the scene with the realities of life on the ground
in the city.

The aerial trajectory of Eastwood's camera, the vision of
an imaginary metaphysical bridge, and Sean's character introduce a vertical dimension to the construction of narrative
identity along with the horizontal narrative progression. The
horizontal narrative maintains continuity, coherence, and
consistency. The horizontal line engages characters and
events in the film according to conventional temporal structures of regular synchronic clock time. Horizontal linear

*Played by Kevin Bacon, state trooper detective Sean Devine has an
elevated view from the bridge of his old neighborhood. (Mystic River,
2003, Warner Bros, Village Roadshow Pictures, NPV Entertainment,
Malpaso Productions, dir. Clint Eastwood.)*

time advances the main narrative lines in the film and incorporates other, ancillary stories.

The vertical dimension strives for transcendence to a diachronic temporality that challenges linearity and the spatial
organization of time. Sean's view from the bridge dramatizes
such an effort for transcendence and contrasts with Jimmy's
attempts for security by fortifying the inner self and Dave's
immersion in the past.

The visual poetics of narrative identity that Eastwood
employs in the bridge scene in *Mystic River* constitutes a film
aesthetic and an ethical project that informs the construction
of Sean's complex ethical subjectivity and parallels the crucial
distinction Levinas famously makes in language between the
"said" and the "saying." For Levinas, "the ontological form
of the said" and "the synchrony of the said" entail "a thematizing, a synchronizing of terms, a recourse to systematic
language, a constant use of the verb being." The said grounds
meaning in the solidity of the moment through the spatially
structured synchronic time of the everyday clock. The said

emphasizes the unity and sameness of consciousness and representation. In contrast, the saying involves the diachronic or disjunctive time of infinity and transcendence and calls for "an infinite responsibility of the one for the other."[15] The saying and the said invariably deceive, betray, and violate each other but ultimately depend upon each other.

As *Mystic River* develops, it becomes clearer that Sean on the bridge embodies the effort to persist in presenting the saying as crucial to the development of ethical subjectivity. At bottom, perhaps the complexities and difficulties of such an ethical endeavor as Sean represents come down to the simple Levinasian gesture of interrupting thought and action to consider the importance of subjectivity in relation to the other. Thus, in his discussion of the said and the saying, Steven Shankman writes:

> Philosophy, Levinas believed, is a betrayal of ethics if it does not interrupt its own demonstration through an openness to transcendence, by which Levinas means an openness to the face of the other person which moves me beyond my allegedly autonomous self and which interrupts philosophy's own dangerously self-contained linguistic games.[16]

Sean performs precisely, as Shankman says, "this gesture of self-interruption, of disrupting its 'said' in the interests of the 'saying,' that is, of my responsibility to the other person."[17]

Eastwood develops Sean's character as consistent with his emerging ethical subjectivity. Eastwood immediately concretizes his portrait of Sean through the state trooper's conversation on the bridge with his African-American partner, Whitey Powers (Laurence Fishburne), who retains the white detective's name in the novel. As a strongly contrasting figure, Whitey sharply accentuates elements in Sean's character. Besides the matter of race, which never emerges, as critics note, as an issue, the men differ dramatically in ways that emphasize other differences. While Kevin Bacon appears intense, taut, and determined and portrays Sean that way as mentally tough and engaged, Fishburne uses his heft and height to impose and intimidate, making his character into a cynical and somewhat jaded foil of a police detective with a sarcastic sense of humor and a studied appreciation for irony.

Significantly, Whitey's speech and personality tend to connect him to the "said." Firm, direct, and immediate in his speech and manner, Whitey offsets the "saying" nature of the more introspective, sensitive, and intellectually inquisitive Sean.

Eastwood develops the immediate contrast between Sean and Whitey by triangulating with a brief insertion of a third figure into the mix as a way of surfacing and highlighting elements of Sean's identity and character. A friendly and attractive female state trooper (Celeste Oliva) approaches the men and first offers to help them complete their work and then invites Sean to join her and some friends for drinks. Sean's rejection of an obvious invitation from an attractive woman arouses Whitey's concern for his partner's mental state as well as his sex life.

Sean's response to the female trooper and his partner dramatizes his current situation and gets to the heart of his identity as a man in ways that distinguish him from others. The conversation quickly reveals that Sean has been separated for six months from his wife, Lauren (Tori Davis). Whitey calls the relationship the "Weirdest fucking thing I ever heard," referring specifically to Lauren's habit that persists throughout the film of calling Sean but not speaking to him. In spite of this behavior from his estranged wife, Sean insists that because of his marriage, he cannot acquiesce to what Whitey sees as the female trooper's overt sexual interest in him. Whitey says, "She is trying to bed you and you don't even blink." Sean simply explains, "I'm married, Whitey."

Whitey's further comment regarding the state trooper that "she worships at the body of Sean Devine" articulates most specifically Sean's status in *Mystic River* as a special spiritual and ethical figure. Elevated on the mystical and physical bridge with his own vision of his environment and with a woman wishing to be with him, Sean transforms a sexual invitation into an ethical statement that instantiates his special metaphysical position in the film.

While the bridge scene looks forward to encapsulating what distinguishes Sean in thought, mindset, and actions from Dave and Jimmy, the discussion of sexual attitudes between Sean and Whitey refers back to *Unforgiven*. In *Unforgiven*, William Munny justifies and bases his attitudes toward sex, religion, and just about everything upon the influence of his deceased wife, Claudia. In sharp contrast, Sean in the face of his partner's teasing frustration, makes his own decisions about sexual relationships and his behavior in general. Still, both Sean and Munny advocate and practice faithfulness in marriage. Both men suggest the virtues of restraint, discipline, and self-control. For Sean and Munny as well, such attitudes about marriage partners, sexuality, and character form part of a larger project of relationships that they articulate as much in their behavior as in the verbal expression of them.

A non-diegetic transfer from *Unforgiven* to *Mystic River* involves the use of strong black male actors in roles as part-ners for men who have lost their spouses. Morgan Freeman, of course, on the journey to Big Whiskey, Wyoming, plays a temporary supportive substitute for Munny's departed wife, while Fishburne acts as a friend and supporter to Sean in Lauren's extended absence. Black actors in such nurturing and partnering secondary and supportive roles remain controversial either in spite of or because of the absence of substantive discussion of race regarding these characters, an unusual treatment of race and an unusual example of color-blindness in mainstream films.

Lauren's strength as a character comes from her absence, from her lack of complete visibility. To Whitey, a man of objects and things and facts, of the said, such absence constitutes a nothingness. It closes the book on her. She becomes an open-and-shut case. Nothing remains, as he sees it, so he thinks Sean should move on to newer and better things. For Sean, her absence means negation and openness. Her absence motivates his search for meaning and understanding. The difference between the two men parallels Kristeva's observation on Heidegger regarding "a distinction between the negation internal to judgment and a Nothingness that annihilates differently from how thought does."[18]

The negation in thought and judgment that Lauren represents becomes part of a greater process of truth-seeking and soul-searching for Sean. Significantly, when Lauren calls, she remains silent. Sean accepts her speechlessness in a way that Whitey fails to understand. She prefers silence as she seeks the right words, the silence of negation that invites the saying. It speaks directly to the credit of Eastwood, his art, and his production that a basic, visceral move such as an absence has considerable meaning in the film. Lauren's absence works as not just a motivating force for Sean in *Mystic River*; it also structures an underlying philosophical purpose to the film of the search for a meaning to experience greater than the sum total of life's individual and collective parts.

Similarly, it proves significant that throughout the film shots of Lauren on the telephone in silence with Sean do not fully reveal her face but focus on what Cornell sees as her "infinitely desirable" and "beautiful" and "fetishistic" lips.[19] This form of visual poetics again emphasizes Lauren's absence. Such shots suggest that in contrast to Dave's wife, Celeste, and Jimmy's second wife, Annabeth, who is also Celeste's cousin, Lauren exists in a condition of incompleteness. Lauren still needs to operate in freedom to construct her own identity in relation to Sean, while Sean must participate in a working and changing relationship with his estranged wife to save his marriage and reconsider his identity.

Lauren's absence and her incomplete construction as a character emphasize her difference from Sean. She functions as a challenge to him in a process of mutual reinvention and renewal. Although as a wife Lauren represents continuity with her husband and baby, she also imposes the other in their relationship. This contrasts sharply with the primary roles of Annabeth and Celeste as secondary figures to their husbands.

Both Annabeth with Jimmy and her cousin Celeste with Dave tend to be dependent figures. Their independence as separate and free individuals suffers in their marriages. Annabeth finally will encourage and support Jimmy's totalistic view of his own power and identity, thereby affirming and advancing their mutual ethical and moral self-centeredness. She will celebrate his murderous work as a sign of his masculine paternal authority and his superiority over others. At the other end of the ethical and dramatic spectrum, Celeste out of confusion over Dave's increasingly unstable and erratic behavior will reach the wrong conclusion that some perversion led him to murder Sean's daughter, Katie. Moved by uncontrollable fears and guilt, she will betray Dave to Jimmy, mirroring Dave's weakness and insecurity and triggering Jimmy's revenge murder of Dave in the same way that he had killed Brendan's father.

Celeste and Annabeth in their relationships with their husbands function as elements of the same. They represent and repeat in their own ways their husbands' psyches, values, and attitudes. Neither Celeste nor Annabeth can stand alone to form a vital and independent ethical position in their marriages. They, thereby, both contribute to the social chaos and ethical collapse that lead to tragedy in the film. Only the absent and estranged wife, Lauren, operates as the other to compel an ongoing dialogue of thought, engagement, and change. The film suggests that this tension of the other between Lauren and Sean strengthens their individual humanity, their ethical positions, and their marriage after their reconciliation at the end of the film.

The Marker: Murder, Mystery, and Tragedy

The three narrative tracks of *Mystic River* proceed at an accelerated pace following the three opening sequences that reintroduce Dave, Jimmy, and Sean as adults. Dave Boyle gets home at 3 a.m., injured and soaked in blood, after drinking at the bar where Katie and her friends had danced. His story of a mugging starts to fall apart as soon as he begins telling it to Celeste who seems sympathetic but fearful. Robbins turns Dave's face into the puffy, crying, frightened visual appeal of a child as Celeste rocks him soothingly in her arms. The close-up of Celeste's face as she holds Dave, however, indicates her doubts.

The film cuts then to the sounds of a 911 operator taking a call about a car with blood all over it. The aerial shot that accompanies the sound starts over the river and points toward the Tobin Bridge again. The shot moves toward the location of the abandoned car near Sydney Street and the so-called Flats by Pen Park, a state facility that immediately will require the police work of state troopers Sean and Whitey rather than the Boston city police.

A simple thing like the aerial shot in this scene exhibits the director's intelligence guiding this film. The aerial shot continues to open onto what appears to be a police helicopter presumably participating in a search. This action not only blends the times of the phone call to the 911 operator with the searching helicopter; it also discreetly contrasts with previous aerial shots that project transcendent significance from an invisible source. The police helicopter in an investigation and the previous aerial shots suggest searches in different realms of meaning and reality.

The camera cuts to locate Jimmy in bed with Annabeth. He awakens to learn that Katie has failed to show up to work at the grocery and has not been home. The tension and concern over Katie's mysterious absence from work on the day of her stepsister's first Communion immediately expose the recurring conflict between Jimmy and Annabeth over his apparent favoritism toward Katie. In this brief scene, Eastwood's practice of paying close attention to detail manifests itself in the brilliant way Laura Linney plays Annabeth. Her voice and tone, with a strong Boston accent, and even her appearance complement and reinforce the hard-edged roughness that Jimmy evidences from his first moments on the screen as an adult.

With resonances and echoes of Montgomery Clift, John Garfield, and Marlon Brando, Penn conveys a pressure under restraint that ticks away slowly until the inevitable explosion. The tension builds at St. Cecilia's Church for Nadine Markum's (Celine du Tertre) first Communion. The soulful, sad chords of Eastwood's theme music introduce the scene and the parade of young children at the service. Jimmy's face erupts in absolute fatherly pride and joy over the sight of the little girl. Jimmy as father and husband lovingly and sincerely also shares this precious moment with Annabeth. Moved by her daughter and the ceremony, Annabeth says, "My God,

Jimmy, our baby." The invocation of God also portends the nature of things to come that will require inner faith and belief and a search for understanding.

The excitement, pleasure, and pride on Jimmy's face as he looks at Nadine contrasts with the very different expression on his face as he repeatedly looks back at the church door for Katie who never appears there. The first time he looks, he checks his watch before looking. The second time he looks, the camera shows him from behind slowly stop his movement. The timing of the movement of his head to look behind him at the church door expresses his deepening anxiety. He moves his head ever so slowly and carefully and then holds the movement. The delay externalizes the inner tension. Moving his head again, ever so slightly, and stopping as though suspending his chin in mid-air like a diver off a board caught in a photograph, he then moves his head a bit more until holding his chin still by his left shoulder. He turns his head to the door. Nothing! In close-up, without any physical or facial gesture, his face shows utter darkness, stillness, helpless foreboding.

Penn starts, holds, and completes his movements. Minimal gestures become acts of psychological significance balancing inner turmoil and outer restraint. Penn moves fluidly between the two roles and positions of doting, loving father with a silly grin for a face for the youngest daughter, and the troubled, worried, and loving father with a death mask for a face for the absent older daughter. Penn's performance, including his repeated looks at the door of St. Cecelia's Church, demonstrates his poise and the acuity of Eastwood's direction.

Eastwood intercuts to the narrative line of Sean and Whitey as they begin their investigation of the abandoned car on Sydney Street. Accentuating the charged attitude of the detectives, Whitey addresses Sean with "Hey there, bad boy!" Eastwood cleverly shows Sean and Whitey at the scene by Pen Park conspicuously wearing sunglasses and strutting like hot-shot state trooper detectives before the uniformed state troopers. Whitey looks flamboyant in a trench coat like a movie detective, while both men wear ties and jackets as signs of their status and distinction. When the identity of the victim as Jimmy's daughter becomes clearer, however, Sean's sensitivity to the situation for his old friend takes over. Similarly, Whitey evidences compassion, saying, "Fuck! He's in for a world of hurt." Eastwood also cuts systematically into the Boyle home to reveal increasing signs of Celeste's deepening concerns about the truth of Dave's story.

Eastwood pulls these disparate events together smoothly and convincingly, including accumulating touches that subtly add to felt experience in the film. He directs little and bigger moments of feeling and action like musical beats, bursting to a crescendo that eventually will explode with violent loss and pain. He builds these tensions steadily to create a test for his characters under the pressure of impending tragedy. Eastwood's camera also maintains the suggestion in the film of a view of events from a transcendent sphere of ethical responsibility and obligation, as well as judgment from the social and cultural realm.

In the scene outside the church after the Communion ceremony, Eastwood brilliantly creates a psychological moment of utterly painful anticipation by using important details to balance the known from the unknown in Sean's mind. Again with perfect timing, the camera takes a moment of sheer pleasure for Sean and his family as they leave the church to set up a shock of horrible recognition outside the church.

Holding Nadine in his arms outside the church and getting warm smiles back from his wife and family, the mood changes in an instant when Jimmy's attention shifts to the sight and sounds of a police car turning the corner onto Buckingham

Avenue at a dangerous speed. On its tail, an unmarked black car, obviously also a police car, follows the first car at the same frantic speed, both cars blaring sounds of alarm and terror. More cars follow the first two, moving at a similar speed with the same frightening sounds. The sounds and sights of sirens shrieking and tires spinning and cars almost out of control on narrow city streets, all heading toward Pen Park, signal impending disaster. Jimmy, the neighborhood boss and gangster and former prison inmate, knows the sounds and looks and meaning of this kind of police activity.

Such details on the street outside St. Cecelia's Church dramatize the precarious balance in Jimmy's mind between the fear of the unknown and the certainty of specific facts such as Katie's absence for a vital family event and the awareness of an emergency nearby in the neighborhood that requires immediate and heavy police attention. The terror of a loving father over the fear for the life and safety of his child registers on Jimmy's face as he slowly and distractedly removes Nadine from his side and puts her back on the ground by the church where she just gave him one of the great joys of his life with her first Communion.

Sequences and scenes culminate in the discovery of Katie's bruised, beaten, and bloodied dead body. The montage that concentrates on the reactions of detectives Sean and Whitey to the discovery of the body involves an absolutely precise temporal and rhythmic organization of filming, editing, and excellent acting. The sequences could be considered a triumph of dramatic montage involving intercutting different figures, places, and moments to reach a powerful emotional, ethical, and dramatic climax.

Driven by fear and drawn by anxiety and dread to the turmoil of police activity at the street entrance to Pen Park, Jimmy leaves his family at the church and walks to the scene of all the excitement. At first, Jimmy must block the sun from his eyes to get a sense of the scene by the park as numbers of police mill around to the crackling sounds of police radios and walkie-talkies. The camera focuses on several uniformed policemen blocking the view. Slowly they separate to reveal the back and rear end of a sedan.

Jimmy looks in horror. He steps forward as the camera zooms in on him. Again, the genius of Penn's acting in this film reveals his ability to do so much with so little time and physical action. With city sunlight drenching the background of this shot and Jimmy's face in close-up in comparative shade, Jimmy sees Katie's car and realizes that his worst fears that have been growing all morning must be coming true. Eastwood structures the scene with two reverse shots by cutting twice between Jimmy's face and Katie's car. In those shots, Penn and Eastwood change the reading of Jimmy's face from the stunning recognition of the worst of all horrors to a terrified reaction to that recognition. As in the church scene, Penn does not overact or show much visible facial or body movement. Just the slightest change in facial composure and a minimal shift in body balance express Jimmy's horror and explosive inner rage.

Eastwood and Penn also punctuate those visual close-up shots of Jimmy's face with Jimmy's repetition of the same spoken line, but just as Penn's face changes so does the intonation and meaning of the line that Jimmy utters. He speaks and repeats the same line but his voice and tone change to match the changing look on his face. As if in shock from a blow to the face, he barely manages to say to no one in particular, "That's my daughter's car." And then again as though dizzy and not believing what he sees and not knowing how to deal with what he thinks he sees, he repeats with a slight uptick in force and volume, "That's my daughter's car."

As this scene develops, Penn vacillates between two different personae, one the near-crazed father filled with fear and
dread and anger, and the other the calm, manipulative boss
and gang leader who immediately starts directing the activities of his crew of low-level ex-cons and mobsters who have
been doing his work for years. Fittingly named Savage, two
brothers, who are related to Jimmy through marriage, will
lead an extra-legal, underground police force under Jimmy's
supervision to find out what happened and who bears responsibility for Katie's death. Even before confirmation of Katie's
death, Jimmy instigates his own search through these brothers in crime.

Calm and deliberate in his directions to the Savage brothers, Jimmy becomes combative, belligerent, and emotional in
confronting the figure of official authority, Sean, at the edge
of the park for information and access to the restricted site
of the police investigation. The brief, tense interaction
between Jimmy and Sean soon becomes a study in contrasting personalities and character types. Jimmy exhibits viciously
intimidating and bullying behavior on the verge of violence
against the police as opposed to Sean who stands as a professional, firm, stolid, and totally aware of all the potential
implications and ramifications of events.

Called away from his encounter with Jimmy on the peri-
phery of the park to go to the location of Katie's body at
the abandoned bear cage in the park, Sean finds a gro-
tesque scene of the beautiful young woman's dead body that
sickens the police. At this point, both Sean and Whitey have
raised or removed their sunglasses. The death obviously
weighs heavily on both men who appear barely capable
of discussing it. In their reactions to the scene of Katie's
death and their awareness of the profound grief to follow it,
Sean and Whitey exhibit extraordinary sensitivity to the
ethical and moral meaning of the situation. In their language,

facial expressions, and body movements, they convey an understanding that having seen the face of death, as an ethical and even a religious demand, they need to directly confront it.

Both men stand above the cage, peering down at the dead body. A camera flashes. Sean says simply, "Oh Christ." A kind of rolling thunder sound segues into Eastwood's musical theme that evokes an almost unbearable sadness. The expressions on Sean's and Whitey's faces show genuine and deep sorrow and incomprehension at the sight of such a loss of life.

Sean then enters into the bear cage below the surface of the ground to examine the corpse. The medical examiner above speaks in painfully detached technical language, describing how Katie was beaten with a stick but also was shot twice, probably by a .38 revolver. Eastwood's music softly plays as a low-angle shot from the perspective of the dead girl shows Sean's clean-cut face above her. In the background of the shot, standing above the cage, Whitey stares down. Sean struggles to hold back his tears. He can hardly speak. As the medical examiner speaks, the camera cuts to Whitey's face. Trying to look and act detached, tough, and professional, Whitey fails because he cannot abide the indifferent drone of the examiner's monosyllabic recitation of the details of the horrible event.

From his position with the dead body in a bear cage in the ground that now serves as a temporary grave for Katie, Sean's eyes glaze over. Bacon portrays Sean as a reverse image of Jimmy in Sean's law-and-order, clean-cut, business-suit style and way. Like Jimmy, however, Sean exudes the tension between impulse and restraint. Strong and determined, Sean conveys a weakness and tenderness toward others that in some ways compare to Jimmy's own feelings toward his family. The difference between the men concerning such feelings and sensitivities involves Sean's expanded horizon of relationships that reaches out to others, while Jimmy retains a tight, enclosed circle of care that excludes people outside of his family and sphere of influence.

Sean's presence and ethical consciousness place Katie's death in a greater context and dimension of meaning. He directs the scene of death and murder toward the vertical dimension of experience that recalls his position on the bridge and that resonates with the symbolism of aerial views of the city. Sean's view of Katie's death incorporates the scene of the visionary bridge over the city as part of a search for a horizon of greater meaning from which to seek some understanding of Katie's death.

The church ceremony of Nadine's first Communion and the mention by Sean of Christ upon seeing Katie's dead body reinforce the mood of *Mystic River*'s hope for a meaning beyond immanent experience. Thus, speaking prophetically, as fits his nature and inclination, Sean leaning over the dead body says in the words and language of a policeman and a Massachusetts state trooper, but also in the spirit of a seeker, "What the fuck am I going to tell him? Hey, guess what, Jimmy? God said you owed another marker. He came to collect."

The sorrowful expression on Whitey's face as Sean speaks complements the prayerful tone of Sean's words. Sean finds words to speak, but the more eloquent expressions on the faces of both men convey a greater sense of wonder over the inexpressible meaning of this death. For Sean and Whitey, the death of Katie becomes a religious moment that demands the struggle to comprehend the incomprehensible. Sean in effect asks what can he tell Jimmy because he cannot find words for himself to conceptualize and explain the useless death of the young girl whose face in death epitomizes the beauty and vulnerability of love and innocence.

In fact, Sean's profanity can be heard as further confirmation of his inability to find the right words for what he feels and what he has to do. Both Sean and Whitey experience the contrast of the saying and the said. Though the words fall short of explaining the encounter with the infinite that occurs at this time of death, they at least express the desire to find such meaning. In Katie's face, Sean and Whitey see and experience the face of the other as the opening to the paradox of the infinite dimension of human engagement.

At the same time, Sean's insight as conveyed in his words over Katie's body that God has called Jimmy for another marker has profound implications. The words themselves mark a trajectory of symbolic images starting from the very opening aerial shot, to the pervert's religious ring, the signifying importance of two bridges, Whitey's description of Sean as a body to be worshipped, Sean's professed beliefs about marriage, the Communion service at church, and on to other resonant scenes of the film. Sean's words constitute a message that will initiate a kind of holy war between him and Jimmy over how to deal with this obscene murder that has been witnessed in several dimensions of meaning, including the transcendent and the immanent.

Pen Park becomes a field of struggle when Jimmy and his pack invade it. The battle with the police over the terrain will determine who will control access to the opening in the earth that holds Katie's body. Sean must leave Katie's side in her temporary gravesite to attend to the pandemonium breaking loose above by Jimmy and his pack, as they rush to fight and overcome the police. The pack wants to break the phalanx of uniformed policemen to find and see Katie's body for themselves.

Eastwood's filming of the wild scene in the park provides a powerful contrast with the solemnity of the detectives with Katie's body. In a long shot, Jimmy and the truly Savage brothers run madly up some steps that will take them to the area of the bear cage. They appear literally like a pack of wolves, like the wolves that haunt Dave's mind. Sadly, this pack of human wolves eventually will take Dave to his death.

The action in this scene of Jimmy's arrival at Pen Park with his pack climaxes all the tensions of *Mystic River* that have developed up to this point. In this park scene, Eastwood films a collision of forces that becomes even more powerful through his specificity as in showing Val Savage (Kevin Chapman) take the lead in the pack's charge. Val hurls himself at the policemen, shouting vile profanities the whole time as he maintains his record of efficient criminal stupidity and incompetence by immediately getting slammed to the ground and covered by the police to assure his uselessness to anyone. Val's face appears in an overhead shot from above the scene. He gets buried in a deep well of police uniforms.

The design and structure of the struggle in Pen Park develop around a powerful center of visual gravity in the eyeline connection between Jimmy and Sean. Throughout the scene, Jimmy's and Sean's eyes will remain interlocked, creating a powerful binding force to help structure the explosive action of the scene.

After rising from the bear cage where he had spoken his version of a prayer over the dead girl that focused on the tragedy facing her father, Sean makes his way to the struggle between Jimmy and the police. Jimmy also has charged into the police, hoping to break through after the distraction of Val's charge. Sean finds him surrounded by officers tightly holding him. Deliberately, in a moderate tone of voice, Sean tells the officers to back off and give Jimmy some room. He says, "Hey, take it easy. That's the father."

Jimmy and Sean look at each other with riveting intensity, while Jimmy remains entrapped within a circle of uniforms. Eastwood's command of the action proves awesome as he uses his arsenal of techniques and ideas to develop the situation. The montage intensifies with close-ups, camera movements, and music. Eastwood balances the fury and chaos on the ground with the unshakeable, gripping tenacity of the eyeline bridge between Jimmy and Sean.

Jimmy's face breaks your heart. He fixes his eyes on Sean as his only hope and his only source of the truth about his daughter that he has intuited but cannot internalize into his already grieving consciousness as a father. Jimmy becomes a raging, crying animal. Sean's eyes stay focused on him, not backing off from confronting the accumulated pain that remains incomprehensible to both men. Sean projects the face and look of his view from the bridge.

The scene becomes a culminating, climactic moment for Penn as a major modern actor in his rendering of the explosion of rage, frustration, and fear that has been churning within Jimmy. In terms of his overall performance, Penn's acting up to these scenes by and in Pen Park has been in anticipation of his violent emotional release. His carefully understated and restrained performance organically connects to his park scenes by setting them up emotionally and psychologically. By not over performing in earlier scenes, Penn anticipates the park scenes of Jimmy's breakdown into mad grief. Thus, the increasing intensity of emotion by the entrance to the park helps time the change to the uncontrollable emotion that follows in the park.

After all the restraint Penn has demonstrated and exercised for Jimmy's character, this eruption of emotion in Pen Park becomes real and terrifying. No longer evidencing the tension between impulse and control in his face and body but only the uninhibited venting of furious energy, Jimmy remains surrounded by a cordon of police. His pain and powerlessness become palpable with his realization that he cannot do anything to correct or alter the situation.

Close-ups, cuts, and movements that close in and pull back sustain a tempo of images that brings out Jimmy's misery and helplessness. While the camera operates primarily on a level plane of action with moves and cuts, Jimmy's struggle never stops. He rises and falls with the swelling and compression of the fluctuating cord of policemen who encircle Jimmy as he pushes and stretches.

As Jimmy twists and turns, his face becomes a bubbling surface of action with lips, teeth, eyes, and cheeks in movement all at once. Penn and Eastwood make Jimmy into a volatile center of wild movements and gestures in all directions, under the penetrating gaze and piercing eyes of Sean Devine. Adding to this mix, Jimmy screams, making terrifying sounds of ultimate pain that come from deep in his throat. He shouts wildly and abusively at Sean.

The camera cuts to Sean and zooms in for a quick close-up. Sean's face and body go absolutely still. He becomes a fixed point of stolid immobility. Echoing the ensnared Val, Jimmy screams, "Mother fucker!" and then screams at Sean, "Is that my daughter in there?" as his face gets even more distorted with pain. His elbows work with his body to break free but to no avail. His voice and screams become a growl. "Is she in there?" he cries at Sean.

In the shot of Jimmy's face, parts of policemen's arms and bodies exert their pressure on him in response to his contortions of useless resistance. Jimmy repeats the question over and over again, "Is that my daughter in there?" The camera then closes in on Sean with another amazing close-up of somber revelation.

Jimmy finally ceases to speak and shout his curses, but just howls in agony like a captured animal, arching his neck back and turning his face to the sky with an uncontrollable shriek of indescribable agony. As the circle of police bodies tightens around Jimmy and one officer pulls his arm tighter around

Sean Penn as Jimmy Markum cries out to his old neighborhood friend detective Devine, "Is that my daughter in there?" (Mystic River, 2003, Warner Bros, Village Roadshow Pictures, NPV Entertainment, Malpaso Productions, dir. Clint Eastwood.)

Jimmy's neck, Eastwood's camera rises to the sound of his musical theme. As the camera rises higher and higher, the musical theme grows stronger. In opposition to the skyward movement of the camera, Jimmy gets pushed lower and lower to the ground by the police. Covered by police bodies subduing him, only Jimmy's face in sharp light can be seen in its expression of horrible torture and complete abandonment as he continues to twist and turn. He cries out, "Oh God! Oh God!"

The elevation of the camera to view Jimmy and the police below, and Jimmy's pleas to God, recall Sean's prophetic words of God's demands upon Jimmy for another marker. The elevated camera, the shot, and the cry continue the trajectory of images in the film that insinuate the search for a transcendent dimension to the film. The scene from the time Sean leaves Katie's body to Jimmy's appeal to God takes about a minute.

In that period of time, it could be argued that Sean's face in close-up epitomizes what Levinas terms the "passivity" before the unknowable and ineffable. In his look, Sean bears

Countering the skyward thrust of the camera, Jimmy gets pushed lower and lower by the police as he cries out in excruciating agony, "Oh God! Oh God!" (Mystic River, 2003, Warner Bros, Village Roadshow Pictures, NPV Entertainment, Malpaso Productions, dir. Clint Eastwood.)

witness to forces greater than himself that impose themselves cruelly on Jimmy, whose response of howls and cries correctly forecasts his demand for blind vengeance. The park scene becomes an encounter of faces that positions Sean and Jimmy against each other. The great action in the park forces an engagement between two different visions of life that lead to very different ethical and moral positions.

In spite of his famous argument concerning the potential idolatry of images, Levinas might see in Sean's look in this scene a fulfillment of the idea of *"il y a"* or "there is."[20] For Levinas, *il y a* entails the search for meaning before the impossibility of achieving total understanding of the infinite through finite human means and experience, especially before the encounter with death and the other. Levinas writes, "The void that hollows out is immediately filled with the mute and anonymous rustling of the *there is* as the place left vacant by one who died is filled with the murmur of the attendants."[21] As attendants to the unspeakable death of Katie, both Sean and Whitey know they can never fill the void of death by simply missing her, grieving for her and her loved ones, trying to replace her with another or seeking formulas and simple answers for her death.

Levinas argues for a transcendence greater than being that fills the emptiness made by death. For Levinas, "the difference of transcendence" entails the relationship of infinite responsibility to the other. Levinas says that given the absence of such transcendence a "factitious transcendence" informs a "Heavenly City gravitating in the skies over the terrestrial city."[22]

Levinas's language elucidates and parallels *Mystic River*'s images and symbols of transcendent meanings and the death of the innocent. *Mystic River* even seriously observes Levinas's caveat about heavenly structures or cities of a "factitious" nature by constructing two kinds of transcendent bridges, one over river waters and another reaching for infinity. Levinas's *il y a* especially enlightens scenes of death, grief, and the search for redemption and meaning in the film. He says, "The *there is* fills the void left by the negation of being."[23]

Confronting the blind emotion and egoism of Jimmy's outrage at the Pen Park scene, Sean's silence and the stillness of his face suggest a reaching out beyond himself to Jimmy's pain. It provides a sharp contrast to Jimmy's self-absorption in his grief.

The depth of Jimmy's pain and grief can be discerned in another amazing scene, this one between Jimmy and Dave that again proves the range and variety of skills and talents of Penn the actor and Eastwood the director. In this scene between Dave and Jimmy that occurs on the day of the wake for Katie, Robbins rather than Bacon helps Penn extract every ounce of emotion and feeling that Penn has for Jimmy's situation and character. The scene takes place in the confines of the porch of Jimmy's house. Robbins continues to play

Dave smartly and with sympathy, keeping him in a kind of fog.

On the porch a kind of psychotherapy takes place for Jimmy. It begins when Dave emerges from the house, ducking his way through overhanging clothes on a line across the porch. Looking lost and distracted even in this narrow space, he starts to light a cigarette and burns his fingers with fright when Jimmy startles him from his seat in the corner of the porch. Soon the camera tightens on Jimmy, capturing the pain of Jimmy's loss on his face as he tries to resist and control his grief. The hurt squeezes out slowly without Jimmy realizing it. He tells Dave how after his first wife and Katie's mother died and he got out of prison, taking care of Katie as a baby frightened him more than anything else in his life. He reveals to Dave how when he and Katie got to know each other on his first night out of prison, "It was like we were the last two people on earth . . . Forgotten and unwanted." Jimmy sniffles and cries, his face breaking into pieces, his arms gesturing as uncontrollable grief moves slowly through his body.

Jimmy then moans that in spite of his loss, he hasn't been able to cry. Shaking his arm and crying, he sobs, "My own little daughter and I can't even cry for her." As Jimmy presses his forehead into his clenched fist, Dave's face registers increasing bewilderment. In a touching gesture and moment, Dave says in a sad voice filled with a sense of concerned confusion, "Jimmy? . . . You're crying now." Jimmy hugs himself with his arms, saying, "I just wanna hug her one more time." With grief and sadness weighing down on both men, they each remain alone in their own domains, still in the kind of mental and social isolation that Jimmy described for himself and Katie.

Alone, later, in a kind of Shakespearean monologue, Jimmy offers a prayer of sorts at home in a way that dramatizes his self-absorption. He says, "I know in my soul I contributed to your death. But I don't know how." Addressing Katie in his prayer rather than God, Jimmy fails to search out an answer other than looking off to the night-time Mystic River, where years before he had dropped the dead body of the father of the brothers Brendan and Silent Ray Harris as punishment for informing on him to the police and causing his imprisonment.

In his sorrowful suffering that Penn expresses so well, Jimmy remains inward-turning and unaware of a dimension of meaning, commitment, and responsibility beyond himself. With all of his street wisdom, intensity of emotion, and charisma, he answers to no one but himself, becoming a study of the ethical and moral smothering of the self-centered autonomous self. In crisis, Jimmy psychologically and ethically has no one to turn to but himself. He never accepts how little he knows.

Sean and Whitey's investigation into Katie's death cleverly persists in dressing the tragedy of *Mystic River* into its credible disguise as a terrific murder mystery. Perfecting his work over several decades on crime, detective, and action films, Eastwood in *Mystic River* brilliantly directs the unraveling of the mystery. Excellent crime laboratory and forensic work, a fortuitous recollection by the victim of a liquor store hold-up years before (played by veteran Eli Wallach in a fine cameo performance), and good basic police instinct and work ultimately identify the murder weapon as the gun that belonged to Brendan's father. A clue on the tape of boys calling 911, which led police to Katie's abandoned car and then her body, sends the two detectives to Brendan's brother, Silent Ray Harris (Spencer Treat Clark), who turns out not to be quite as deaf as he previously seemed, and his inseparable friend John O'Shea (Andrew Mackin).

Sean and Whitey get to the Harris home to find the O'Shea boy holding a .38 revolver to shoot Brendan for beating him and breaking his nose. Brendan had learned that the boys found the hidden gun and used it to kill Katie when their original intention to scare her went out of control. Enraged over discovering how his girlfriend died, Brendan brutally beat both boys until John pulled the gun on him.

The unraveling of the story also ties Jimmy to the murder of his daughter, since his execution of Brendan and Silent Ray's father years before for betraying him ultimately helps set events in motion for the fatherless boy to have access to the gun that killed Katie. In the investigation, Sean learns that the blood on Dave the night of Katie's murder belonged to a man Dave saw getting oral sex from a boy prostitute. Seeing him and the boy together ignited memories for Dave of his kidnapping and molestation 25 years before. In his rage, Dave beat and killed the man and hid his body on the same night as Katie's death. The dead man became the fictitious mugger that Dave invented and kept using as his excuse for his condition after he got home to Celeste.

A Matter of Love: Families in Crisis

Eastwood structures the concluding portion of *Mystic River* as a life-and-death race between Sean and Jimmy. Not only Dave's life hangs in the balance. The network of ideas and values of law, justice, and ethics that turns separate individuals into a society also hangs in suspension as Sean and Whitey discover Katie's killers, while Jimmy undertakes his own underground police action and justice.

In a well-executed montage, Eastwood contrasts Sean and Whitey's investigation of Katie's murder with Jimmy's private vigilante trial of Dave in the evening darkness by the Mystic

River. Jimmy institutes an extra-legal process as Dave's judge, jury, and executioner. The Savage brothers also participate as enthusiastic witnesses to the perversion of justice and the violation of human and sacred law that Jimmy undertakes and leads.

Thus, under cover of darkness in the foggy evening during Dave's impromptu illegal trial, Jimmy confesses how years before he had killed Harris at this very place by the river. He tells the story to further intimidate and frighten Dave into confessing. The torture and lies Jimmy inflicts on Dave that he will spare Dave's life in exchange for a confession powerfully contrast with the detailed police and legal procedures Sean and Whitey follow, especially given Sean's insistence with Whitey on adhering to such laws and rules.

Jimmy brings God into the story. He describes in lurid detail how he made Harris kneel down in the same spot by the river and how Harris had begged to live because of his son Brendan and his wife's pregnancy. Jimmy says both men were crying at the time, and Jimmy also says he could feel God watching him as he shot Harris and held him under the water.

Jimmy says, "The whole time I was holding him under the water, I could feel God watching me, shaking His head." Jimmy pauses for a beat and makes an amazing judgment on his understanding of God and his relationship to God. He says, "Not angry, but like you do if a puppy shit on the rug."

Jimmy's humanization and trivialization of God suggest his displacement of God in his own mind. Jimmy puts himself before both man and God. Jimmy says to Dave, "Admit what you did and I will give you your life," empowering and anointing himself to take and give life.

As he proceeds with his execution of Dave, he says, "We bury our sins here, Dave. We wash them clean." With those words, he appropriates for himself a religious ritual of purification and asserts his own exculpation of guilt for avenging his daughter's death with his own hands. Jimmy bestows forgiveness upon himself and incorporates all ethics and morals within his own domain. He reduces transcendence to his own immanence, being, and identity.

After Jimmy thrusts his knife into Dave's stomach, one of the Savage brothers says that Dave's lips still move. Jimmy responds, "I got eyes, Val." Ironically, from the beginning of the film, Jimmy can see but lacks vision, insight, and understanding.

Significantly, this scene of a deep, insidious darkness for Dave's mob-style trial and execution by the river has only a distant hazy outdoor light to expose the faces of the participants. As in his films over the years, Eastwood uses darkness, shadow, and light to intensify mood, feeling, and drama but also to suggest moral meaning and emphasis in a scene.

In this darkness, Dave whispers his last words, "I wasn't ready." Dave pleads for his life so that he can return to Celeste, the wife who had betrayed him to Jimmy out of fear, and to his son who depends on him. He realizes too late his lost time of life and his lack of readiness for the infinity of death.

Unfortunately, he faces Jimmy who treats time like a commodity on his grocery shelf. By going to prison, Jimmy had done "time." Harris by "ratting" out Jimmy took from Jimmy's time with his first wife Marita and daughter Katie, so Jimmy took time back. Now Jimmy will take Dave's time on earth. He concludes the execution by firing his gun into Dave.

In response to the murder and firing, Eastwood's musical phrase also bursts forth with its own explosive emotion and pain as the camera surges skyward into sudden heavenly light, repeating *Mystic River*'s powerful religious imagery and suggesting a greater transcendent time.

The film then cuts to the light of the morning and a drunk and dazed Jimmy, gripping a depleted bottle of sour-mash whiskey, as he sits on the sidewalk on Gannon Street where the boys wrote their initials in the cement. When Sean arrives and convinces Jimmy that his daughter's killers have been found, another scene of amazing tension and compression occurs as Jimmy must sober up to the brutal details of Katie's death and the fact that he has just murdered the wrong man.

Sean in turn must move gracefully and quickly from informing Jimmy to indicating his intuitive awareness of Jimmy's crime. Eastwood's sharp cuts and reverse shots propel the intensity of Penn's and Bacon's acting in an exchange of painful fatality. Sensing the truth, Sean asks Jimmy what he has done. Jimmy says, "Thanks for finding my daughter's killers, Sean. If only you'd been a little faster." Jimmy again sees life as finite measurements of being and power as he places responsibility for his actions on time and Sean.

Jimmy also says the last time he saw Dave was 25 years before in a car with the kidnappers. Sean says "all three of us got in that car" and have been living with it ever since. Jimmy then simply walks up the street, shrugging his shoulders and extending his arms outward and parallel to the ground as though on a cross.

As the story unwound, Eastwood had dramatically altered the screenplay with the accelerated pace of the montage of intercuts connecting Jimmy's execution of Dave, Brendan's fight with his brother and the O'Shea boy, and the frantic efforts of the police to crack the case. The accelerated montage of cuts tied the stories together ever more tightly with the importance of love. Thus, when Brendan asked his brother if he loves him, Silent Ray nodded that he loves his brother but does not love their mean-spirited, crass mother. Brendan then demanded that Ray speak his love for him. When Ray not only remained silent but held up his middle finger, Brendan exploded in rage and accused his brother of loving him so much he killed Katie so he should be killed in turn. Brother against brother; killing makes more killing.

The melding of the storylines gives special prominence to the question Brendan raises with his brother about love. Eastwood suggests the absence or misuse of love as a source for the problems in both Jimmy's and Brendan's lives and families. In the end, *Mystic River* maintains that a family without love and responsibility for others breeds violence and hate and the kind of indifference that leads to murder between brothers.

Mystic River returns to Eastwood's theme in his body of work of violence as a response to the void at the core of being and identity. Violence fills the abyss of the word and meaning; violence erupts before the ambiguities and fears of our origins in and dependence upon parental figures of love and discipline.

A kind of epilogue that includes children to balance out the prologue concludes *Mystic River*. Eastwood segues into the conclusion with a cell-phone call to Sean from the future in the form of his wife, Lauren (Tori Davis), calling to come home. Sean finally apologizes for pushing her away. For the first time, the camera shows her beautiful face, and for the first time in the film, Sean smiles broadly and handsomely when she announces her hope to get past being "so messed up. Loving you, hating you." She also reveals the name of their daughter, Nora, a name meaning honor and light and therefore a hope for their future lives.

Soon thereafter, as the Buckingham Day Parade starts up with a fire engine, police cars, floats, and a color guard, the film cuts to the interior of Jimmy and Annabeth's house. The camera moves slowly through a narrow foyer and into their bedroom, revealing Jimmy with his naked back to the door and the camera. He looks out the window. Eastwood again adds to the original novel and the screenplay in the way he emplaces an imposing tattoo cross on Jimmy's back. The top of the cross starts from Jimmy's neck and goes between his shoulder blades. The cross could suggest the burden on Jimmy's shoulders, the cross he thinks he bears, and the sacrifice he thinks he makes of himself for others. On the other hand, as Kristina Eugenia Hamner-Yonke suggests, Jimmy turns his back on the cross.

As the camera focuses on his back and Jimmy confesses about the previous night of killing Dave, Annabeth interjects herself between the camera and Jimmy, interceding on behalf of her husband to help him in assuaging his guilt. She stands between him and the omniscient witnessing vision of the camera, attempting to shield him from higher authority and meaning.

Annabeth chillingly reports that she put their children to bed the night before with a story about how Jimmy loved Katie and now loves them and would do whatever was necessary to protect and care for them all. She says, "It's like I told the girls. Their daddy is a king. And a king knows what to do and does it even if it's hard. And their daddy will do whatever he has to for those he loves. And that's all that matters."

She also confesses that she knew about the danger facing Dave from Jimmy because Celeste called the night before. Annabeth says, "She told me about Dave. Told me what she told you. What kind of wife says those things about her husband? And why'd she run to you?" To Annabeth, Celeste's weakness as a wife and woman proves Annabeth's argument about Jimmy's superiority. She says, "Because everyone is weak, Jimmy. Everyone but us. We will never be weak. And you. You could rule this town." Annabeth installs and venerates Jimmy not only as a savior figure and religious leader, but also as a political leader to rule and dominate. The scene fades out with Annabeth moving on top of him, presumably giving herself to him in a sexualized religious ritual.

Annabeth's words, the tattoo cross on Jimmy's back, his extended arms as he earlier went up the street before Sean, and his appeals to God all suggest Jimmy as a Christ figure, but a special image of Christ as the King. As stated in John 18:37 and 19:17–19, Jesus answers in the affirmative to Pilate's question if Jesus considers himself the King of the Jews. Jesus answers, "Thou sayest that I am a king. To this end was I born, and for this cause came I into the world, that I should bear witness unto the truth." The idea of Christ the King as a sovereign compares to Annabeth's vision of Jimmy as a king who carries, suffers, and sacrifices for her and the family by ruling and dominating through his superior strength and will.

In contrast to Annabeth's vision and adoration of Jimmy as a kingly and sovereign Christ figure, Eastwood proffers an alternative with a radically different conception of the divine, transcendent, and ethical. Frankie Dunn in *Million Dollar Baby* and Sean Devine in *Mystic River*, it can be argued, stand in strong opposition to the idea of a ruling God of absolute command and authority. Instead, they can be seen to represent what Richard Kearney and others describe as a kenotic surrendering and emptying of the self and the ego in love and responsibility for the other, "a recovery of the divine within the flesh, a kenotic emptying out of transcendence into the heart of the world's body, becoming a God beneath us rather than a God beyond us." Kearney articulates a "refusal of triumphal sovereignty" that Annabeth proclaims and Drucilla Cornell suggests for Jimmy. He says, "The greatest danger for religion is to assume sovereign power. And this can mean both sacred sovereignty and political sovereignty." He maintains that "the concept of God as absolute Monarch of the Universe stems from a literalist reading of the Bible along with unfortunate misapplications of a metaphysics of causal omnipotence and self-sufficiency."[24]

Annabeth secures her place at Jimmy's side with her argument to him that he can justify and excuse his murder of Dave and any of his other crimes because of his special powers and strengths that she apparently shares. Her statement to her daughters on the previous night about the love and strength of their father the king anticipates the beginning of her own reign of power. Her awareness of the possible outcome of events makes her at least morally and ethically complicit in Jimmy's sacrificial slaying of Dave. They each put themselves and their children and their family first before other people, before the law and community, before a sense of the transcendent and infinite in the relation to others. Like Jimmy's ritualistic washing of his hands after the murder, the implied sex between Jimmy and Annabeth on the morning of his confession to her suggests a ritual and ceremony of forgiveness, sharing, and mutual empowerment. They absolve and sanctify each other. Afterward, they assume their elevated place as king and queen on the steps of their home with their family as a kind of court to watch the parade pass.

In addition, the patriotic exhibitionism of the parade suggests a possible extension of Jimmy's and Annabeth's imperial posture to the sphere of American politics, history, and culture. Such a concern recalls the flag behind William Munny in *Unforgiven* after the slaughter at Greely's. A similar sensitivity about politics and history occurs in the remarkable and transformative film venture to come, with the making of both *Flags of Our Fathers* and *Letters from Iwo Jima* as a joint effort and statement about culture and war.

Out on the street as the Buckingham Day parade proceeds in *Mystic River*, Celeste wanders desperately, looking guilty and lost, searching for her son on a baseball-team float. When the float appears, she calls out his name. All the boys look happy and smile, while he sits glumly in a kind of self-enclosed solitude, a young boy missing his father, already giving up on himself and his dreams. Sean and Lauren also attend the parade, a couple on the mend with their baby.

When Jimmy emerges from his house amidst his wife, daughter, and the Savage brothers, he and Sean again face off. Sean looks coldly at Jimmy, and Jimmy cannot resist an expression between a smirk and a smile, looking like a kid who got away with murder, two murders in fact. In a final ambiguous gesture, Sean holds his fingers like a gun and drops his thumb as though firing. The action may allude to Jimmy's crimes but also suggests the possibility of ultimate justice for Jimmy. The scene closes on Jimmy's look back to Sean of indifference.

For one last time, the Eastwood musical motif bursts forth as the camera elevates again over the neighborhood and then cuts to the initials on the sidewalk. In an overlapping image, the letters on the sidewalk blend into a final, fast-moving aerial shot of the Mystic River that goes over the water toward the bridge. The camera flies over the river and seems to bow down to the water, perhaps out of respect for the dead, searching for the bodies that have been disposed there as the screen grows darker.

Mystic River ends by solving one mystery while leaving another open, the question of meaning. Eastwood does not seek closure as in the usual crime or detective story. At the end, the film throws off its disguise as a mystery story to emphasize its more complex and confounding implications. While the murder mystery *Mystic River* uncovers Katie's killers, the moral and ethical drama *Mystic River* ends with a prophecy through the persona of Sean Devine of the significance and inevitability of witnessing in the relationship of the self to the other in transcendence and responsibility.

5

FLAGS OF OUR FATHERS/LETTERS FROM IWO JIMA: HISTORY LESSONS ON TIME AND THE STRANGER

Iwo Jima: Introduction to Hell

In contrast to the transcendent aerial shot that opens *Mystic River*, Eastwood in *Flags of Our Fathers* begins with a ground-level shot of the feet of a terrified lone man in combat fatigues running on a thoroughly barren and blackened volcanic landscape. Lost and desperate, he runs frantically, trying to respond to echoing distant shouts for a corpsman, the Navy medics who go into battle with the Marines and at great risk to themselves attend to the wounded. The camera swirls around the man, replicating his confusion as he tries to identify the location of the voice calling to him, and then the camera circles around from his perspective, showing the stark emptiness of the landscape. The cries persist, "Corpsman! Corpsman! Corpsman! For God's sakes! Corpsman!" Smoke rises everywhere over the blackened grounds, indicating the smoldering devastation of an area that has been consumed by fierce, deadly fire. The nerve-wracking sounds of artillery firings, explosions, and unseen airplanes intensify the panic, terror, and confusion. The corpsman appears to be the only living being in an environment of death. The thoroughly drained coloring of the scene accentuates the impression of lifelessness. Such drained coloring will persist in the film's battle scenes.

Significantly, the desperation on the man's face apparently comes as much from failing to locate the calls for help as from concern over his own situation of loss and abandonment. The camera then moves in ever more closely on his face. In this close-up, the tight strap of the helmet on the head of the corpsman further distorts his dirt-encrusted, frightened face. The corpsman, John "Doc" Bradley (Ryan Phillippe), invariably shows his caring concern and sense of responsibility for others.

A cut then reveals that in fact the camera has intruded into and been reporting from the mind of Doc Bradley as a seventy-year-old man (George Grizzard) who has this recurring

In a recurring nightmare of the Battle of Iwo Jima, John "Doc" Bradley (Ryan Phillippe) hears the cries of a wounded Marine, "Corpsman! Corpsman! Corpsman! For God's sakes! Corpsman!" (Flags of Our Fathers, 2006, DreamWorks SKG, Warner Bros, Amblin Entertainment, Malpaso Productions, dir. Clint Eastwood.)

dream of his experiences at the Battle of Iwo Jima in World War II. The trauma of the dream of loss and separation suggests that the nightmare originates from a place deep within Doc's mind and memory that compels repeated symbolic expression in his sleep. The man turns out to be the father of the co-author of the source book for the film with the same name as the film. The book by the son, James Bradley (Tom McCarthy), and his co-author, Ron Powers, quotes a correspondent who describes the terrain of Doc Bradley's nightmare scene on Iwo Jima. The correspondent described the "rocky plateaus abutting on steep cliffs" and "shallow ravines" of the west coast of Iwo Jima as being " 'like hell with the fire out.' "[1] As John Bradley's wife gently strokes his arm and shoulder to help him go back to sleep, the scene fades out.

An Unprecedented Project

Eastwood's *Flags of Our Fathers* and *Letters from Iwo Jima* made world film history for their unprecedented coordinated release by the same director and producer to give two different sides of the same battle and war, in this case the terrible Battle of Iwo Jima. The films came out over a period of about three months in the fall and winter of 2006. As Robert Sklar says, "It may take some time to absorb the implications and potential influence of this remarkable pairing." Describing "the rarity of Eastwood's endeavor," Sklar asks, "What precedent exists in film history for a director to make and release more or less simultaneously two feature films on the same subject, each telling the opposite side of a cruel, brutal, and immensely destructive battle?"[2]

What began as James Bradley's retracing of his father's experience as one of the Marines raising the American flag on Mt. Suribachi on Iwo Jima became a thoughtful, well-written, and rigorously researched history by Bradley and Powers of the battle, the flag-raising, a bond drive at home, and the Pacific campaign. The book and the film deal seriously and sympathetically with the situation of the surviving Marines of the famous flag-raising event, who were exploited for the government-directed campaign at home to sell war bonds. Similarly personal and intimate in tone, *Letters from Iwo Jima* builds on actual letters that were written and then hidden by the Japanese at the time of the battle and were discovered in 2005.

Flags of Our Fathers and *Letters from Iwo Jima* conceivably also may make history by influencing history not only by projecting the world view of Eastwood, the iconic film and public figure, but also by signifying a changing national consciousness. Eastwood's movement from seemingly embodying classic American values and attitudes of the autonomous self to becoming the avatar as a director of an individual and national ethics of the responsibility to the foreign other could both reflect and signal a shift in ethical perspective in American culture.

A Time Experiment: Ethics, History, and the Other

As a sign of Eastwood's creative independence and intellectual confidence regarding his "Iwo Jima Saga," in much of *Flags of Our Fathers*, he films in the mode of a disruptive temporal regime that departs dramatically from the coherent, orderly, and systematic construction of the source book. Bradley and Powers' book provided Eastwood and the screenwriters William Broyles, Jr., and Paul Haggis with an intelligently conceived, clearly designed, and solidly constructed work to help them with the making of the film version of *Flags of Our Fathers*. Instead of following this guide, Eastwood frequently engages in an experiment with time and narrative in a context of national meaning and identity. Moving fluidly between different time periods and perspectives in the opening sequence and throughout the film, his narrative employs a non-linear, disjunctive temporality of repeated interruptions. Such a narrative structure invites self-reflection about the art form itself and its subject matter.

The process of temporal and spatial disruption in turn encourages investment in new perspectives and new ways of thinking about events. A new way of looking creates the possibility for a different way of relating to others in the development of ethical subjectivity and meaning.

In this experiment in time, history, and ethics, as the elder Bradley falls back to sleep after his Iwo Jima nightmare, Eastwood's camera opens on the dark cellar of the funeral home that has been Bradley's place of business since the end of the war. The soft piano refrain of Clint Eastwood's original musical composition accompanies a voice-over that comes from Captain David Severance (Harve Presnell) during his interview as an older man about the war with James Bradley, co-author of the source book for the film. As reported by Bradley and Powers, "Easy Company's boss was Captain David Severance, a tall, lean Wisconsin native; a ramrod Marine of exceptional judgment who had shown his mettle in battle, who expressed his authority through calm understatement and unflinching example" (*FF*: 103).

As the elderly Doc Bradley walks past several open caskets in the basement and toward and then through a hallway and to some stairs, the senior Severance in voice-over says, "Every jackass thinks he knows what war is. Especially those who've never been in one. We like things nice and simple: good 'n evil, heroes and villains. And there's always plenty of both.

Most of the time they are not who we think they are." Eastwood's piano phrase gently expands into a strong thematic
variation with strings and wind instruments as a sudden
stroke stops the elderly Bradley halfway up the stairs. As he
collapses on the stairs, he calls out in confusion – "Where is
he?" "Where did he go?" "Where is he?" – obviously once
again returning in his mind to his nightmare of the war.

Exploiting the multidimensional visual and audial artistic
power of film, Eastwood's narrative art form continues to
occupy different temporalities and spaces at once in the
sequence. Severance's voice-over bridges across to a shot of
James Bradley, the author of his father's story, *Flags of Our
Fathers*, entering a hospital to see his father following his
stroke. Severance continues to speak, saying, "Most guys . . .
certainly didn't think of themselves as heroes."

The camera then cuts to a darkened study with no obvious
interior light, just soft light that comes through the windows
and shines on a wood-paneled wall covered with pictures, war
memorabilia, and a framed picture of the raising of the American flag on Mt. Suribachi on Iwo Jima. Elderly Dave Severance sits on his couch and speaks to James Bradley, continuing
his commentary about the war.

Without relying on the device of conventional flashback
to represent history and the past in these early scenes, Eastwood's camera shows Bradley occupying two temporalities
and spaces at once, the hospital and the study, consequently
disrupting classic linear narrative form. Severance says,
"They died without glory. Nobody's takin' their pictures.
Only their buddies knew what they did. I tell their folks they
died for their country. But I'm not sure that was it." Thus,
Eastwood breaks from the linearity of tightly structured time
to rewrite and renarrate time to establish complex creative
constructions of biography and history with serious ethical
and philosophical implications.

The Stranger

In *Flags of Our Fathers* and *Letters from Iwo Jima*, Eastwood returns once more to the theme of the stranger. The return, however, comes with a new artistic, historical, and ethical dimension. As the internal stranger among the Marines, Ira Hayes (Adam Beach), the Pima Indian who participated in the famous and celebrated second flag-raising on Mt. Suribachi on Iwo Jima, becomes an indispensable player on multiple levels of the film's meaning and work. Along with Doc Bradley (Ryan Phillippe), Rene Gagnon (Jesse Bradford), Ira finds himself suddenly entrapped in a historical drama that brings close scrutiny to him and the other participants. Until the flag-raising, they were unknown Marines and an unknown Navy corpsman. As a result of being the survivors in the group in the front-page photo of the flag-raising, they immediately lost their anonymity, becoming freshly minted celebrities and heroes and key players in the vital campaign at home to raise money for the war by selling bonds. As a Native American, Ira's ethnic identity singled him out as different and interesting and therefore quite valuable for publicity purposes to the campaign. Ira's alcoholism that ultimately led to his ruin also contributed to his notoriety. Eastwood nurtures Ira's differences to make him a moral, ethical, and psychological sign of the stranger and the other. Largely immune to the insults inflicted upon him from his fellow Marines who aggressively and ceaselessly ride, razz, and torment each other with a stinging barracks and battlefield humor, Ira especially suffers marginalization, insult, and humiliation on the home front during the war bonds tour.

Thus, the embodiment in *Flags of Our Fathers* of the stranger and the foreigner within and at home, Ira becomes a study of the fear of the other. He also becomes a test and measure for the film of the strength of democracy at home. The film assumes the sacrifice of so many in the war compels making the country a home for everyone.

Eastwood makes Ira's place as the stranger a fundamental ethical imperative for *Flags of Our Fathers*. As the stranger whose foreignness becomes so important to many, Ira compares to the foreignness and strangeness that many Americans felt about the Japanese enemy. Ironically, Ira's situation somewhat resembles the place and role in society of the ordinary Japanese soldiers, Saigo (Kazunari Ninomiya) and Shimizu (Ryo Kase), in *Letters from Iwo Jima*.

Eastwood embraces Ira's otherness of the stranger, as Julia Kristeva might describe it, to bridge the time of the other to what Emmanuel Levinas terms "the time of the nations."[3] Ira as the stranger connects *Flags of Our Fathers* and *Letters from Iwo Jima* with an underlying current of the other and the struggle for a greater ethical consciousness of the other. The extraordinary melding of the films, with Ira as a key player and transitional figure, makes the time of the other and the nations intrinsic to the project. After the necessary achievement of victory over the Japanese in the war, Eastwood's film project advocates and envisions an ethics of the stranger in a time of redemption and transcendence.

Film and History

In addition to being a time experiment, an ethical project, and a historical vision, *Flags of Our Fathers* and *Letters from Iwo Jima* also make an important contribution to the subgenre of the historical film, works that blend film art and history. Eastwood evidences great vision in the films not only as ethical and moral insight, but also vision in the sense of historical reporting and perspicacity. He shows himself to be fully aware of his multiple commitments by adhering like a documentary film-maker to the historical record as much as possible while also working as a creative modernist and a moral visionary. In these films, battle scenes exhibit historical and psychological realism, while Eastwood projects the prescience of his social imagination and the intelligence of his social and cultural criticism. His educated exposure of the home-front public relations drive for war-bonds sales reinforces his sympathetic portrayal of Ira Hayes.

In terms that inform Eastwood's efforts in these films, Robert Rosenstone discusses the significance of the advent of film as a multidimensional medium for portraying and representing history. Rosenstone's insights into this film form of historical representation help to explain the kinds of issues Eastwood faced in making *Flags of Our Fathers* and *Letters from Iwo Jima*. Rosenstone says,

> For hundreds of years, the only mode for historical representation has been what we call naïve "realism," the attempt to make the world on the page seem as much as possible like the world we imagine we encounter each day – linear, regular, with a clear sense of cause and effect. History on film has generally adapted the same mode of presentation: the codes of representation that mark the classic Hollywood motion picture – camera position, continuity editing, lighting, acting, story – are all designed to make it seem as if the screen is a window through which we observe a world that replicates our own.[4]

Rosenstone, however, emphasizes how film's creative and unique powers of visual and audial representation can influence film's documentary function. The dramatic expressiveness of film can enhance but also can distort its truth-seeking purposes in historical representation. Rosenstone notes that "some films carry the process of revisioning further as they foreground their own construction and point to the arbitrary nature of knowledge or move beyond 'realism' to embrace innovative modes of representation such as surrealism, collage, expressionism, mythic rumination, and postmodernism." The ability of film images to operate on different levels of meaning can prove especially important in a film's representation of historical reality.

Rosenstone emphasizes that film "provides a layered experience of moving images enhanced by language and sound" through a variety of techniques.[5] Over the years, Eastwood certainly cultivated Rosenstone's idea of the "layered experience of moving images" to engender greater complexity and significance in his work, including in the Iwo Jima films.

Also exemplifying Rosenstone's observation about the capacity of some films to "foreground their own construction," Eastwood often brings attention to his own artistic processes in his films. Gaining from the experience of Steven Spielberg's *Saving Private Ryan* (1998), Eastwood begins *Flags of Our Fathers* with a complexity that constitutes a form of self-reflection that eschews standard Hollywood direction for popular films and conventional Hollywood narrative styles. Such self-reflection elucidates truth-seeking processes and the problematic nature of truth in general in both historical films and works of fiction.

The Photo

Eastwood brilliantly creates a mini-history of the significance of the Iwo Jima flag-raising photo as an encapsulation of the interweaving of time and history in a public image so as to compel a rethinking of the ethical and historical meaning of the event. As the elder Severance expatiates for writer Bradley upon the importance of a vivid photograph in capturing world attention during the Vietnam War, Eastwood's camera moves in closer on them in Severance's study. The music builds and the camera shifts to a montage that starts with a photo editor looking at an image that appears in a pan of darkroom chemicals. The emerging photograph shows the iconic image of Marines raising the American flag on Mt. Suribachi in what history will clarify as a second raising of the flag. The montage then dramatizes the picture's domination of the front pages of newspapers all over the country, including the *New York Times* on February 25, 1945, as seen on a typical city news-stand.

The montage also shows newspapers being delivered in suburban and rural areas throughout the country, including one to the home of one of the men in the picture. Severance comments in words that resonate throughout the film and pointedly pertain to America today. He says, "The country was bankrupt. People were becoming cynical and tired of war." As he speaks and the screen shows people looking at the image of the Marines on the front pages of their newspapers, Eastwood's music becomes ever more vibrant with horns and brass playing an emotional, sentimental watch-the-country-coming-together theme.

When the paper gets delivered to the family farm home of Belle Block in the Rio Grande Valley of Texas, Belle immediately recognizes her son Harlon on the front page even though none of the faces can be seen in the famous photograph. She recognizes his backside. Unfortunately, in what will become a major issue in the film, in the confusion of all the excitement over the photograph, Harlon's name got dropped from the list of flag-raisers, an oversight that will be part of the controversy surrounding the flag-raising and the publicity and fund-raising tour that follow it.

The film also cuts to the delivery of the paper to the White House and into the hands of Franklin Delano Roosevelt, who apparently saw it as a great opportunity to reignite enthusiasm for fighting the war. Along with many others, President Roosevelt immediately understood the potential of the image for helping to sell war bonds.

In a brilliant touch, Eastwood then cuts from FDR's hands holding the *New York Times* at the White House to what appears to be a flashback to the Marine assault on Mt. Suribachi. Marines struggle up the mountain to the sounds of gunfire and artillery explosions. Artillery bursts in the air. The camera shows their assault under enemy fire from below and above. When the three men, Bradley, Hayes, and Gagnon, reach the top, it becomes obvious that the scene has been staged. Instead of flashing back to the actual battle, the story has moved ahead to a staged battle with a papier-mâché mountain constructed for a packed stadium at Soldier Field in Chicago. Magnificent fireworks burst over the sky to the great cheers of the appreciative crowd.

The three survivors of the second replacement flag-raising, who will become the focus of *Flags of Our Fathers*, wave to the wildly cheering crowd from the top of the fake mountain they just pretended to capture in the make-believe battle. As the three face the crowd at Soldier Field, Doc Bradley turns to the camera, thinking he hears a voice in the darkness behind him.

The shot brilliantly isolates and encircles Doc in an interior mental darkness. Fascinatingly, as an example of multi-layered film-imaging, the close-up captures the difference between this clean-shaven, clean-cut, wholesome-looking face and the close-up of the face in the opening nightmare, a face distorted by fear, terror, and pain, the face of a helpless, teary Navy corpsman desperately looking for a wounded Marine who needs his help. At Soldier Field, a voice from inside Doc's mind calls out for a corpsman. Over the tumult at Soldier Field, Doc once again hears, "Corpsman!" The voice and dream remain with Doc. The film then cuts once again to the actual scene of the real battle.

In the real battle scene, Doc and his friend Ralph "Iggy" Ignatowski (Jamie Bell) shared a miserable bombed-out shell hole as their only protection against enemy fire in the darkness of the night on Iwo Jima. Over Iggy's frightened objections, Doc went off to help another wounded Marine calling for a corpsman. In the midst of tending to that wounded Marine, Doc in a gruesome fight kills a lone Japanese attacker. Returning to his shell hole, he found Iggy gone. Years later, he recounts to his son for his book how Iggy had been captured, mutilated, and killed. He said, "The Japanese had pulled him underground and tortured him. His fingernails . . . his tongue . . . It was terrible. I've tried so hard to forget all this" (*FF*: 344). In the film, Eastwood cuts again from Doc and Iggy's shell hole to go back ten days to the group of Marines on Iwo Jima, looking younger and cleaner, including Iggy brought back to life by virtue of Eastwood's godlike powers as a director.

Thus, a sequence that begins with the development of an iconic photo becomes a study in the complex interrelations of truth and fiction, time and space, present reality and history. By following through in much of *Flags of Our Fathers* with the shock of temporal innovation in the opening nightmare scene, Eastwood achieves a new intensity and originality of expression. Diachronic interruption disrupts the narrative's orderly pattern of presenting and explaining matters. By continuing a diachronic temporal regime that ranges over the past, present, and future, Eastwood counters the comfort of the film's consistent linear construction of events, thereby raising questions about the meaning of those events and the sacrifice of the lives and blood lost in them. The employment of disruptive, diachronic time internalizes within the structure of *Flags* itself a process of examining and rethinking that Severance proposes and undertakes in his account to Bradley.

Eastwood's artistic form challenges easy answers to questions of time, narrative identity, and national purpose. Severance's pontifications during an interview on the proclivity toward oversimplification and glamorization about war occur while the screen shows other events in other times and places that reposition the person Severance addresses, the book's author. Also, a montage shows FDR looking at the picture of the flag-raising on Mt. Suribachi, and then a cut demonstrates the mutability of time by moving forward to a staged event that reflects back on the complex doubleness of the real event in the past on Iwo Jima, the truth of which remains permanently jumbled in the public imagination because of being frozen as the seemingly fixed and final truth of the photographic image in the President's hands.

The decision to construct a very different modernistic temporal regime for the film *Flags of Our Fathers* has important implications not only for the historical and artistic meaning of the film, but also perhaps for its reception by general movie audiences and some notable critics. Eastwood's experiment with time in the film suggests an explanation for some of the dissatisfaction with the film for some critics. Thus, Manohla Dargis called the film "an imperfect addition" to Eastwood's development of "a fascinating body of work that considers annihilating violence as a condition of the American character, not an aberration," while David Denby also had a mixed reaction to the film, saying "it lacks an emotional payoff."[6] At the same time, Dargis affirms that in the film Eastwood "suggests metaphysics" and expresses "moral certitude" regarding the cost of war in lives.[7]

In contrast to the mixed feelings of these reviewers, Drucilla Cornell asserts that "*Flags of Our Fathers* should be considered an American masterpiece, but it has not received the critical praise that it deserves." She then adds:

Another masterpiece, *Letters from Iwo Jima* crosses the battle lines to discover the stories that animate the lives of Japanese soldiers who are hopelessly defending the island against the American invasion. *Letters from Iwo Jima* has received more critical acclaim than *Flags of Our Fathers*, perhaps because, on a surface level, it presents the more conventional story of a dedicated general in impossible straits.[8]

Similarly, Sklar notes that *Letters from Iwo Jima* has proven more accessible to reviewers and critics than *Flags of Our Fathers* because of its more "conventional" structure. Comparing the two films, Sklar writes, "*Letters from Iwo Jima* is structurally and thematically more conventional, hence more appealing to audiences and more highly regarded by critics, yet made radical by its imaginative presentation of the enemy's side."[9]

To help make the point regarding the complexity of the temporal regime and project of *Flags of Our Fathers*, eminent scholars disagree over the "time periods" and the "temporal points of view" of the film. Cornell writes that "the film proceeds through three subjective temporal points of view." She describes these three points of view as "James Bradley's contemporary encounters with the history of his father's traumatic past, shot in color; flashbacks to war scenes, which are almost always shot in black and white; and color depictions of the publicity tour of the men who raised the replacement flag at Mount Suribachi."[10]

Sklar, on the other hand, writes:

The film challenges nearly all the expectations of blockbuster viewing. Its story unexpectedly moves back and forth among at least four different time periods – the early 1945 Iwo Jima battle itself, the subsequent exploitation of the three surviving flag raisers, with glimpses of their later lives and deaths, and scenes of the author Bradley interviewing for and working on the book.[11]

The fluidity and fluctuations between points of view explain how Sklar can say "at least four" for the number of time periods and Cornell can claim three subjective views. The discussion makes Eastwood's case for the ephemerality, mutability, and complexity of the truth.

Heroes

Eastwood's filming and editing must set a new standard for the realism of the violence of war. The violence explodes so closely to the camera, so rapidly, and from so many directions that the film convincingly conveys the horror of the situation for the troops. Montage at a radically accelerated pace and rapid, irregular, jarring movements of hand-held cameras as well as intense intercuts of flashbacks and memory flashes re-create the disorder of the battle. Eastwood repeatedly plants mortar and artillery explosions at places that create a felt sense of immediate danger. The rapid fire of rifles and machine guns tear through bodies that seconds before seemed safe. The head of a veteran Marine named Lundsford (Scott Eastwood) gets blown off his body by a mortar and rolls like a "coconut shell or something" down the back of another Marine and lands on the ground (*FF*: 159). A close-up of the Marine's head severed from its body shows shocked eyes. This explosive violence occurs at such a rapid pace as to challenge the mind's ability to organize it. The men seem inured to the filth, dirt, mud, and blood that pervade the battle scenes and become almost palpable on screen. Skin darkened by dirt and grime and fatigues drenched in sweat and covered in dirt and boots caked with mud all become common. Through it all, Eastwood shows men, most especially the extraordinarily calm and composed Sgt. Mike Strank (Barry Pepper), acting decisively with inordinate bravery and concern for each other's survival. Under fire, the men continually gesture signals and directions and shout orders and actions to each other.

As *Flags of Our Fathers* advances, Eastwood balances his artistically innovative narrative form for rendering the chaotic time and experience of battle with a narrative time of coherence and cohesion that structures the chronological progression of events. He creates such a balance, for example, with an extensive scene of the men in the mess deck of the transport U.S.S. *Missoula* before the island invasion. In the shadows and dimness of the scene with the Marines in their quarters, each man seems deep into his own solitude and darkness, trying to grapple in individual ways with the fear that grips every one of them. Men stare into the shadows, sit in silence, avoid contact with each other, or seek busy work like Ignatowski repeating his offer to sharpen the bayonets and knives for other Marines, some of whom want to be left alone. This sequence of steady filming establishes a soft contrast and an even tempo with the accelerated and energetic filming to follow in the impending battle.

Accordingly, once having established an unconventional, non-linear temporal regime for the beginning of *Flags of Our Fathers*, Eastwood also projects a more conventional supportive and parallel narrative structure to provide a solid foundation for the development of his film. As a representation of historical events that have been documented and analyzed empirically and become part of America's historical consciousness for around 70 years, Eastwood's film version of Iwo Jima necessarily acknowledges the record of events even in the film's fractured temporality. Working from the excellent Bradley and Powers text, Eastwood, his writers, and his production crew also necessarily and correctly felt obliged in their film to respect the fighters on both sides of the battle by portraying them and events as accurately as possible, as based on available sources.

Thus, following the opening of *Flags of Our Fathers*, Eastwood introduces the basic group of Marines who will constitute the bulk of the story for his film. The introduction of the Marines comes in a carefully designed narrative pattern for conveying as much information as possible, as quickly and entertainingly as possible, to make the men recognizable and sympathetic. In doing so, Eastwood actually follows a classic Hollywood style and convention of simplifying narration and character in presenting a group by focusing on specific qualities for each member of the group, most often defining characteristics that at once seem very particular and universally recognizable.

In *Flags of Our Fathers*, amazingly enough, fact, so to speak, proves as strange as fiction. The actual, real-life men portrayed in Eastwood's film version of the Marine saga strongly resemble the composite portrait of a cross-section of American society that Hollywood still enjoys presenting, especially in its war films, with at least one famously important exception of the absence of a significant number of actively involved African-Americans.

Without feeling it necessary to defend his history of using African-Americans in his films and of his awareness of African-American issues, Eastwood responded angrily to Spike Lee's attack on *Flags of Our Fathers* for not including more blacks, criticism that recalled Lee's earlier attack on Eastwood for his film about jazz great Charlie Parker, *Bird*. Shots of African-Americans as harbor masters do indicate their limited presence and participation in the battle that

Eastwood filmed without purposely depreciating or deprecating their contribution to the overall effort.

Eastwood, as Richard Schickel says, asserted blacks "had not been present in the part of the battle that concerned him." Eastwood concluded his contribution to the discussion by telling Lee " 'to shut his face.' "[12]

In their description of the group of Marines who raised the second flag on Iwo Jima, Bradley and Powers write, "Six boys. They form a representative picture of America in 1945: a mill worker from New England; a Kentucky tobacco farmer; a Pennsylvania coal miner's son; a Texan from the oil fields; a boy from Wisconsin's dairy land, and an Arizona Indian" (FF: 12). The authors add that "only two of them walked off the island." They report that since "three were buried there" and "one was carried off with shrapnel embedded up and down his side," namely Doc, the group provides "a representative picture of Iwo Jima" where two out of three American fighters were either killed or wounded (FF: 12).

Eastwood picks up on the details of the written account to introduce and portray the Marines in the film. Mike Strank (Barry Pepper), the sergeant from Pennsylvania and the immigrant son of immigrant Czech parents, stood at the head of the group, considered, as the authors say, "the protector . . . a Marine's Marine" (FF: 48), the one they all looked up to as the most senior. He will be dead before his twenty-fifth birthday. For all his strength of character and poise under fire, in the film his gregariousness and his sense of humor help explain his leadership skills. Sgt. Strank initiates much of the teasing in the film of Franklin Sousley (Joseph Cross) of Hilltop, Kentucky, the youngest in appearance and behavior of the group who was considered the country boy. In the sequence that introduces the men, Strank teases Sousley that they all are in the South Pacific on a volcano preparing to go to the desert to fight Bedouins. The sergeant tells him that when Marines get trained for desert warfare "they do it on a volcano." True to his youthfulness and lack of experience, Sousley asks, "What's a Bedouin?," and when Harlon tells him, "It's a guy with a camel!" gullible Sousley responds, "Jeez-Louise, maybe we are going to the desert."

Soon after the joke about desert training on a Pacific volcano, to the amusement of everyone except Franklin, the sergeant announces that they all must have their "masturbation papers" signed in order to go overseas. While the others urge him on, the sergeant tells Sousley to find the officer in charge of records to get those papers signed. He tells him that if the officer calls him an idiot then "take it like a man, but don't leave without signing them." Others in the group include Harlon Block (Benjamin Walker), another country-farm boy from Texas, a natural athlete and the second in command after Mike Strank; and the three survivors who appear early into the film, including Hayes, the Pima Indian and Marine paratrooper; Rene Gagnon, who was teased for his good looks and for joining the Marine Corps because the uniforms made him look good and like a hero; and Doc Bradley who gave haircuts to the men that made them look, people thought, like corpses because Doc had practiced at home on bodies in the funeral parlor where he worked.

Of the men who raised the flag on Mt. Suribachi only Bradley, Gagnon, and Hayes live to see how significant the event becomes in the American imagination, and only they will endure the guilt of feeling singled out as heroes while so many of their buddies died unsung or continued to fight without the recognition they deserved. Harlon Block dies gruesomely when his body gets literally blown up. Franklin Sousley dies from a bullet in his back, and Henry "Hank" Hansen (Paul Walker) dies as Doc holds him in his hands. Hansen raised the first flag, but mistakenly gets identified for being in the second famous flag-raising and thereby replaces

Block for a time in the record of the event. Sgt. Strank gets killed by a shell that "tore a hole in his chest and ripped out his heart" (*FF*: 231) while trying to protect and lead his men who were under fierce assault from Japanese snipers.

In *Letters from Iwo Jima*, Eastwood clearly attempts to follow the pattern established in *Flags of Our Fathers* of portraying the men as individuals with important characteristics and traits that separate them from each other but that also help define how they form a vital group and military unit under nearly impossible stress. As in *Flags of Our Fathers*, he endeavors in *Letters from Iwo Jima* to present a cross-section of Japanese culture and society.

In rendering the Japanese story, however, Eastwood was hindered by several factors in trying to represent Japanese culture at this point in its national history, especially under the conditions of Iwo Jima. These factors include the limitations of his basic source material of Japanese letters. Eastwood also was hindered by the restrictions of the setting for the Japanese in caves and underground shelters that naturally determined the actions, interactions, and the numbers of Japanese participants.

In addition, Eastwood had to face one of the major challenges that made his whole venture so compelling in the first place, namely the lack of familiarity in America, including his own, with Japanese culture and language. He had to overcome the difficulty of making his representation of the complexities of Japanese culture authentic but also accessible and understandable for American audiences.

Especially given these challenges, Eastwood's achievement in making *Letters from Iwo Jima* becomes truly exceptional in terms of both film art and film history. His decision to film *Letters from Iwo Jima* in Japanese with English subtitles in itself entails a revolutionary concept and action for an American director. With a wonderful sense of irony and amazement, A. O. Scott writes that *Letters from Iwo Jima* "might just be the best Japanese movie of the year." That comment, coming from the film critic for *The New York Times* about Clint Eastwood, seems quite astounding as a tribute to Eastwood's development as a director over so many years. Scott amplifies his argument that Eastwood made a great Japanese movie. He writes, "This is not only because the Japanese actors, speaking in their own language, give such vivid and varied performances, but also because the film, in its every particular, seems deeply and un-self-consciously embedded in the experiences of the characters they play."[13]

While a lack of familiarity with Japanese culture presented one problem for Eastwood with *Letters from Iwo Jima*, by contrast, in *Flags of Our Fathers*, he faced the opposite problem of the universal recognition of the flag-raising as a moment of mythic importance in American history. He certainly wanted to avoid glamorizing or romanticizing that moment as had occurred in John Wayne's *The Sands of Iwo Jima* (1949), a film in which Bradley, Gagnon, and Hayes reluctantly appeared at Wayne's side. He needed to build to the drama of the flag-raising but without making the subsequent part of the film about the events at home seem like an after-thought or anti-climactic. Mostly, Eastwood clearly did not want the historic symbolism of the flag-raising to overshadow the bravery, strength, and fortitude of the men who fought the battle and who suffered and lost so much in winning that battle.

Eastwood sustains an effective tempo and pace in the film as he anticipates the re-enactments of both flag-raisings. As the men move toward the base of Mt. Suribachi to attempt the assent up the mountain, Col. Chandler Johnson (Robert Patrick), the battalion commander, spontaneously decides to reach for an American flag that had been taken from the U.S.S. *Missoula*. He then hands it to a new officer, Lt. H.

"George" Schrier, saying, "If you make it to the top, put this up." Having heard the colonel, young Capt. Severance will remember the resonances of the word "if" for the rest of his life, with its seeming casualness about the distinct possibility of imminent death (*FF*, 202). When they get to the top, the men who are photographed raising the first flag include Schrier, Hank Hansen, and Ernest "Boots" Thomas (Brian Kimmel), while others add drama to the shot by being placed near the site of the raising. Staff Sgt. Louis R. Lowery (David Hornsby) stages that shot.

Eastwood maintains a serious tone and attitude for the flag-raisings. He dramatizes both events as the combined actions of men working together, rather than as some kind of mythic, superhuman occurrence. He humanizes the happenings by concentrating on the details of individual and group activity. The film also captures the pride and excitement of the Marines on land and Navy personnel on ships over the sight of the first flag-raising. The sounds of whistles and horns from the ships in the harbor fill the air as men on ships and land wave their arms and cheer in excitement.

The tone changes, however, as the film shows commanding General Holland M. "Howlin' Mad" Smith (Gordon Clapp) and Navy Secretary James Forrestal (Michael Cumpsty) come ashore and notice the flag flying on the Japanese stronghold. Forrestal insists that he wants that flag and the order goes out to put up another one. Enraged over what he considers an insult to his brave troops, Col. Johnson gives the order to replace the first flag with another one so that the original could be saved for the battalion.

For the second flag-raising, Sgt. Strank takes charge as usual with a cigarette dangling from his mouth, his sign of casual resolve. He tells the men to find a pole, while off-screen Marines call out to get the job done. People work busily. When Sgt. Strank fixes the new flag – the second flag

– to the pole, Eastwood's music and visualizations epitomize respect for the moment, the flag, the men, and the country.

Arriving late to the scene on Mt. Suribachi so that he missed taking a picture of the first flag-raising, but just in time to make history, Associated Press photographer Joe Rosenthal (Ned Eisenberg) was not sure if he managed to get a good photograph of the second flag-raising, what turned out to be the photograph of a lifetime or even of a century. The flag-raisers had found a heavy drainage pipe to use for a pole. As they started to maneuver to raise it, Rosenthal aimed his bulky Speed Graphic Camera as best he could, not knowing until days later what he had caught in his shot. He was concerned that he got nothing and wished that he had been able to get their faces. He was sure that the photograph should have faces. It did not.

D-Day for the invasion and amphibious landings on Iwo Jima took place on February 19, 1945. The flag-raisings took place on February 23, and many saw the waving flag on top of Mt. Suribachi as a sign of victory, but it would not be until March 14, 1945, that Admiral Chester W. Nimitz, Commander of the Pacific Fleet, declared the island conquered. The battle lasted 36 days with 25,851 American casualties and almost all of the 22,000 Japanese defenders killed, making it "the only battle in the Pacific where the invaders suffered higher casualties than the defenders" (*FF*, 246).

Anticipating the Japanese side of the story, one ominous series of shots in *Flags of Our Fathers* foretells the view of the war that will be presented in *Letters from Iwo Jima*. As the Marines land on the beaches and enter the island, Eastwood films them from the perspective of hidden, underground Japanese bunkers. The Japanese train their long artillery guns, rifles, and machine guns on the Marines who remain unaware of the enemy buried in the ground just a few feet and seconds away.

Flags of Our Fathers relied primarily on exterior battle and troop scenes, involving terrifying images of death and destruction, but Eastwood also used other exterior scenes of interest to vary and develop the story, including amazing recreations of the vast American armada sailing toward the island. Even shots of relatively basic troop exercises such as practicing going over the side of the high transports on rope ladders to the launching vessels below could prove dangerous, as one Marine falls into the water from the ladder.

In contrast, the Japanese remain underground in their caves and bunkers to fight to the last man, and die not for the victory they know cannot be achieved but only to delay the attack on Japan itself. Considering Iwo Jima part of their homeland rather than only conquered territory such as the Philippines that had been retaken by the Americans, they fight for their native soil and for the honor of dying either in combat with the enemy or by their own hand for the Emperor. Eastwood, as noted earlier, tells this story in a fairly conventional manner without the innovations that prove so compelling in the telling of the American side of the story. As Sklar says, "*Letters from Iwo Jima* fulfills standard genre expectations in ways that *Flags of Our Fathers* refuses. It tells a straightforward chronological story with only a few clearly demarcated flashbacks."[14] Eastwood leaves seamless transitions between scenes and shots with overlapping temporalities primarily but not exclusively to *Flags of Our Fathers*.

Some basic elements of Eastwood's style of filming and editing carry over to *Letters from Iwo Jima* such as parallelisms in story development and an enclosed narrative frame. Thus, the film opens and closes in 2005, a year before its actual release, enveloping the film within a certain contemporaneity. Also, widely known performers in Japan and elsewhere have leading roles. Ken Watanabe, who received praise for his work in Edward Zwick's *The Last Samurai* (2003) with

Tom Cruise, plays Lt. Gen. Tadamachi Kuribayashi. Kuribayashi's letters to his wife and children along with letters from
other troops fill a suitcase that gets discovered at the film's
opening. The voice-over of the Japanese reading the letters
immediately personalizes and humanizes the Japanese side of
the story. Eastwood apparently came across the letters for the
film when they were published in Japan and then translated
into English, as noted by Sara Anson Vaux, by Tsuyuko
Yoshida as *Picture Letters from Commander in Chief* and col-
lected in another work by Kumiko Kakehashi as *Letters from
Iwo Jima*.[15] The letters became the basis for a screenplay by
Iris Yamashita along with the collaboration of veteran screen-
writer Paul Haggis.

In addition, the character of Saigo, a down-to-earth Japanese version of "GI Joe" or the ordinary, everyday common
man in battle, achieves status and prominence as played by
Kazunari Ninomiya, apparently, according to Sklar, a widely
known star of popular music in Japan. Accordingly, Eastwood
chose at least two prominent Japanese figures for the leading
roles in *Letters from Iwo Jima*, in contrast to the relatively
lesser-known actors in *Flags of Our Fathers*, as though to
emphasize for Japanese, American, and world audiences the
seriousness of his endeavor in the Japanese film, while making
the point for the American film that the word "hero" belongs
to the universal and generic American Marine, thereby
keeping to the spirit of the source book and the screenplay.

Watanabe plays Kuribayashi with great dignity, poise, and
self-restraint, the farthest characterization from the stereo-
typing of Japanese military personnel during the war. Kuribayashi has an historic role in the film in the Battle of Iwo Jima
for ordering the strategy of having his troops dig into defensive positions as opposed to trying to confront the Americans
directly on the beaches. Understanding that without any air
protection or reinforcements his troops could never defeat

the Americans, he devises the defensive strategy of underground tunnels and shelters from which to fight. Watanabe makes Kuribayashi thoroughly credible as a man of sensitivity and devotion with a clear conscience and a strong sense of common humanity who rejects the fanaticism of his generation of Japanese military leadership without giving up his loyalty to Japan, the military, and the Emperor. Eastwood and Watanabe also show Kuribayashi to be an exemplification and embodiment of military leadership in any culture, making him charismatic in his own reserved way with qualities of patience, endurance, self-sacrifice, and even a sense of irony and humor.

Eastwood's early concentration on Saigo and Kuribayashi establishes a range and depth of representation for the Japanese. Saigo cultivates sympathy and identification. Kuribayashi creates a quality of dignity and seriousness for *Letters from Iwo Jima* as a whole.

Kuribayashi's visit as an officer and student to the United States helps to account for his sophistication and cultivated gravitas. Like other Japanese in the film, his time in America left him with fond memories and positive feelings toward the country. This experience instilled a certain ambiguity of feelings for him and a troubling question about politics and psychology for the film. In a flashback, he remembers that after receiving a goodbye present of a pearl-handled .45 caliber pistol from American friends, he is asked how he would choose between his feelings toward Americans and his loyalty to Japan in a war. He hopes not to have to choose. He does.

Kuribayashi's dilemma in *Letters from Iwo Jima* highlights one of the great issues of totalitarianism during the last century. Decades after fascism in Europe, Stalinism in the Soviet Union, and imperialism in Japan, the questions persist about the ability of such regimes to maintain the absolute devotion of their people. Kuribayashi's ultimate loyalty to the point of believing completely in the necessity of sacrificing himself and his soldiers remains embedded in his psyche and character. Such loyalty to totalitarian regimes and systems of belief by sophisticated and ethically mature people remains troubling in the film.

Saigo provides a dramatic and convincing contrast with Kuribayashi. Without any advanced training, education, worldly experience, and travels, Saigo exhibits strong loyalties and deep beliefs that stay close to home. A baker at home, Saigo was called into the military. Survival becomes Saigo's obsession rather than the heroics of the professional military. Saigo's basic motivational force concerns managing to find his way home to his wife and to his baby that he has never seen. In a moving scene in which Saigo's innocence runs against his wife's more realistic fears and pessimism, Saigo places his head on his wife's stomach imagining intimate contact with his unborn child. Saigo has a kind of schlemiel-like quality, a form of dramatic humor that perhaps gives him an inner source of strength and durability to go with his considerable amount of luck.

In a similar vein, one powerful example of a form of inner moral courage and independence occurs with another ordinary everyman Japanese character, Shimizu (Ryo Kase). Stationed at home in relative security, Shimizu could not bring himself to follow orders from the military police to kill a dog whose endless barking at night was deemed dangerous to security. Shimizu refused to add to a Japanese family's misery and unhappiness by killing the offending beloved pet dog. The terrifying authoritarianism and blind discipline of the military police present a frightening portrait of this aspect of Japanese society at the time. Shimizu's refusal to obey the orders to kill the dog gets him sent to Iwo Jima, a punishment that amounts to a death sentence. He could die for giving a dog some additional moments of life and for providing some comfort to a family under horrible stress, thereby proffering a concrete example in the film of individual human courage and integrity on an imaginable scale and in a tangible form.

Eastwood continues to develop this pattern of contrasts between ordinary people and educated and elite characters. Baron Nishi (Tsuyoshi Ihara), like General Kuribayashi, overcomes his warm memories of visiting America to maintain his loyalty to the Japanese cause while also retaining his sense of honor and humanity. Baron Nishi visited America as an equestrian medalist at the 1932 Olympics in Los Angeles, where he also met movie stars Mary Pickford and Douglas Fairbanks. Baron Nishi provides the lead, as Sklar and others note, for one of the key emotional moments of the film involving a wounded Marine, Sam from Oklahoma (Lucas Elliott). Japanese soldiers bring the wounded Marine into a cave. A Japanese soldier asks if he should "finish him off." Baron Nishi insists that the American should be treated for his wounds. He says, "You would expect the same, wouldn't you?" Sitting next to him, Baron Nishi enjoys talking to the Marine and telling him stories about his American experience with movie stars.

In sharp contrast to stories about Japanese torture and atrocities performed against enemy soldiers, the wounded Marine under Baron Nishi's authority suddenly becomes simply another human being as he spends his last moments in life situated among the Japanese soldiers.

When the Marine dies, Baron Nishi reads and translates for his troops a letter found on the Marine from his mother. The letter reports ordinary details of everyday life that resonate with the Japanese troops. As Baron Nishi reads the letter, Eastwood's close-ups of the faces of the Japanese soldiers, including Saigo and Shimizu, become a heartbreaking dramatization and visualization of the common plight and

Baron Nishi (Tsuyoshi Ihara), who knew English and visited America, reads and translates for his troops a letter that was found on the body of a dead American Marine from his mother, a moment that establishes a powerful sense of shared pain, fear, and loss for all of the combatants in Letters from Iwo Jima. *(Letters from Iwo Jima, 2006, DreamWorks SKG, Warner Bros, Malpaso Productions, Amblin Entertainment, dir. Clint Eastwood.)*

destiny of soldiers at war. Mostly, the words of the dead Marine's mother about how to live his life strike a powerfully responsive chord with the Japanese. She tells her son in the letter to "always do what is right, because it is right."

Doing what is right based on conscience becomes one of the film's fundamental themes. The American mother's compelling hope for her son Sam to see, know, and do what is right, under conditions when it becomes so difficult to recognize the right and then to act upon it, articulates the ethical crisis for all of the war's participants in both films. The fact that the letter comes from an American and resonates with the Japanese universalizes the ethical and moral challenge.

The blindness that Baron Nishi suffers in battle becomes a rather obvious way for the film to dramatize the difficulty of seeing and knowing what is right. Before he dies at his own hands, he repeats the mother's words to her son about doing what is right that become words for all the sons after the Japanese troops have heard them. Nishi, however, has provided his own best example of doing what is right in his treatment of the dying American Marine with care and respect, which clearly contrasts with the immoral and inexcusable murder for convenience by Marines of Shimizu and another Japanese prisoner after Shimizu surrenders. Eastwood unmistakably makes the inescapable point that atrocities and criminal acts as well as acts of kindness and mercy occur on both sides of war, including on Iwo Jima.

Considering the strangeness of the Japanese side of the Iwo Jima story to most Americans, Eastwood finds ways to make the story increasingly accessible to audiences, one of which involves condensing the Japanese effort to the relationship between Saigo and Kuribayashi. As Sklar and Cornell, among others, emphasize, circumstances of battle repeatedly bring these two men together, overcoming their great differences of origin and class. Their paths cross at crucial points. When fanatical officers challenge Kuribayashi's order to retreat then continue fighting after the loss of Mt. Suribachi, rather than dying on the spot, Saigo follows his instinct for survival and his dream of his return to his family. Choosing to obey the general's original order, he faces being beheaded for disobeying the subordinate officer's command to die. General Kuribayashi intervenes and saves Saigo's life. In an earlier scene, as a lesson for his officers on leadership, the general saves Saigo from punishment for complaining about poor rations and horrible conditions.

Toward the end, the general orders Saigo to stay back for the final Japanese assault in order to destroy any information of possible use to the Americans. Gravely wounded during the hopeless battle that he leads, the general needs Saigo's help to die. He apparently sees and feels the irony of once again confronting the unhappy, reluctant soldier. Reassured by Saigo that they remain on Japanese soil and not in

Kazunari Ninomiya as Saigo, a representative of the ordinary Japanese soldier, assists the dignified and kindly commanding General Kuribayashi (Ken Watanabe) during the general's last moments of life on the Iwo Jima beach. (Letters from Iwo Jima, 2006, DreamWorks SKG, Warner Bros, Malpaso Productions, Amblin Entertainment, dir. Clint Eastwood.)

American hands, so that he can die on his own terms, Kuribayashi shoots himself with the Colt .45 from America.

The bond between Saigo and the general on the beach at the end insinuates a touch of poetry into the film for the possibility of finding purpose and meaning in human relationships, even in the face of great differences of class and character under the worst conditions. Sklar wisely compares them to "Lear and his Fool." Saigo the survivor goes home.

The Home Front: The Society and Culture of "The Spectacle"

The home front of America during World War II, as depicted in glorious, even raging color by Clint Eastwood in *Flags of Our Fathers*, proves to be an embarrassment. Eastwood provides a searing, scathing vision of the country for which the Marines of Iwo Jima fight, bleed, and die. The stark contrast of the colors accentuates the two different worlds of the battle and home. Only the combatants and the mothers seem to sacrifice and suffer. Eastwood depicts a home front of relative comfort and self-indulgence that does not let any information about the realities and conditions of the battlefield lower the priority given to entertainment and pleasure.

Amazingly, in fact, in Eastwood's gut-wrenching masterpiece duo of war with its unprecedented presentation of two sides of the same battle, he also manages to create a sharply critical and perceptive representation of the society to emerge out of the war. Like Melville's *Battle-Pieces* (1866) about post-Civil War America, *Flags of Our Fathers* describes the emergence of a lost culture committed to living a false reality. While the source book dramatizes the crisis of heroism and loyalty for the three men at its center, the film *Flags of Our Fathers* transforms their journey home on the bond-raising tour into a visual and audial documentation of a sick society. Eastwood does more than simply impugn the public relations aspects of the bonds tour for its exploitation of the three men and for its patriotic hucksterism as perpetrated by political, military, business, and community leaders. He suggests a source of the social illness that goes deeper than the vulgarity, greed, and selfishness of opportunists who wish to gain and benefit from the pain and suffering of others.

Eastwood depicts in his film the emergence of a new America, a culture that Kristeva and Guy Debord dub the "society of the spectacle." Eastwood's rendering of the bond and publicity tour in *Flags of Our Fathers* can be viewed as dramatizing the beginnings of such a modern society and culture.[16]

On their tour through America to raise bonds, Ira Hayes, Rene Gagnon, and John "Doc" Bradley become crucial players in the building of the new society of images, starting with the image of the flag-raising. The charged emotional appeal of the image of the Iwo Jima Marines, the power of media and marketing forces, and the war-weary public hungry for good news all made it difficult to resist capitalizing on the power of the image to sell bonds. The enthusiasm over the image stifled genuine efforts of the three men to temper the excitement by setting the record straight about the circumstances surrounding the flag-raising and their involvement in it, especially in the face of questions that began almost immediately about the possible staging of the photograph. So, while word from the battlefield and theater of action about the event soon reached home, the power of the image dominated another theater, that of public opinion.

Eastwood finds a near-perfect figure and actor to embody and personify the emergence of Kristeva's "mediatic universe of the image."[17] In this case, the unique merging of character and actor exemplifies the layering power of the film image that Rosenstone finds so fascinating in film.

Accordingly, much of the action and meaning of the home-front phase of *Flags of Our Fathers* focuses on this representative individual of a changing America, Bud Gerber of the Treasury Department, the publicity man for the bond drive, as portrayed by John Slattery of the prize-winning television series *Mad Men* about the rise of the modern-day advertising industry and culture. Slattery makes his character almost interchangeable with the figure he plays on the television series, Roger Sterling. Slattery easily could move in and out of both roles without changing many of his gestures, speech patterns, and physical actions, including his cigarette smoking, heavy drinking, glib speech, tenaciousness, and bullying. In both roles he conveys an incipient danger and decadence beneath a manner of cool insouciance and indifference. He plays the master of the word and the pitch. When he works to assuage the resistance of the Marines to conquering the fake papier-mâché Mt. Suribachi at Soldier Field in Chicago, he emphasizes that they should regard it as just "show biz."

John Slattery (a star of television's Mad Men *series) as Bud Gerber of the Treasury Department stands before a papier-mâché Mt. Suribachi that serves as a prop for a re-enacted assault at Soldier Field in Chicago during the bond drive. (*Flags of Our Fathers, *2006, DreamWorks SKG, Warner Bros, Amblin Entertainment, Malpaso Productions, dir. Clint Eastwood.)*

Slattery's work on the television series adds special depth and impact to his role in *Flags of Our Fathers* as the personification of a new age of spectacle, advertising, and media.

The America that Gerber seeks to manipulate with the bond-raising tour anticipates the America that makes Walt Kowalski so angry in *Gran Torino* (2008) when he looks at his sons and his grandchildren and sees a society of spoiled children, weak fathers, self-indulgent families, consumerism, media, instant gratification, and commodification, in which values of work, family, discipline, and community decline. In this cultural vacuum, Kowalski overcomes his racism and prejudice and finds redemption.

Gerber becomes the architect and builder for this culture that Kowalski, the Korean War veteran, hates as a senior citizen after making a good life for himself and his family as an automobile assembly-line worker during the boom years of the industry in Detroit. Words and images serve as the concrete and steel for Gerber's construction of the spectacle. He designs what Daniel Boorstin famously termed "pseudo-events" that occur solely for publicity and media attention.[18] Such pseudo-events do not exist for anything of intrinsic value or meaning to the events themselves. In the society and culture of the spectacle and image, a McLuhan-esque atmosphere emerges of media and technology as a basis for cultural and informational assembly lines for the production of celebrities, events, mindless distraction, entertainment, and ultimately for the manipulation and control of the political process and system.[19]

Early into their home tour, the participants, especially Ira Hayes, balk over the exaggeration of their roles in the Battle of Iwo Jima as uniquely heroic for their involvement in the flag-raising, an event which was misrepresented in the media from the beginning. Gerber vociferously and effectively defends his project of the bond drive. His rhetorical defense of the bond drive occurs after Hayes calls the plans for publicity a "farce," especially concerning the general disregard for the true identities of the actual participants in the two different flag-raisings in which Hansen and Block were switched. In response, Gerber gives a speech that describes the situation at home that necessitates the raising of money to finish the war against the Japanese. His words could apply to America today in the debate over the cost in lives and money that seriously diminished willingness to support and continue the wars in Iraq and Afghanistan.

As portrayed so convincingly by Slattery, Gerber very persuasively and powerfully goes into a tirade for the three men, saying that instead of dubbing the bond drive after the Marine Corps' "The Mighty Seventh," "They might have called it the 'We're Flat Fucking Broke and Can't Even Afford Bullets, So We're Begging for Your Pennies' bond drive, but it didn't have quite the ring." Gerber explains that the last four bond drives failed to raise money for the war and that on Wall

Street everyone knows the American dollar has become worthless.

Gerber passionately argues that the lack of funds for the war could result in failing to win it. He insists that because of the image of the flag-raising, people now want to give their money to the drive. If people feel the image proves false and the identity of the participants incorrect, then "that's all anybody will talk about, and that will be that." The detail, length, and passion of Gerber's oration suggest Eastwood's sympathy for the significance of what he says.

In spite of the remarkable achievement of showing both sides of the Battle of Iwo Jima as well as the banality of much of the American home front, Eastwood evidences unqualified certainty about the absolute necessity for the ultimate American victory. History informs both of his films in terms of facts and moral sensibility. At one point, after Sousley and Lundsford had been teasing Ira, he shows them famous photographs of the Japanese beheading prisoners of war. Shocked, they grow silent as they look over the pictures. Ira says, "If I were you, cowpokes, I wouldn't think about waving a white bandanna." The Marines knew the history of the Japanese in China, at Nanking, at Bataan, and the Philippines. Bradley and Powers report:

> Japanese treatment of defenseless prisoners of war alarmed the American fighting man. All armies commit atrocities against their opponents, but these are usually isolated incidents not condoned by higher officials. But Japanese authorities in Tokyo, including the Emperor, condoned a different set of rules to fight their war. Rules that permitted, among other startling actions, slavery, systematic torture, barbaric medical experiments, even cannibalism. (*FF*: 138)

Hayes, Gagnon, and Bradley consequently acquiesce readily to Gerber's appeal to go on the tour.

The publicity and bond tour in *Flags of Our Fathers* becomes a nostalgic visit in color to a romanticized past of clean, efficient, and comfortable trains; massive train stations; great ball parks packed with cheering and patriotic throngs; luxurious and glamorous hotels; charming towns and stores; a rustic countryside; thriving cities that are still active and vital urban centers. Eastwood shows few signs of a post-Depression America in black and white or a segregated America or a country suffering from major social and economic problems. Eastwood concentrates on American glitz at the home front during the war.

Eastwood creates a visualization of a national mental state. He contrives a kind of colorized consciousness of escapism to portray the American psyche. The color of the home front in contrast to the drained colors of grayish-white and black of the fighting on Iwo Jima connotes a frivolous and superficial people. Eastwood dramatizes a tour through an American consciousness of self-serving avarice and self-centered politics. Incidents abound of commercialism, materialism, exploitation, opportunism, all under the guise of involvement in a national war effort. A businessman named Tennack tries to persuade Gagnon to join him in selling prefab homes. He tells Rene, "They're not gonna build homes anymore, they're gonna deliver them." The image of prefab homes supports the symbolism of an America of manufactured needs and tastes that cultivate the superficial and artificial. As the "largest furniture wholesaler in Illinois," another businessman urges Gagnon to work with him. Gagnon's later efforts to take advantage of such offers all end in painful rejection. Even Gagnon's girlfriend and future wife exploits the situation of the tour to gain attention for herself.

Interestingly, President Harry S. Truman (David Patrick Kelly) apparently becomes part of the project of manipulating the three men. At the beginning of the tour, Gerber takes them to meet the President. President Truman greets them warmly but singles out Ira Hayes for special attention. Ira had protested to Gerber most aggressively about the tour. The President looks at Ira and beams. President Truman says, "Ira, you're off the Gila River Reservation in Arizona, am I right?" As the President speaks and engages Ira, a quick cut to Gerber and the Marine public relations officer Keyes Beech (John Benjamin Hickey) suggests the President may have been prepped to placate Ira and encourage him with special recognition. The President says, "Being an Indian, you are a truer American than any of us. . . . Bet your people are proud to see you wear that uniform." Radiating personal and ethnic pride over President Truman's words, Ira assures him that his people also feel a great deal of pride in him.

Incidents of corruption, exploitation, and personal gain at great cost to others occur in all war situations and go back to our earliest conflicts. The mixing of money, politics, and corruption during both wartime and peace can be considered as old as the country itself and probably as old as humankind. In its modern version in America, such harsh realities can be found in the writings of Mark Twain, Henry Adams, and John Dos Passos, among many others. Eastwood's portrayal of a glitzy America fits into this category of criticism.

The depiction of Gerber and his work in *Flags of Our Fathers*, however, suggests a new dimension of manipulation, opportunism, and exploitation in his system of public relations and marketing. Gerber institutes a new apparatus for marketing celebrity images and pseudo-events. He implants new processes for public relations for advancing his project.

Thus, at the beginning of the tour, Gerber's reluctant heroes find themselves at Griffith Stadium in Washington, D.C., for their first real exposure to the public, at a baseball game between the old Washington Senators and the New York Yankees. Overwhelmed by the roaring jubilant crowd, the great spotlight, the band music, and the announcer calling them "the heroes of Iwo Jima" and then introducing them individually to the crowd, the three enter the ball field. In a great shot, they walk past the Yankees and baseball Senators who stand and applaud enthusiastically. The beaming faces of the baseball stars show genuine admiration, even awe, of these new heroes.

In the context of this moment, two Marines and a Navy corpsman become freshly manufactured heroes like the ballplayers, only without the ability to play a sport for longer celebrity status. Along with genuine pride and joy for the Marines, the moment epitomizes the production, embellishment, and marketing of celebrity image, in this case to sell a special product, war bonds. Later, at Soldier Field in Chicago, as previously described, time enables the construction of a fake Mt. Suribachi for a make-believe assault of the mountain to re-enact the flag-raising, all as a matter for Gerber of entertainment for the public to advance the campaign.

It could be argued that Buffalo Bill, P. T. Barnum, and maybe even the Romans used the same techniques as Gerber. Gerber, however, has the capacity to employ a national media and public relations apparatus to intensify and amplify the whole process of spectacle creation and image propagation. His apparatus extends from the White House to the homes of the Gold Star mothers. Using a word for money that recalls *Unforgiven*, Gerber explains to an incredulous Doc during their first meeting, "That's what we're calling the mothers of the dead flag raisers; you present each mother with a flag; they say a few words, people will shit money, it will be so moving."

So Gerber capitalizes on the Marine image to manipulate the needed emotion to raise money. The three men realize they have become part of a process of exploitive representation that perpetuates itself, precisely what Gerber wants and what they hate but succumb to, until it eats away at their integrity and selfhood. When Ira and Gerber exchange words and attitudes about the confused identities of two of the flag-raisers, Harlon Block and Hank Hansen, the point also becomes clear that actual identities do not matter, only images.

So Ira barks back at Gerber when the public relations man exclaims, "Are any of you in the goddamn picture?" Ira growls, "Yeah, we're in the goddamn picture." As Gerber attempts to deal with the situation of the misplaced identities, Ira grows angrier, saying to Doc, "Can I hit this guy?" and then saying to Gerber, "Are you deaf? Hank isn't in the picture! Harlan is in the picture!"

The Politics of the Stranger and the Time of the Other

Like King Philip and Annawon, early Native American chiefs in New England who entered into "discourse" with Puritan leaders such as Benjamin Church, Ira Hayes, a member of the Pima tribe of Arizona, senses that by becoming part of the language of the spectacle with the leaders of the modern United States government, he also has lost the war.[20] The first serious film to tell the Hayes story had the appropriate title of *The Outsider* (1961) and starred Tony Curtis in one of the best performances of his long career. Veteran director Delbert Mann, who won an Oscar for the surprise hit and critical success *Marty* (1955), directed it. Hayes remains an outsider in *Flags of Our Fathers*. As in the Curtis-Mann film, in Eastwood's film, the other Marines also tend to refer to Hayes as "Chief." *Flags of Our Fathers* provides multiple examples of the Marines addressing Hayes with language that by today's standards would be considered slurs indicative of racist attitudes.

On the evening before the attack, Marines notice Ira looking at some photos. They joke with him in a way that appears to be meant as friendly teasing. One says, "That your girlfriend, Chief. Bet she's a pretty damn good-looking squaw," while Franklin Sousley implies Ira would like to be with her in their "wigwam." Ira indicates no sign of offense and, as previously noted, just shows them the photographs of the Japanese beheading a blindfolded Australian prisoner. When it comes to teasing, Hayes has proven himself as aggressive as the other Marines, joining the teasing of Sousley about getting his masturbation papers signed, and telling him they were "running short" of such papers. In another incident, flamethrower Corporal Chuck Lindberg (Alessandro Mastrobuono) bristles over Ira's winning a big pot of poker money. Lindberg accuses Ira of getting back at him for Sitting Bull, and Ira points out that "The Pimas fought on the side of the white man." Other examples of such language and attitudes occur when Gagnon asks if Ira had done anything else besides play cards on the reservation. Also, on the publicity tour, Lt. Beech, the public relations officer, says, "You okay, Chief?" regarding Ira's drinking.

On the surface, Ira seems indifferent to such comments as part of Marine teasing even in light of the racist intention and ignorance of some. Interestingly, Ira in *Flags of Our Fathers* hides whatever offense he feels about language, seeing it as part of the regular interaction with other Marines much like his own teasing of Sousley. He never shows signs in the film of feeling alienated or abused or mistreated at the hands of fellow Marines. In addition, in any physical aggression between himself and the other Marines, Ira initiates such action for reasons unrelated to identity. Such incidents do not stem from any inference regarding race, ethnicity, or heritage. While troubling for contemporary sensibilities and taste, Ira evidences little concern in the film for being seen

Ira Hayes (Adam Beach) threatens fellow Marine Rene Gagnon (Jesse Bradford) not to let officials know that he participated in the second flag-raising on Iwo Jima in order to avoid being separated from his buddies on the island. (Flags of Our Fathers, *2006, DreamWorks SKG, Warner Bros, Amblin Entertainment, Malpaso Productions, dir. Clint Eastwood.)*

by his buddies as a Native American or even being called by what today would be deemed by many to be a pejorative epithet, Chief.

Rather than appearing distraught or alienated as a Native American in *Flags of Our Fathers*, Ira's strongest and most passionate identification comes from being a Marine among Marines, and he remains fervently devoted and committed to his fellow Marines and the Corps. In a strong demonstration of the depth of Ira's loyalty to the Marines in his unit, he resists admitting that he helped with the flag-raising because he does not want to be separated from his fellow Marines to return home for the publicity tour. For doing that, Gagnon calls him a "dumb redskin." Chastised by his superiors for Ira's failure to respond to orders, a visibly angry young Capt. Severance (Neal McDonough) cuts sharply through busily working Marines to order Ira to pack up and leave for his new assignment on the tour. The captain tells Ira to move his "red ass." In the film,

Severance significantly then adds, "We are going to miss you, around here."

Persisting in his identification with and loyalty to the Marines, Ira complains to Doc Bradley early into the home-front tour that they belong back with their buddies in the battle rather than on a train speeding to a bonds rally. Indicating deep psychological trauma and insecurity, Ira, somewhat under the influence, embarrasses himself at a reception for Gold Star mothers when he persists in hugging the mother of his Marine hero, Sgt. Strank. Like a child sharing her grief, Ira appears to want to take the place of her deceased son to be part of a bigger Marine family.

The word Ira dreaded about himself that he found repellent and ran from had nothing to do with his blood and his heritage, but with publicity and the spectacle. He hated being called a "hero" by people who do not know what they are talking about and, even worse, manipulate the term and corrupt its meaning to exploit the very Marines they supposedly wish to honor and celebrate. After learning that he has been ordered by the Marine Commandant himself to return to the war, Ira articulates his feelings to Lt. Beech, the Marine public relations officer, about being called a hero and about his relationship to the other Marines.

Emotionally fighting back and giving way to tears, Ira says, "But I can't take them calling me a hero. All I did was try not to get shot." He says, "Some of the things I saw done, things I did. . . . They weren't things to be proud of, you know." Soft strains of Eastwood's music accompany Ira's words. Ira calls Mike Strank the real hero. Beech tries to console Ira by telling him that even Sgt. Strank would deny being a hero, but Beech cannot quite find the words to convince Ira not to be ashamed of himself for his alcoholism. He only confirms that Ira will not have time to see his mother before returning to the front. Ira also tells Beech he thinks going back to the war would be "good." He says, "That's what I want." He also emphasizes that he appreciates the necessity for the bond drive. He says, "It's a good thing, raising the money and that, 'cause we need it."

At home on tour in America, Ira becomes homeless and displaced. Apparent instances of felt insult, abuse, and alienation that Ira experiences as a Native American occur with Americans outside of Ira's group of Marine buddies. Contact with influential Americans proves demeaning and humiliating. One senator greets Ira by trying to speak Ira's native language. The senator says to Ira, "Pappoo gomma sush medyaha." When Ira has no idea what the man and his words mean, the senator repeats, "Pappoo gomma sush medyaha! That's Pima Indian talk, boy, don't you know your own language." The befuddled senator then tells another senator, "Took forever to memorize the damn gibberish." Another senator says, "I hear you used a tomahawk on those Japs, that true, Chief?" Ira's one expression of outrage over being mistreated as a Native American occurs when a bartender in Chicago refuses to serve him a drink. Ira has to be extricated by Doc from an altercation with the police over the incident.

Ira Hayes rages against police in Chicago when a bartender refuses to serve him a drink because the bar does not serve "Indians." (Flags of Our Fathers, *2006, DreamWorks SKG, Warner Bros, Amblin Entertainment, Malpaso Productions, dir. Clint Eastwood.)*

Again in Chicago, Ira suffers the most degrading treatment and language in the film from a fellow Marine, the Commandant of the Marine Corps, Alexander Vandegrift. Seeing Ira sick and drunk outside Soldier Field, the Commandant shouts, "Jesus Christ, he's drunk. Goddamn Indians," and later orders Ira sent back to the front, as he wishes, as punishment for his drinking and general behavior. Vandegrift says, "He's an embarrassment to the uniform." In *Flags of Our Fathers*, the Commandant, the first four-star general in the Marine Corps who helped save the corps from being disbanded at the end of the war, overreacts in Eastwood's depiction in his unsympathetic treatment of a sick Marine.

As the representative outsider, Ira Hayes in *Flags of Our Fathers* marks Eastwood's revivified view of the stranger. Eastwood alters the context for the idea of the stranger in this film to develop a powerful ethical and political vision that becomes a major purpose of *Flags of Our Fathers* and *Letters from Iwo Jima*.

Ira's role in *Flags of Our Fathers* as the stranger internal to the society of his fellow American Marines becomes important as a paradigm and framework for dramatizing the advent of the external foreigner in *Letters from Iwo Jima*, as well as for highlighting the universal position of internal and external strangers. As such, Hayes can be seen as a scapegoat figure who engages other Marines to accommodate the external stranger while also learning to confront what Kristeva considers their own inner foreigner of uncertainty. She writes, "Strangely, the foreigner lives within us: he is the hidden face of our identity, the space that wrecks our abode, the time in which understanding and affinity founder. By recognizing him within ourselves, we are spared detesting him in himself" (*SO*: 1).

Kristeva connects the otherness of the stranger and the foreigner to the unconscious operations of the Freudian

Unheimliche or the uncanny as "the return of a familiar repressed," meaning what at first seems unfamiliar actually manifests embedded fears and phobias so that "uncanniness occurs when the boundaries between *imagination* and *reality* are erased" (*SO*: 188). She asks, "Are death, the feminine, and drives always a pretext for the uncanny strangeness?" (*SO*: 185).

In his interactions with other Marines, Ira, so often called Chief as a sign of otherness and the foreigner, makes his buddies aware of the otherness they face in the forms of death and the enemy. In fact, Ira may have sensed this latent power when he showed his teasing buddies the photos of the Japanese torturing and beheading prisoners. In that instance, he became an emissary of fear, of what Kristeva terms the "other of death," but he also provides a means as the other for the Marines to deal with and structure their fear. Thus, Kristeva asserts the other's power resides in the innermost fears of the subject. She writes, "In the fascinated rejection that the foreigner arouses in us, there is a share of uncanny strangeness in the sense of the depersonalization that Freud discovered in it, and which takes up again our infantile desires and fears of the other – the other of death, the other of woman, the other of uncontrollable drive." She says, "The foreigner is within us" (*SO*: 191). Interestingly, Ira's alcoholism can be seen as part of Ira's difficult engagement with his own inner demons of otherness in relationship to other Marines and society.

For Kristeva, the relationship between "the foreigner" that resides "within us" and the other returns her to the interest she shares with Eastwood in borders and boundaries. The porous borders between the self and the other create the possibility for both regenerative and destructive encounters. Kristeva writes, "The clash with the other, the identification of the self with that good or bad other that transgresses the fragile boundaries of the uncertain self, would thus be at the source of uncanny strangeness whose excessive features, as represented in literature, cannot hide its permanent presence in 'normal' psychical dynamics" (*SO*: 188–9). Ira represents such borderline interaction that Kristeva describes between the inner foreigner and the other/stranger, in the construction of a fluid self with great potential for creative diversity.

Thus, Kristeva proposes the Freudian foreigner – *Unheimliche* – connection for recognizing the foreigner in the self as a basis for stronger intersubjective relationships. She says, "Freud does not speak of foreigners: he teaches us how to detect foreignness in ourselves. That is perhaps the only way not to hound it outside of us" (*SO*: 191). Arguing that "Freud brings us the courage to call ourselves disintegrated," Kristeva says, "By recognizing *our* uncanny strangeness we shall neither suffer from it nor enjoy it from the outside. The foreigner is within me, hence we are all foreigners" (*SO*: 191–2).[21]

As the stranger on the psychic and social border, Ira embodies the differences that constitute the diversity of the fabric of America as largely seen in the cross-section of Marines in *Flags of Our Fathers*. From Kristeva's psychoanalytical perspective, Ira the foreigner and other proffers the possibility for unity based on difference.

A New "Consensus" and "Community Bond"

Ira's role in *Flags of Our Fathers* as the foreigner and the other sets the stage psychologically and ideologically for the history-making pairing of *Flags of Our Fathers* with *Letters from Iwo Jima*. The bridging of the films initially shocks, with their meaning together as a counter-intuitive rejection of conventional one-sided views of war, especially World War II, the "good war" that produced "the greatest generation."

Adhering to such views of America's role and history in the war, Eastwood still found the moral and aesthetic courage and imagination to look through and beyond the time of the war to make his Iwo Jima Saga.

Eastwood's purpose in his two Iwo Jima films parallels what Kristeva in her project on the foreigner and stranger sees as lacking and needed today – "a new community bond – a saving religion that would integrate the bulk of wanderers and different people within a new consensus, other than 'more money and goods for everyone'" (*SO*: 195). She says:

[W]e are, for the first time in history, confronted with the following situation: we must live with different people while relying on our personal moral codes, without the assistance of a set that would include our particularities while transcending them. A paradoxical community is emerging, made up of foreigners who are reconciled with themselves to the extent that they recognize themselves as foreigners. (*SO*: 195)

Eastwood does not simply promote or preach such an argument, but literally enacts it with the linkage of the two films as they are individually and collectively made and presented. In his art, Eastwood realizes Kristeva's ethical and political call for a new time of the foreigner and the stranger. Eastwood's union of *Flags of Our Fathers* and *Letters from Iwo Jima* instantiates the abstraction of Kristeva's argument for community and consensus. It is not just a matter of dramatizing the other side, but the way Eastwood does it. He changes the nature of the discussion by how he presents it. Rather than simply thematizing and articulating foreignness, the two films together structurally see and engage the other. The art of the films affirms difference and otherness.

Thus, Eastwood transforms his time experiment in *Flags of Our Fathers*. He goes from the time of the Marines to a new inter-temporality and subjectivity. The time of the narrative opens to the other and the infinite of the other. In the Iwo Jima films, time and the other in history become part of the art form. The art form structures the idea that history can change and be reborn by envisioning a new time of the other.

An example of film as history and history as film, *Flags of Our Fathers* and *Letters from Iwo Jima* also can be seen as philosophy and ethics. Eastwood's films incorporate in their art form a transformation in what Kristeva terms the "psychological or even metaphysical realm" (*SO*: 195). Eastwood's openness to the time of the other and his rejection of closure and totalization constitute his artistic processes of ethical transcendence in relation to difference and the other. Thus, Sara Anson Vaux correctly proposes that "Eastwood reaches for transcendence" but not as she suggests "from the inside of a cosmic heart," at least not the kind of transcendence or cosmic heart that she imagines as justifying her use of such words as "murder" and "crime" to describe the killing of the enemy by Marines in battle on Iwo Jima.[22] Transcendence in Eastwood establishes a complex set of relationships with the other for an ethical vision that requires dialogue with difference, not its consumption as a form of moral narcissism.

Thus, Eastwood's war saga dramatizes a crisis of values and belief in the midst of a life-and-death battle that both sides deem as absolutely necessary and justified. His ethical position resonates with Lincoln's observations in his Second Inaugural Address of March 4, 1865. Even as the leader, the voice, the embodiment, and the spirit of the Union cause, Lincoln could say of the North and the South in the Civil War: "Both read the same Bible, and pray to the same God; and each invokes his aid against the other." Lincoln understood that "the prayers of both could not be answered," but he saw that impossibility with sorrow as the inherent limitation of the moral and ethical vision of the human condition, even when striving to do the right "with firmness in the right, as God gives us to see the right."[23] Lincoln's words enlighten the ethical and aesthetic search in Eastwood's *Flags of Our Fathers* and *Letters from Iwo Jima*, including as represented by Ira Hayes, Sam's mother, Saigo, Shimizu, and Baron Nishi, among many others.

The project Kristeva articulates and Eastwood insinuates in his films would suggest the biblical ideal of a land that welcomes the stranger and the foreigner with the same love that the native born receives. This would compel answering the demand from Leviticus, "And if a stranger sojourn with thee in your land, ye shall not do him wrong. The stranger that sojourneth with you shall be unto you as the home-born among you, and thou shalt love him as thyself; for ye were strangers in the land of Egypt" (Leviticus 19: 33–4). Justice would be the same for the stranger, the foreigner, and the native born in this land.

The time of the stranger ultimately carries its greatest weight as the time of ethics, not just because obeying the moral law requires treating the stranger as a family member and one of our own, but also because from a Levinasian perspective ethics means a time of ultimate responsibility that exceeds the boundaries of beginnings and endings. The stranger comes as nobody from nowhere and demands total commitment. Only that kind of commitment for Levinas entails maintaining ethical responsibility as a human being – an infinite responsibility before and beyond any chronological order of time. The time of ethics for Levinas "concerns the duration of time as a relation with the infinite, with the uncontainable, with the Different." Such time, as previously stated, involves "a deference of the immemorial to the unforeseeable." He says, "Time is at once this Other-within-the-Same and that Other who cannot be together with the Same; it [time] cannot be synchronous."[24]

Accordingly, for Levinas, the parental relationship entails the ethical paradox of the same and the other in its most intimate form. That relationship of parent and child dramatizes in the extreme the perplexities of sameness and difference in time. If Ira Hayes in *Flags of Our Fathers* serves as a vehicle and an agent for the meanings of the stranger and the foreigner, then John and James Bradley impart the significance of the relationship between fathers and sons and between parents and children. At the end of *Flags of Our Fathers*, Doc Bradley tells his son, "I wanted to tell you I'm sorry I wasn't a better father." Shocked at such a thought, James can hardly believe his father could imagine such inadequacy and failure. He says, "Sorry? You were the best father a man could have." Doc Bradley, who never told anyone that he had received the Navy Cross for his service on Iwo Jima so that it went unknown until his son found the medal neatly tucked away in a carton in the attic, relates a story of how after coming down from Mt. Suribachi "they took us swimming." He says, "It was the funniest thing, all this fighting and . . . and we were jumping around in the water like kids. That's the way I remember Iggy now." Eastwood's camera then goes back in time to the vision of the boys swimming in the ocean water, just being themselves, boys, not heroes, as James Bradley's voice-over asserts, for "They may have fought for their country, but they died for their friends."

The Bradley and Powers account, Eastwood's films, and the historical record, however, secure our memory of them as heroes, in part because they did not see themselves that way but acted as men with ultimate responsibilities for each other. Doc Bradley's story for his son of the boys swimming in the Pacific Ocean conveys the transmission of meaning between generations and a legacy of parental and family love, care, and responsibility. As the Hebrew song says, *"L'Dor V'Dor,"* from generation to generation.

Eastwood and his work also represent a generational bridge. Martin Scorsese, in Richard Schickel's documentary *Eastwood Directs: The Untold Story*, calls Eastwood "the last vestige of the Golden Age of Hollywood." The bridge between movie generations links more than movie-making sensibilities and style, however, and extends to questions of values, beliefs, and meaning. On such issues, Eastwood clearly also looks to the future. Eastwood's ethical consciousness in *Flags of Our Fathers* and *Letters from Iowa Jima* proffers a hope for future generations. With the Bradleys in *Flags of Our Fathers* and with Saigo in *Letters from Iwo Jima*, Eastwood revisits his perennial theme in his films of parental responsibility and family relationships as the basis for a healthy society. In his dual creation of the films that engenders a dialogue between them, he expounds a view for the future of a society and culture, as Kristeva proposes, of care, of balancing the tension of the same and the other in order to nurture the foreigner in ourselves and to love the stranger among us. As Kristeva writes, *"Caritas* is infinite, it grows, goes beyond itself and ourselves, thus welcoming foreigners who have become similar in their very distinction" (*SO*: 85).

Eastwood's films look to such a time of a nation of strangers in a union of love and care based on difference.

NOTES AND REFERENCES

Introduction: Eastwood's America – From the Self to a World View

1 See Edward Buscombe, *Unforgiven* (London: BFI Classics, 2004), for an essential comprehensive and thorough analysis and interpretation of *Unforgiven*, especially in the context of the development of the Western genre. See also Christopher Frayling, *Spaghetti Westerns: Cowboys and Westerns from Karl May to Sergio Leone*, rev. edn (London: I. B. Tauris, 2006), and Jim Kitses, *Horizons West: Directing the Western from John Ford to Clint Eastwood* (London: British Film Institute, 2004). See also, for a classic study of the Western that remains relevant today, John G. Cawelti, *Six-Gun Mystique* (Bowling Green: Bowling Green Press, 1969), as well as Will Wright, *Six Guns and Society: A Structural Study of the Western* (Berkeley, CA: University of California Press, 1975).

2 See Emmanuel Levinas, *God, Death, and Time*, trans. Bettina Bergo (Stanford, CA: Stanford University Press, 2000), pp. 19, 162.

3 See Dennis Bingham, *Acting Male: Masculinities in the Films of James Stewart, Jack Nicholson, and Clint Eastwood* (Piscataway, NJ:

Rutgers University Press, 1994); Drucilla Cornell, *Clint East-wood and Issues of Masculinity* (New York: Fordham University Press, 2009); Adam Knee, "The Dialectic of Female Power and Male Hysteria in *Play Misty for Me*," in Steven Cohan and Ina Rae Hark, eds., *Screening the Male: Exploring Masculinities in the Hollywood Cinema* (London: Routledge, 1993), pp. 87–102; Christine Holmlund, "The Aging Clint," in Holmlund, *Impossible Bodies: Femininity and Masculinity at the Movies* (London: Routledge, 2002), pp. 141–56, and Holmlund, "Sexuality and Power in Male Doppelgänger Cinema: The Case of Clint Eastwood's *Tightrope*," *Cinema Journal* 26 (Autumn 1986): 31–42; Judith Mayne, "Walking the *Tightrope* of Feminism and Male Desire," in Alice A. Jardine and Paul Smith, eds., *Men in Feminism* (London and New York: Methuen, 1987), pp. 62–70; Tania Modleski, "Clint Eastwood and Male Weepies," *American Literary History* 22 (Spring 2010): 136–58. See also Peter Lehman, "In an Imperfect World Men with Small Penises are Unforgiven: The Representation of the Penis/Phallus in American Films of the 1990s," in *Men and Masculinities* 1 (October 1998): 123–37; Janet Thumim, "Maybe He's Tough, But He Sure Ain't No Carpenter: Masculinity and Incompetence in *Unforgiven*," in Gregg Rickman and Jim Kitses, eds., *The Western Reader* (New York: Limelight, 1998), pp. 341–54. On Eastwood and *Tightrope*, see Richard Schickel, *Clint Eastwood: A Biography* (New York: Vintage, 1997), pp. 390–1.

4 See Julia Kristeva, *Intimate Revolt: The Powers and Limits of Psychoanalysis* (New York: Columbia University Press, 1997), pp. 10, 63–80, 139–40.

5 Richard Schickel, *Clint: A Retrospective* (New York: Sterling, 2010), p. 206.

6 John Belton made this statement in correspondence proposing Eastwood for an award on July 21, 2009. See also Drucilla Cornell, *Clint Eastwood and Issues of American Masculinity*, p. 1, and Sara Anson Vaux, *The Ethical Vision of Clint Eastwood* (Grand Rapids, MI: Wm. B. Eerdmans, 2012).

7 Pauline Kael, "Saint Cop," *The New Yorker*, January 15, 1972, rpt. Deeper Into Movies (Boston, MA: Little, Brown, 1972),

p. 388, says of *Dirty Harry* that "this action genre has always had fascist potential and it has finally surfaced." She also said "Clint Eastwood is a totally unprincipled killer" to Iain Johnstone, *The Man With No Name: The Biography of Clint Eastwood* (New York: Morrow Quill, 1981), pp. 50–1, quoted in Dennis Bingham, *Acting Male: Masculinities in the Films of James Stewart, Jack Nicholson, and Clint Eastwood* (New Brunswick, NJ: Rutgers University Press, 1994), p. 168.

8 See Cornell, *Clint Eastwood and Issues of American Masculinity*, pp. 7, 11, 121, 122, 123, 146.

9 Schickel, *Clint Eastwood: A Biography*, pp. 16, 117.

10 See also Kristeva, *Strangers to Ourselves*, trans. Louis S. Roudiez (New York: Columbia University Press, 1991), and *New Maladies of the Soul*, trans. Ross Guberman (New York: Columbia University Press, 1995).

11 Shickel, *Clint Eastwood: A Biography*, p. 16.

12 See Adam Knee, "The Dialectic of Female Power and Male Hysteria in *Play Misty for Me*," in *Screening the Male: Exploring Masculinities in the Hollywood Cinema*, pp. 98–101.

13 Richard Kearney, *Anatheism (Returning to God After God)* (New York: Columbia University Press, 2010), pp. 182, 183.

14 See Michael Barbaro and Michael D. Shear, "Before Talk With Chair, Clearance from the Top," *The New York Times*, September 1, 2012, A1, 13. See also Eastwood's image on the cover of such magazines as *AARP The Magazine*, *GQ*, and *The Costco Connection*, magazines with very different targeted readers, plus his carefully chosen media interviews, which all attest to his high public standing as a figure with a strong and definite national identity. See "Badass of the Year: Clint Eastwood," *GQ* (December 2009): 262–7, 308; David Hochman, "Clint Eastwood," *AARP: THE Magazine*, (January–February 2010): 32, 64; "Eastwood's Odyssey," *Costco Connection* (June 2010): 26–8.

15 See Jeremy W. Peters and Jim Rutenberg, "Republicans See Politics in Chrysler Super Bowl Ad," *The New York Times*, January 2, 2012, A13, A17.

16 Sara Anson Vaux, *The Ethical Vision of Clint Eastwood* (Grand Rapids, MI: William B. Eerdmans, 2012), p. 114.

17 Geoffrey O'Brien, "Fallen World," *The New York Review of Books*, December 18, 2003, pp. 67, 70.

18 David Denby, "Out of the West," *The New Yorker*, March 8, 2010, pp. 52–9.

Chapter 1 The First Twenty Years: Borderline States of Mind

1 Julia Kristeva, *Intimate Revolt: The Powers and Limits of Psychoanalysis*, trans. Jeanine Herman (New York: Columbia University Press, 2002), pp. 7, 9, 10. All subsequent references to this work will be to this edition and will be included parenthetically in the text as *IR*.

2 Kristeva, *New Maladies of the Soul*, trans. Ross Guberman (New York: Columbia University Press, 1995), pp. 7, 178. All subsequent references to this work will be to this edition and will be included parenthetically in the text as *NMS*.

3 On Mark Twain and the transcendent hero, see Henry Nash Smith, *Mark Twain: The Development of a Writer* (New York: Atheneum, 1967).

4 Drucilla Cornell, *Clint Eastwood and Issues of American Masculinity* (New York: Fordham University Press, 2009), p. 13, says, "the Stranger appears, outlined in flames that make him the very Devil raised from the pit of Hell," perhaps a variation of the Stranger's transcendence and a suggestion of the dual nature of the Stranger.

5 Kristeva, *Desire in Language: A Semiotic Approach to Literature and Art*, ed. Louis S. Roudiez, trans. Thomas Gora, Alice Jardine, and Leon S. Roudiez (New York: Columbia University Press, 1980), p. 154. All subsequent references to this work will be to this text and will be included parenthetically in the text as *DL*.

6 Kristeva, *Powers of Horror: An Essay on Abjection*, trans. Leon S. Roudiez (New York: Columbia University Press, 1982), p. 97.

All subsequent references to this work will be to this edition and will be included in the text as *PH*.

7 Richard Schickel, *Clint Eastwood: A Biography* (New York: Vintage, 1997), p. 292.

8 Schickel, *Clint: A Retrospective* (New York: Sterling, 2010), p. 176.

9 Schickel, *Clint Eastwood: A Biography*, p. 403.

10 Emmanuel Levinas, *Totality and Infinity: An Essay on Exteriority*, trans. Alphonso Lingis (Pittsburgh, PA: Duquesne University Press, 1961), p. 155.

11 For additional discussion of the theme of the dwelling and feminine space in John Ford and Michelangelo Antonioni, see my *Levinas and the Cinema of Redemption: Time, Ethics, and the Feminine* (New York: Columbia University Press, 2010).

12 Kristeva, *Black Sun: Depression and Melancholia*, trans. Leon S. Roudiez (New York: Columbia University Press, 1989), p. 62. All subsequent references to this work will be to this edition and will be cited in the text as *BS*.

13 Kristeva, *Hatred and Forgiveness*, trans. Jeanine Herman (New York: Columbia University Press, 2010), p. 73. All subsequent references to this book will be to this edition and will be included parenthetically in the text as *HF*.

14 Kristeva, in *New Maladies of the Soul*, p. 230 n.2, cites Sigmund Freud, "Observations on Transference-Love" (1915), in *Standard Edition*, 12: 157–72.

15 Kristeva, *Revolution in Poetic Language*, trans. Margaret Waller, introduction Leon S. Roudiez (New York: Columbia University Press, 1984), p. 198. All subsequent references to this work will be to this edition and will be included parenthetically in the text as *RPL*.

16 Kristeva develops insights into the comedy of modernist writers such as Baudelaire and Lautréamont. Kristeva writes: "Lautréamont makes laughter the *symptom of rupture* and of the heterogeneous contradiction within signifying practice when he requires that poetry *bring about an explosion of laughter within metalanguage* at the same time he *refuses the laughter* that is a phenomenon of psychological decompression (or compensation) or narcissistic compromise" (*RPL*: 223).

Proposing laughter as an act of negativity and rejection in the service of independent identity, Kristeva calls such laughter "an act of aggression" (*RPL*: 223). She writes, "Laughter is what lifts inhibitions by breaking through prohibition (symbolized by the Creator) to introduce the aggressive, violent, liberating drive" (*RPL*: 224). For Kristeva, the aggression, contradiction, and even violence of laughter and comedy can be harnessed to become a source and force for renewal. She writes: "The pleasure obtained from the lifting of inhibitions is immediately invested in the production of the new. Every practice which produces something new (a new device) is a practice of laughter: it obeys laughter's logic and provides the subject with laughter's advantages. When practice is not laughter, there is nothing new; where there is nothing new, practice cannot be provoking: it is at best a repeated, empty act" (*RPL*: 225).

17 Kristeva, *Intimate Revolt*, p. 27, describes her semiotic-symbolic philosophy as a kind of energy hermeneutic of the transformation of undifferentiated instinctual impulses into symbol and language. The semiotic and the symbolic operate in a relationship of dependence and need. To exist they require each other in their mutual opposition and tension. The gap between them becomes a major force field. The tension that separates and connects the semiotic impulse and the symbolic promotes heterogeneous meaning. Kristeva writes: "If it is true that in the course of analysis there is a 'becoming conscious' of the instinctual impulses that control the desire of the subject and his/her identifications, this becoming conscious depends on an unfillable breach between drive and meaning, the energetic and the hermeneutic."

18 Schickel, *Clint: A Retrospective*, p. 139.

19 Gene Siskel, "Eastwood Acts as a Mere Plot Device in *Honkytonk Man*," *Chicago Tribune*, December 20, 1982, p. E4.

20 See Janet Maslin, "Film: Eastwood Stars and Directs 'Bronco Billy,'" *The New York Times*, June 11, 1980, p. C24, where she called *Bronco Billy* both "disarmingly boyish" and "an emphatically American fable," while Siskel, "Clint Eastwood Shows the Range of his Talents in Top-notch 'Bronco,'" *Chicago Tribune*,

June 12, 1980, p. B10, said, *"Bronco Billy* should be an immensely pleasing movie to Eastwood's fans, as well as to those who consider him a one-note, violence-freak actor." Siskel said, "Eastwood seems to be moving his powerful screen persona into more gentle territory." Maslin, "Film: Eastwood's 'Honkytonk Man,'" *The New York Times*, December 15, 1982, p. C29, was less convinced of the success of *Honkytonk Man*. She wrote, "The film comes across sympathetically but unconvincingly, as an attempt by a well-established movie tough guy to reveal his tender side. When Mr. Eastwood has tried this before in 'Bronco Billy' or even in 'Play Misty for Me,' he had much more of a story to carry him along." Similarly, Siskel, "Eastwood's 'Honkytonk Man,'" *Chicago Tribune*, December 20, 1982, p. E4, also expressed some disappointment in *Honkytonk Man* as a flawed work that lacked "credibility" for both the star and the film.

Such reviewers sometimes discerned the possibility in the Eastwood comedies of a future for him as a significant director. Thus, Maslin described Eastwood in *Bronco Billy* as "almost playing a very large Peter Pan" in what she dubbed a kind of "fairy tale," while Siskel saw the film as "a little bit of fable."

21 Maslin, "Film: Eastwood Stars and Directs 'Bronco Billy,'" p. C24.

22 Schickel, *Clint: A Retrospective*, p. 158.

23 David Robinson, *Chaplin: His Life and Art* (New York: Da Capo, 1994), p. 146.

24 Siskel, "Eastwood's 'Honkytonk Man,'" p. E4.

25 See Paul Smith, *Clint Eastwood: A Cultural Production* (Minneapolis, MN: University of Minnesota Press, 1993), pp. 80–3. See also Gary Arnold, "Play Misty for Me," *The Washington Post, Times Herald*, October 29, 1971, B11; Roger Greenspun, "Play Misty for Me," *The New York Times*, November 4, 1971, B1; Dennis Bingham, *Acting Male: Masculinities in the Films of James Stewart, Jack Nicholson, and Clint Eastwood* (New Brunswick, NJ: Rutgers University Press, 1994), pp. 197–8; Schickel, *Clint Eastwood: A Biography*, pp. 57–8, 246–8.

26 Kenneth Patchen, "O Fiery River," in *Selected Poems* (New York: New Directions, 1957), p. 14.

27 For a discussion of the idea of "wonder" and the feminine as developed in the work of Luce Irigaray and applied to film, see my *Levinas and the Cinema of Redemption*, pp. 74–5, 211.

28 Cornell, *Clint Eastwood*, p. 3.

29 See Kelly Oliver, *Reading Kristeva: Unraveling the Double-bind* (Bloomington, IN: Indiana University Press, 1993).

Chapter 2 *Unforgiven:* The Search for Redemption

1 See Levinas, *God, Death, and Time*, trans. Bettina Bergo (Stanford, CA: Stanford University Press, 2000), p. 105. All subsequent references to this work will be to this edition and will be included parenthetically in the text as *GDT*. For further discussion of the meaning of the face and the face-to-face for Levinas, see my *Levinas and the Cinema of Redemption: Time, Ethics, and the Feminine* (New York: Columbia University Press, 2010).

2 Levinas, *Proper Names*, trans. Michael B. Smith (Stanford, CA: Stanford University Press, 1996), p. 77.

3 See Levinas, *Outside the Subject*, trans. Michael B. Smith (Stanford, CA: Stanford University Press, 1993), pp. 94, 95.

4 See Edward Buscombe, *Unforgiven* (London: British Film Institute, 2004), p. 7.

5 Julia Kristeva, *Hatred and Forgiveness*, trans. Jeanine Herman (New York: Columbia University Press, 2010), p. 298. All subsequent references to this work will be to this edition and will be included parenthetically in the text as *HF*.

6 On Freeman and Hackman about violence in *Unforgiven*, see Buscombe, *Unforgiven*, p. 72. See also John C. Tibbetts, "Clint Eastwood and the Machinery of Violence," *Literature/Film Quarterly* 21 (Fall 1993): 10–17; William Beard, "*Unforgiven:* Anatomy of a Murderer," in *Persistence of Double Vision: Essays on Clint Eastwood* (Alberta: University of Alberta Press, 2000), pp. 45–65; Dennis Bingham, *Acting Male: Masculinities in the Films of James Stewart, Jack Nicholson, and Clint Eastwood* (New

Brunswick, NJ: University of Rutgers Press, 1994), pp. 163–245. See also Paul Smith, *Clint Eastwood: A Cultural Production* (Minneapolis, MN: University of Minnesota Press, 1993). See also *Tightrope* (1984).

7 See John Belton, *American Cinema/American Culture*, 3rd edn (New York: McGraw-Hill, 2009), p. 262.

8 Buscombe, *Unforgiven*, p. 77.

9 For example, see Mary Whitlock Blundell and Kirk Ormand, "Western Values, or the Peoples Homer: *Unforgiven* as a Reading of the *Iliad*," *Poetics Today* 18 (Winter 1997): 533–69.

10 See Paul Smith, *Clint Eastwood: A Cultural Production* (Minneapolis, MN: University of Minnesota Press, 1993), pp. 38, 213, 223, 239. See also Levinas, *Time and the Other*, trans. Richard A. Cohen (Pittsburgh, PA: Duquesne University Press, 1987), p. 73 n.50, and "Thinking About Death on the Basis of Time," in *God, Death, and Time*, pp. 106–12.

11 For further discussion of the history and meaning of these terms in the context of Kristeva's philosophy, see Kelly Oliver, ed., *The Portable Kristeva*, updated edn (New York: Columbia University Press, 2002); Oliver, *Reading Kristeva: Unraveling the Double-bind* (Bloomington, IN: Indiana University Press, 1993); and Toril Moi, ed., *The Kristeva Reader* (New York: Columbia University Press, 1986).

12 For Levinas's discussion of diachronicity, see Levinas, *Time and the Other*, pp. 31, 32, 103, 137. For the weather and snow in the filming of *Unforgiven*, see Schickel, *Clint Eastwood: A Biography* (New York: Vintage, 1997), pp. 463–4.

13 Steven Shankman, *Other Others: Levinas, Literature, and Transcultural Studies* (New York: SUNY Press, 2010), p. 9.

14 Levinas, *Totality and Infinity: An Essay on Exteriority*, trans. Alphonso Lingis (Pittsburgh, PA: Duquesne University Press, 1969), pp. 74, 75, 79–81.

15 Ibid., p. 75.

16 Ibid.

17 Norman O. Brown, *Life Against Death: The Psychoanalytic Meaning of History* (New York: Vintage, 1959), p. 179. All

NOTES TO PAGES 118–121 293

subsequent references to this work will be to this edition and will be included parenthetically in the text as *LD*.

Chapter 3 *Mo Cuishle:* A New Religion in *Million Dollar Baby*

1 See F. X. Toole, "Million $$$ Baby," in *Rope Burns: Stories from the Corner* (New York: HarperCollins, 2000), p. 84. All subsequent stories from this collection will be from this edition and will be included parenthetically in the text as *RB*. For recent stories on women in boxing, see "Bout Time: America's Fighting Women Set Their Sights on an Olympic Debut," photographs by Sue Jaye Johnson, *The New York Times*, January 29, 2012, pp. 30–5, and Barry Bearak, "The Living Nightmare," Sports Sunday, *The Sunday New York Times*, February 12, 2012, pp. 1, 6–7.
2 See Bob Sklar, in *"Million Dollar Baby*: A Split Decision," by Sklar and Tania Modleski, in *Cineaste* (Summer 2005): 6.
3 Sara Anson Vaux, *The Ethical Vision of Clint Eastwood* (Grand Rapids, MI: Wm. B. Eerdmans, 2012), p. 112, in her sensitive and informed discussion of the scene, reports this quote from Michael Henry Wilson, *Clint Eastwood: Entretiens avec Michael Henry Wilson* (Paris: Cahiers du Cinéma, 2007), p. 173.
4 See Sharon Waxman, "Groups Criticize 'Baby' For Message on Suicide," *The New York Times*, January 31, 2005, p. B1, and Frank Rich, "How Dirty Harry Turned Commie," Arts and Leisure Section, *Sunday New York Times*, February 13, 2005, pp. 1, 4. For an attack on the film from a Christian perspective, see Maurice Timothy Reidy, "Clint's World: The Trouble with 'Million Dollar Baby,'" *Commonweal*, April 8, 2005, p. 6.
5 A. O. Scott, "3 People Seduced by the Bloody Allure of the Ring," *The New York Times*, December 15, 2004, B1, B5; and David Denby, "High Rollers," *The New Yorker*, December 20 and 27, 2004, pp. 186, 187.
6 Waxman, "Groups Criticize 'Baby' for Message on Suicide," B1.

7 See Emmanuel Levinas, *Otherwise than Being, Or Beyond Essence*, trans. Alphonso Lingis (Pittsburgh, PA: Duquesne University Press, 1997), p. vii.

8 Steven Shankman, *Other Others: Levinas, Literature, Transcultural Studies* (New York: State University of New York Press, 2010), p. 119.

9 Levinas, *Otherwise than Being*, p. 92; J. Aaron Simmons, *God and the Other: Ethics and Politics After the Theological Turn* (Bloomington, IN: Indiana University Press, 2011), p. 78.

10 Levinas, *Otherwise than Being*, pp. 92, 93. See also Shankman, *Other Others*, p. 49.

11 Levinas, *Otherwise than Being*, p. 146.

12 Vaux, *The Ethical Vision of Clint Eastwood*, p. 98.

13 See James Naremore, *Acting in the Cinema* (Berkeley, CA: University of California Press, 1990), p. 15.

14 Sklar, "*Million Dollar Baby:* A Split Decision," *Cineaste*, p. 8.

15 See Sklar, *City Boys: Cagney, Bogart, Garfield* (Princeton, NJ: Princeton University Press, 1992), for an extended demonstration of how these various elements of performance, public personality, biography, and history as well as social, cultural, and political history all operate together in the making of the work of three figures of enormous importance to film history and American culture.

16 Sklar, "*Million Dollar Baby:* A Split Decision," *Cineaste*, p. 8.

17 See Ernest Hemingway, *The Sun Also Rises* (1926 rpt: New York: Scribner's, 1954), p. 113.

18 Wes Davis argues that the connection between Gaelic and Yeats in the film is problematic. See Davis, "Fighting Words," *The New York Times*, February 26, 2005, A27.

19 Levinas, *Outside the Subject*, trans. Michael B. Smith (Stanford, CA: Stanford University Press, 1993), p. 148.

20 See Tania Modleski, in "*Million Dollar Baby*: A Split Decision," by Sklar and Modleski in *Cineaste*, p. 10, for another perspective on these relationships in the film.

21 See Charles Murray, *Coming Apart: The State of White America, 1960–2010* (New York: Crown, 2012), and some of the discussion surrounding it, including David Brooks, "The Great

Divorce," *The New York Times*, January 31, 2012, A23, and W. Bradford Wilcox, "Values Inequality," *The Wall Street Journal*, January 31, 2012, A13.

22 Richard Kearney, *Anatheism (Return to God After God)* (New York: Columbia University Press, 2010), pp. 113, 57. All subsequent references to this work will be to this edition and will be included parenthetically in the text as *RK*.

23 Kristeva, *Hatred and Forgiveness*, trans. Jeanine Herman (New York: Columbia University Press, 2010), p. 279.

24 Ibid., p. 302.

25 Kristeva, *New Maladies of the Soul*, trans. Ross Guberman (New York: Columbia University Press, 1995), p. 120.

26 See Vaux, *The Ethical Vision of Clint Eastwood*, p. 104.

27 For a discussion of redemption in *Raging Bull*, see Girgus, "*Raging Bull:* Revisioning the Body, Soul, and Cinema," in Girgus, *America on Film: Modernism, Documentary, and a Changing America* (Cambridge: Cambridge University Press, 2002), pp. 67–86, and on *Body and Soul*, see Girgus, *Levinas and the Cinema of Redemption; Time, Ethics, and the Feminine* (New York: Columbia University Press, 2010), pp. 34–8.

28 Kristeva, *New Maladies of the Soul*, pp. 121–2.

29 Ibid., p. 122.

30 See Wes Davis, "Fighting Words," *The New York Times*, February 26, 2005, A27, and Richard Ellmann, *Yeats: The Man and the Masks* (New York: Dutton, 1948), p. 80.

31 Levinas, "Loving the Torah More than God," in *Difficult Freedom: Essays on Judaism*, trans. Seán Hand (Baltimore, MD: Johns Hopkins University Press, 1997), p. 143. All subsequent references to essays in this work will be to this edition and will be included parenthetically in the text as *DF*.

32 Levinas, *Proper Names*, trans. Michael B. Smith (Stanford, CA: Stanford University Press, 1996), p. 73. All subsequent references to this work will be to this edition and will be included parenthetically in the text as *PN*.

33 See Søren Kierkegaard, *Fear and Trembling and The Sickness Unto Death*, trans. Walter Lowrie (New York: Doubleday Anchor, 1954).

34 J. Aaron Simmons, *God and the Other: Ethics and Politics After the Theological Turn* (Bloomington, IN: Indiana University Press, 2011), p. 70. See also J. Aaron Simmons and David Wood, eds., *Kierkegaard and Levinas: Ethics, Politics, and Religion* (Bloomington, IN: Indiana University Press, 2008), and Shankman, *Other Others*, pp. 1–22, on Abraham and Isaac.

35 Ibid., pp. 178–9.

36 Ibid., p. 70.

37 Ibid., pp. 166, 177–8.

38 Maurice Yacowar, "The Tender Pugilist: Clint Eastwood's *Million Dollar Baby*," in *Queen's Quarterly* (Spring 2005): 123.

39 Drucilla Cornell, *Clint Eastwood and Issues of Masculinity* (New York: Fordham University Press, 2009), pp. 118, 189.

Chapter 4 Cries from Mystic River: God, Transcendence, and a Troubled Humanity

1 Sara Anson Vaux, *The Ethical Vision of Clint Eastwood* (Grand Rapids, MI: Wm. B. Eerdmans, 2012), p. 89.

2 Emmanuel Levinas, *Otherwise Than Being or Beyond Essence*, trans. Alphonso Lingis (Pittsburgh, PA: Duquesne University Press, 1998), pp. 147, 148, 150.

3 David Denby, "Dead Reckoning," October 13, 2003, *The New Yorker*, p. 113, and A. O. Scott, "Dark Parable of Violence Avenged," *The New York Times*, October 3, 2003, pp. B1, B28.

4 Geoffrey O'Brien, "*Mystic River*," *The New York Review of Books*, December 18, 2003, p. 67.

5 Ibid., p. 68.

6 Richard Schickel, *Clint: A Retrospective*, intro. Clint Eastwood (New York: Sterling, 2010), p. 230.

7 Paul Ricoeur, *Time and Narrative*, vol 3, trans. Kathleen Blamey and David Pellauer (Chicago, IL: University of Chicago Press, 1988), pp. 241, 242. All subsequent references to this work will be to this edition and will be included parenthetically in the text as *R*.

8 See Sam B. Girgus, *Levinas and the Cinema of Redemption: Time, Ethics, and the Feminine* (New York: Columbia University Press, 2010), pp. 52–6, 61–2, 157, 182, 225 n.29.

9 Scott, "Dark Parable of Violence Avenged," p. B1.

10 See Drucilla Cornell, *Clint Eastwood and Issues of American Masculinity* (New York: Fordham, 2009), pp. 136–7.

11 See Christopher Lasch, *The Culture of Narcissism: American Life in an Age of Diminishing Expectations* (New York: Norton, 1978).

12 Levinas, *Totality and Infinity: An Essay on Exteriority*, trans. Alphonso Lingis (Pittsburgh, PA: Duquesne University Press, 1961), p. 199.

13 Cornell, *Clint Eastwood and Issues of American Masculinity* also uses a scheme of discussing each of the three main characters in separate sections in her chapter on *Mystic River*.

14 Dennis Lehane, *Mystic River* (New York: Harper, 2001), p. 53.

15 Levinas, *Otherwise Than Being or Beyond Essence*, trans. Alphonso Lingis (Pittsburgh, PA: Duquesne University Press, 1998), pp. 155, 156, 160, 161.

16 Steven Shankman, *Other Others: Levinas, Literature, Transcultural Studies* (Albany, NY: SUNY Press, 2010), p. 100.

17 Ibid., pp. 100–1.

18 Julia Kristeva, *Intimate Revolt: The Powers and Limits of Psychoanalysis*, trans. Jeanine Herman (New York: Columbia University Press, 2002), p. 8.

19 Cornell, *Clint Eastwood and Issues of American Masculinity*, p. 135.

20 On Levinas and images, see Levinas, "Reality and Its Shadow," in Seán Hand, ed., *The Levinas Reader* (Malden, MA: Blackwell, 1989), pp. 129–43, and my *Levinas and the Cinema of Redemption*, pp. 77–81.

21 Levinas, "Essence and Disinterestedness," in Adriaan T. Peperzak, Simon Critchley, and Robert Bernasconi, eds, *Basic Philosophical Writings* (Bloomington, IN: Indiana University Press, 1996), p. 110.

22 Ibid.

23 Ibid.

24 Richard Kearney, *Anatheism (Returning to God After God)* (New York: Columbia University Press, 2010), pp. 53, 91. See also Cornell, *Clint Eastwood and Issues of American Masculinity*, pp. 131–3.

Chapter 5 *Flags of Our Fathers/Letters from Iwo Jima*: History Lessons on Time and the Stranger

1 James Bradley with Ron Powers, *Flags of Our Fathers* (New York: Bantam, 2000), p. 230. All subsequent references to this work will be to this edition and will be included parenthetically in the text as *FF*.

2 Robert Sklar, "Film Reviews: *Flags of Our Fathers*; *Letters from Iwo Jima*," *Cineaste* (Spring 2007): 44.

3 See Kristeva, *Strangers to Ourselves*, trans. Louis S. Roudiez (New York: Columbia University Press, 1991), p. 1. All subsequent references to this work will be to this edition and will be included parenthetically in the text as *SO*. See Emmanuel Levinas, *In the Time of the Nations*, trans. Michael B. Smith (Bloomington, IN: Indiana University Press, 1994).

4 Robert A. Rosenstone, "Introduction" to Rosenstone, ed., *Revisioning History: Film and the Construction of the Past* (Princeton, NJ: Princeton University Press, 1995), p. 11.

5 Ibid., pp. 11, 10. The variety of techniques Rosenstone notes includes "the different kinds of shots, the movement of the camera, the ability to juxtapose divergent sorts of footage – black and white, color or tinted, sharp or grainy, documentary or staged" to "aural elements – music, dialogue, narration, and sound – and how they can underscore, question, contradict, intensify, or lead away from the image."

6 Manohla Dargis, "Ghastly Conflagration, Tormented Aftermath," *The New York Times*, October 20, 2006, p. B21, and David Denby, "Battle Fatigue," *The New Yorker*, October 30, 2006, p. 102.

7 Dargis, "Ghastly Conflagration, Tormented Aftermath," *The New York Times*, B21.

8 Drucilla Cornell, *Clint Eastwood and Issues of American Masculinity* (New York: Forham University, 2009), pp. 162, 163.

9 Sklar, "Film Reviews," *Cineaste*, p. 44.

10 Cornell, *Clint Eastwood and Issues of American Masculinity*, p. 153.

11 Sklar, "Film Reviews," *Cineaste*, p. 44.

12 Richard Schickel, *Clint: A Retrospective*, introduction by Clint Eastwood (New York: Sterling, 2010), p. 261. For more on the Spike Lee controversy over *Bird*, see Cornell, *Clint Eastwood and Issues of American Masculinity*, pp. 179–81.

13 A. O. Scott, "Blurring the Line in the Bleak Sands of Iwo Jima," *The New York Times*, December 20, 2006, B1–10.

14 Sklar, "Film Reviews," *Cineaste*, p. 46.

15 As noted in the concluding credits to the film but also by Sara Anson Vaux, *The Ethical Vision of Clint Eastwood* (Grand Rapids, MI: William B. Eerdmans, 2012), p. 155, provides the information about the Yoshida collection and translation and on p. 155 n.2 cites, Kumiko Kakehashi, *Letters from Iwo Jima*, trans. Giles Murray (London: Phoenix, 2007), for a collection of eyewitness accounts from Iwo Jima that includes Kuribayashi's letters.

16 Julia Kristeva, *Intimate Revolt: The Powers and Limits of Psychoanalysis*, trans. Jeanine Herman (New York: Columbia University Press, 2002), p. 140. See also Guy Debord, *Society of the Spectacle* (Detroit: Black and Red, 1983).

17 Kristeva, *Intimate Revolt*, p. 140.

18 See Daniel J. Boorstin, *The Image: A Guide to Pseudo-Events in America* (New York: Harper Colophon, 1964).

19 See Marshall McLuhan, *The Mechanical Bride: Folklore of Industrial Man* (Boston: Beacon Press, 1951).

20 For some additional discussion and information, see my *Hollywood Renaissance: The Cinema of Democracy in the Era of Ford, Capra and Kazan* (Cambridge: Cambridge University Press, 1998), pp. 36, 43, 47.

21 Kristeva's Freudian view provides a psychoanalytical and philosophical study of the stranger as part of a philosophy and

politics of difference. She writes that "differences in love are not to be erased but forgiven" (*SO*: 84). She proposes a psychoanalytical basis for an ethical philosophy of people coming together through their differences as opposed to attempting homogeneous assimilation. She writes, "The ethics of psychoanalysis implies a politics: it would involve a cosmopolitanism of a new sort that, cutting across governments, economies, and markets, might work for a mankind whose solidarity is founded on the consciousness of its unconscious – desiring, destructive, fearful, empty, impossible" (*SO*: 192).

Kristeva sees Freudian ethics as making difference a condition of community. She says, "Freud, the one of *Beyond the Pleasure Principle*, sets the difference within us in its most bewildering shape and presents it as the ultimate condition of our being *with* others" (*SO: 192*).

22 See Vaux, *The Ethical Vision of Clint Eastwood*, pp. 145, 161. On imputations of murder and crime by the Marines, see pp. 145, 147, 152.

23 John Grafton, ed., *Great Speeches: Abraham Lincoln* (New York: Dover, 1991), pp. 107, 108.

24 Emmanuel Levinas, *God, Death, and Time*, trans. Bettina Bergo, ed. Jacques Rolland (Stanford, CA: Stanford University Press, 2000), p. 19.

INDEX